Sociobiology and the
human dimension

Contents

v

Foreword

by Mary Midgley

It is surprisingly hard to discuss human evolution fairly and without rancour. Time has not done as much for us here as we might have hoped. The issues which Darwin laid open – but certainly did not invent – still, even today, seem to many people intolerably threatening. Can we find unbiassed ground from which to approach them? Looking back, we can now see much that was wrong about the tribal approach of Darwin's contemporaries. Some treated their religion as a science, others treated their science as a religion. Many who accepted Darwin joyfully did not understand him at all. Everyone tended to find what they were already looking for. Today the tribal divisions have shifted: different groups, different ideals, different hatreds are involved. But the animus is scarcely less, and – what is really surprising – the name of Darwin is still in use as a tribal rallying-cry. Can it still be right to treat him as a war-leader, for or against whom we should take sides? What is to be done about all this?

Georg Breuer's book is a solid attempt to do the first thing needful – to keep one's head and one's temper, get rid of irrelevancies and sort out the different issues involved in the current form of the dispute. His subject is the recent vigorous attempt to apply Darwinist principles to mankind, which is known as Sociobiology. This movement has been met with a small tornado of controversy in America which, on the usual principles of intellectual weather, is now reaching Europe. On those same principles, the tornado has picked up a surface layer of controversial grime which obscures the original complexity of the issue. Breuer begins by putting this aside and expounding the theory itself, clearly and sympathetically, for non-specialists. He then considers – also with great sympathy – the general moral, political and psychological objections that have been brought against it. He accepts some of them, but suggests that others are excessive or misplaced. He also brings some very interesting criticisms of his own. On the whole he concludes that sociobiological thinking can indeed be useful, and is certainly not illicit. It is, however, a tool with a much more limited use than its champions have sometimes suggested.

This conclusion is, of course, not very surprising; it is the sort of verdict that one might expect to reach when moral and political charges are being brought against what seems, on the face of it, to be a branch of physical science. But it is not so easy to get the details right, particularly on a matter like this on which all of us are more or less engaged. Breuer thinks – I am sure rightly – that the tone or what some of its critics call the 'atmosphere' of sociobiology has been faulty as well as its excessive claims, and is involved in those claims. By over-simplifying human affairs, by constant brashness of language and occasional brutality of examples, sociobiologists have sometimes allowed the admission of hereditary elements in human behaviour to look like the acceptance of moral and emotional meanness. There has too, at times, been a triumphantly reductive tone, even a defiant quasi-religious exaltation of dubious entities such as the 'selfish gene'. This sort of fault can be a serious nuisance, even when it does not really form part of the theory that it deforms, because it can discredit scientific work which is itself harmless and, if harmless, then useful.

That it might be useful is a dominant consideration with Breuer, and in that he is surely right. We do not have so full and satisfactory an understanding of human conduct that we can afford to throw away unexamined what might be a useful tool for it, just because we do not like the wrapping or the manners of the postman who delivers it. It is essential to see how deep the damage really goes. Breuer seems to me to do this very well, carefully distinguishing first what sociobiologists actually say from what they are merely suspected of meaning or implying, and then sorting out, within what they do say, the central theses from more optional and discardable elements. In its wide and minimal definition, Sociobiology sounds inoffensive enough. Its best-known exponent defines it as simply 'the systematic study of the biological basis of all social behaviour' (E. O. Wilson, *Sociobiology* p. 3–4). To apply this to man, however, is to accept that human behaviour has such a biological basis. And even this apparently modest thesis has been widely resisted on political grounds. Left-wing critics have denounced it as illicitly deterministic, as implying an immoral acceptance of the status quo, and as amounting to racism and fascism. Breuer takes this argument apart link by link, and succeeds, I think, in making it clear that the alarm is unfounded, and is inconsistent with any intelligible left-wing position. He rightly points out how much this denunciation of physical determinism, and in particular of the biological sciences, would have surprised Marx and Engels. Determinism is the tool of every scientist. The difficult task of reconciling it with free-will has not been noticeable more neglected in the biological than in the social sciences. About racism, Breuer speaks from the informed position of an Austrian who experienced himself the intellectual climate of the pre-Nazi time and Hitler's advent to power, and who had to leave his country after its annexation by Germany to avoid political and racial persecution. In general, as he justly remarks, it is never relevant to cite the *misuses* that have been made of doctrines as evidence against them. The large question of whether human behaviour has some genetic causes is a factual one, to be settled by the evidence. Moral questions about what we should then do about it are separate.

A total absence of genetic causes is in fact so hard to argue for, or even conceive, that thoughtful opponents in the social sciences usually prefer now to say, more subtly, that these causes do indeed exist, for man as for other animals, but that in man nothing can be known about them. Human life, then, can be studied only by the social sciences; it is entirely opaque to biology. Thus a rather precarious truce was for some time maintained, by which social scientists agreed not to deny the reality of human evolution, so long as nobody attempted to make any intellectual use of it. That truce was radically disturbed by the far-reaching ethological discoveries of Konrad Lorenz and Niko Tinbergen, which showed parallels between animal and human behaviour much more profound and important than had previously been suspected. Many social scientists have welcomed these insights and have used them admirably, showing that co-operation with biology is entirely possible – as indeed one might expect. Others, however, closed ranks and denounced the whole development. To them, sociobiology comes as a deeper shock. It renders the truce so far maintained even more awkward and unconvincing, because it is carried on in terms far more familiar to the social sciences (particularly in America) and has been so promoted as to catch the attention of a wide scientific public. Yet it seems to contain much that is alarming.

There are two ways out of this predicament. One is to retreat into a general scepticism about evolution itself. To some extent this can indeed be done. Apart from the pathological phenomenon of 'creationism', there seem to be good scientific reasons for thinking that 'neo-Darwinists' (or Haldanists, as they should perhaps be called) have indeed been far too confident in recent years about our knowledge of the actual mechanisms of selection. But this is a minor matter. However little we may know about these mechanisms, selection itself is not in doubt, and would not be even if some mechanism for the inheritance of acquired characteristics did eventually turn up as well. (And the discovery of such a mechanism would of course make biological issues even more central to the discussion.) There is therefore really no choice but to take the other way and examine the issues which sociobiology lays before us properly, one at a time and without prejudice. If this is done, it should be possible to spot fairly quickly what are its actual strengths and faults in method. Breuer is an admirable guide here, and particularly in the shrewd attention which he gives to the topic of what sociobiologists do *not* say. Their fascination with small, particular behaviour-patterns makes them, as he remarks, singularly blind to certain large and crucial emotional patterns that are characteristically human. But because these *are* characteristically human, there should, one would suppose, be nothing objectionable about admitting that the capacity for them is a part of our genetically determined human constitution. On this topic, as on many hereabouts, it is a mistake to take sides too quickly. Breuer sets an excellent example in avoiding the tribal feuds which have dogged this controversy, and in treating this most difficult issue fairly. Yet he has zest and enthusiasm enough to carry through it even those who are inclined to groan at the very name of sociobiology. Because he is not a specialist, he can get the issues in proportion, and so convey the real fascination of the topic. This is a book to learn from, and also one to enjoy.

Sociobiology – between the Two Cultures

If man is a descendant of animal ancestors, human behaviour must have evolved from animal behaviour. Of course, this proposition should not be taken as a basis for far-reaching speculations. Man, after all, is unique on earth and basically different from even those species which biologically are most closely related to him. Yet in spite of all these differences our descent cannot be denied. Biochemically we are more similar to chimpanzees than a dog is to a fox. Every one of us has certain bones, tendons and other organs that have no recognizable function in the human organism. Their existence can only be explained if they are considered as relics of organs that served a useful purpose in our animal ancestors a long time ago. It is therefore not absurd to assume that there might be similar relics in human behaviour as well.

Karl Marx thought of dedicating to Charles Darwin his main work, *Das Capital*. Darwin did not like the idea; apparently this was because he did not want his scientific work to be rubber-stamped politically. Nevertheless the descent of man was soon hotly debated – not only by biologists but even more in philosophical and political circles. To simplify somewhat, one could say that in such disputes it was, as a rule, the progressives who supported Darwinism whilst the conservatives violently rejected it.

Today it seems that the tables are turned. Scientists wanting to explain the evolution of human behaviour and particularly of social behaviour in Darwinistic terms are attacked from the left. Progressives of our generation denounce the attempt to unify modern biological knowledge in the new scientific branch of sociobiology as giving support to reactionary and even fascist ideas. And many scholars of anthropology, sociology, psychology and philosophy –

not necessarily with left allegiances – also voice considerable reservations about this new trend in biology.

Is such a rejection of sociobiology merely due to prejudices and misunderstandings? Is it due to the narrow-mindedness of social scientists not wanting biological 'intruders' in what they consider to be a field of research reserved for themselves? Can it be attributed to an over-rating of miscellaneous quotations taken out of context, which do not represent the real essence of sociobiological ideas? Or is it really true that sociobiology – and particularly its simplifying popularizations – have an *inherent* tendency to foster and support reactionary ideas?

In this book I want to show that *any one* of these questions is justified; that *none of them* can be answered with a clear and unequivocal 'yes' or 'no'. Even more important in my view is the fact that the discussion on sociobiology has so far avoided what seems to me one of its most basic problems. It is what I call in this book 'the human dimension': the exclusively human ability to identify with *any one* of his conspecifics and feel sympathy with him. I think that basically a considerable part of the uneasiness caused by applying sociobiology to man is due to the fact that it does not take sufficient account of this most human of all human faculties. Moreover, most of its critics do not seem to realize this either; anyway, they do not spell it out clearly.

In this book I want to present a *balanced* view. I am trying to explain the essence of the arguments of supporters as well as critics of sociobiology. I do not think that this new discipline is a mere pseudo-science. It asks reasonable and relevant questions when demanding a Darwinistic explanation for the evolution of social behaviour; and these questions are amenable to scientific research. After talking with quite a number of scientists studying animal behaviour I am convinced that sociobiology has given them many a valuable impetus – even though its ideas are hotly disputed amongst biologists.

On the other hand sociobiology is a very young branch of science. It does not possess as yet a basic stock of assured and thoroughly tested knowledge. It is only just starting to delimit its field of research and to calibrate its tools. Any such new scientific enterprise must start of necessity with preliminary assumptions, hypotheses and model concepts that are still to be tested and then changed, improved and at last perhaps adopted in the course of further research. Popular presentations that do not sufficiently emphasize this *preliminary* character of many of the ideas developed by sociobiology so far are bound to create misunderstandings and distortions.

Moreover, this field of research is of interest to each of the 'Two Cultures'. Yet natural scientists and social scientists both have their own specific and different methods of investigation and thinking arising from their different traditions. All this makes an interdisciplinary exchange of views rather difficult.

Yet even after discounting all such secondary discrepancies and the exaggerations, typical of a heated debate, there remains a hard core of basic divergence which, I think, is not due to mutual misconceptions. One main bone of contention is the question whether and to what extent it is possible to apply insights gained in the study of animal societies to man, whose societies are mainly the result of a cultural and not of a genetic evolution. Moreover there are the apprehensions of the progressives that any investigations of an inborn 'human nature' might be used – or rather abused – to vindicate an unsatisfactory status quo of human society as being 'natural'; for something that is 'natural' need not necessarily be right.

Yet man, after all, is part of nature, even if many people nowadays hardly seem to realize it. Human nature cannot be properly understood unless it is seen as part of nature as a whole, subject to the same laws of heredity and evolution. Therefore it would not appear reasonable to me to ban the question about natural inborn tendencies of man and declare it 'taboo', as it were. Neither would it be reasonable to call everybody a reactionary who is interested in such research. Such an attitude would merely result in surrendering a whole field of investigation to those who do not mind being dubbed reactionaries.

Equally, to me it would seem counter-productive to build up 'fortified positions' in the social sciences so that the concepts of sociobiology could be attacked. In the long-run, social and human scientists cannot restrict themselves to merely denouncing methodological inadequacies in the application of genetics and ethology to man. Rather, sociologists and anthropologists, psychologists and philosophers ought to strive to help scientists from the biological fields to get to grips with what is typically human. Thus many pitfalls and fallacies lurking for researchers in the human realm might easily be avoided. In common interdisciplinary work, with representatives of the human and social sciences, it probably would be easier to find out how human behaviour really did evolve than it would be for sociobiologists, ethologists and geneticists working in isolation.

In the course of evolution natural selection evidently put a premium on behaviour patterns that helped our pre-human and early human ancestors to adapt to the environmental conditions *of their time*. Most probably, comparative ethology and sociobiology are more likely than human and social sciences to uncover behaviour patterns that were useful to pre-humans or men of the early stone-age but which are not necessarily useful now. Whilst we cannot change our genes, the recognition and knowledge of such problems might help us to avoid trouble. We might be able to look for ways and means to ease tension resulting from the fact that we live in a totally different environment today than at the time when our specific genetic make-up was formed. We will understand man better when we know how he became man.

The idea of writing this book first occurred to me when attending the Dahlem workshop on Morality as a Biological Phenomenon in Berlin in December 1977. For a week, a panel of highly distinguished biologists, anthropologists, psychologists, social scientists and philosophers from five countries discussed problems of the evolution of human morality – and I could see for myself the extent of existing misconceptions and diverging views.

By taking part in this conference, and in two further ones on the Evolution of Social Behaviour and on Animal and Human Mind, I had the chance not only to acquaint myself with the present state of knowledge in these fields but also to talk to many of the participants and ask them questions. I am greatly indebted to the Dahlem Conferences and to their organizer Dr Silke Bernhard for giving me this unique opportunity.

At an early stage of writing this book I sent a draft of what are now sections 1.15 to 2.3 to Professor E. O. Wilson of Harvard University, one of the leading promoters of sociobiology, asking him for his comments. As the reader will see these chapters are by no means an uncritical endorsement of Wilson's views. I raised quite a number of objections and reservations. All the more I was striving to present *his* point of view in a fair and undistorted way. Wilson's reply was very encouraging and a confirmation that I had succeeded in this task. He had not found any errors in substance; there were, of course, different philosophical interpretations, but it would not be a fruitful enterprise to try to work them all out in detail. 'Your approach is reasonable,' he wrote, 'and raises issues that ought to be expressed boldly (for example, your opinion on the criteria of what constitutes evolutionary advance among major groups of social organisms).'

I can only hope that the finished volume will find a similar reception by all the scientists to whose works I refer in this book. With many of them I have had personal conversations and/or correspondence, and some of them took the time to read parts of my draft manuscript and let me know their comments. For this valuable aid I am particularly indebted to: Professor Francisco J. Ayala, University of California; Professor Patrick P. G. Bateson, University of Cambridge; Professor John T. Bonner, Princeton University; Professor Stephen T. Emlen, Cornell University; Professor Marcus W. Feldman, Stanford University; Dr Jane Goodall, Dar es Salaam; Dr Paul Harvey, University of Sussex; Professor Bert Hölldobler, Harvard University; Professor Hans Kummer, University of Zürich; Dr Charles J. Lumsden, Harvard University; Professor Hubert Markl, University of Konstanz; Professor Peter Marler, Rockefeller University; Professor Emil W. Menzel, Jr., State University of New York; Professor Charles D. Michener, University of Kansas; Professor Gordon W. Orians, University of Washington; Dr Geoffrey A. Parker, University of Liverpool; Professor Ludwig Prokop, University of Vienna; Dr Hans-Ulrich Reyer, Max-Planck-Institut für Verhaltensphysiologie, Seewiesen; Professor Donald S. Sade, Northwestern University; Dr E. Sue Savage-Rumbaugh, Yerkes Primate Research Center; Dr Robert M. Seyfarth, Rockefeller University; Professor Paul W. Sherman, University of California; Professor Robert C. Solomon, University of Texas; Professor Gunther Stent, University of California; Professor Evelyne Sullerot, formerly of the University of Paris-Nanterre; Dr Christian Welker, University of Kassel; and Dr Richard Wrangham, University of Cambridge.

My special thanks go to Professor Mary Midgley of University of Newcastle upon Tyne who not only wrote the Foreword to this English version of my book but read the whole manuscript through, giving many valuable comments and helping me time and again in expressing my ideas in intelligible English. The interest she took in my work has been a great encouragement to me.

For the views expressed in this book and for all its shortcomings and errors I alone bear the full responsibility.

Vienna, September 1981   GEORG BREUER

1

How could unselfish behaviour evolve at all ?

1.1 *Why does a sheep want to be in the middle of the herd?*

'A sheep kept alone on a farmstead is not a proper sheep at all,' says my son who has been working as a shepherd for several years. 'It will become neurotic and get a disturbed personality structure. Sheep are herding animals. They only feel well when there are other sheep to their right and left.'

I sometimes watched my son leading his herd to the pasture. The sheep graze hastily, as if somebody were hurrying them. All of them are pressing forward, wanting to be in the first row where they can get grass not yet trodden down. Occasionally one or two of them stop at some dainty morsel – to grab some climbing plants from the bushes for instance. But as soon as the others have proceeded a few metres, the stragglers are turning their heads towards them. The tasty morsel can no longer hold them. As if drawn by an irresistible force, they follow the others and push themselves into the middle of the group. They could, one might think, advance to the fringe of of the herd in order to reach the first row and good fresh grass as soon as possible. But no, they crowd in amongst the others where they must push hard and make great efforts to get to the front.

Why does the sheep want to be in the middle of the herd? 'It calls for explanation when a herd animal wants at all costs to be near a lot of other members of its own species', writes the Austrian etholo-gist Konrad Lorenz (1963/66, p. 140). 'The justification for this question will immediately be apparent if we consider the obvious disadvantages of big herds; for instance, the difficulty of finding enough food for so many animals, the impossibility of concealment, the increased predisposition to disease, and many other factors.'

1

If herd animals are to the smallest degree capable of defence against predators, Lorenz continues (*ibid*, p. 141), it is understandable that there should be safety in numbers. Indeed many species that live in herds have well-organized defence systems. The young are kept in the middle surrounded by older and stronger individuals, but even a fully grown animal is much safer in a group than alone.

In species in which only females and their young form herds whereas the adult males live solitarily or in loose groups, the strongest females bear the brunt of defence. In elephants this is mainly the 'matriarch', the oldest female of the herd and hence the largest and strongest, since elephants continue growing past maturity. 'The matriarch is exceptionally altruistic,' writes the well-known zoologist Edward O. Wilson of Harvard University in his standard work *Sociobiology – the New Synthesis* (1975, p. 494). 'She is ready to expose herself to danger while protecting her herd, she is the most courageous individual when the group assembles in the characteristic circular defense formation.'

In mixed groups of males and females, as formed by musk-oxen, buffaloes and many monkey species, defence is mainly a male job. In the Amboseli National Park in Kenya, Jane and Stuart Altmann (1970) observed the attack of a leopard on a group of yellow baboons at the edge of a water hole: 'The baboons sprang away, then turned on the leopard, barking loudly . . . Faced with this mass attack, the leopard turned and ran.' On the other hand the Swiss ethologist Hans Kummer has observed cases of baboons fleeing before wild dogs and relinquishing one of their females, though the males would have been well able to ward off the predators. 'If I were a baboon female,' he told me when I visited him at his institute in Zürich in 1980, 'I would not rely on the males to defend me in any case.'

This episode is an example of a phenomenon to which we will return again and again in this book: generalizing claims that members of a certain species 'always' behave in a certain way, are not usually correct. Animals are not pre-programmed automatons. Their behaviour is variable within certain limits.

A herd of sheep too is capable of self-defence. Mother sheep in particular can be very aggressive when trying to defend their lambs. They even do not hesitate to face the shepherd's dog which does not know how to behave in such a situation.

But why do herding animals crowd densely even if it does not serve common defence? 'What advantage does close herding together bring to the completely defenseless, such as herrings or small birds in enormous flocks?' asks Lorenz (1963/66, p. 142). 'I can think of only one explanation and I offer it tentatively because it seems scarcely believable that a single, small, but widespread weakness in predators could have wrought such far-reaching consequences in the behaviour of their prey: this weakness lies in the fact that many, perhaps all, predators which pursue a single prey are incapable of concentrating on one target if, at the same time, many others are crossing their field of vision.'

Actually predators prefer hunting single animals that have lost contact with their group. Some birds of prey, like falcons, even carry out sham attacks and all sorts of manoeuvres to isolate some of their prey from the flock. The response of the hunted is to draw close together in case of danger, for, according to Lorenz, even as formidable a predator as a lion or a tiger tries to avoid obtaining its prey from a dense crowd.

When it does attack a herd, a predator has the best chance if it can concentrate on a certain animal that is conspicuous by its size (e.g. a young animal), its different behaviour (e.g. a sick animal) or its colour. Field ecologists have repeatedly noted that the marking of some individuals of a herd with coloured patches or bright collars greatly reduces their chances of survival (Wickler and Seibt, 1977, p. 150).

Thus, Lorenz's conjecture that predators have considerable difficulty in singling out prey from a dense and hastily moving crowd is well founded. Yet, it seems that he himself is not quite satisfied with this explanation. And indeed, as we shall see, it is only part of the answer to the question of why animals form herds.

For sociobiology, a behaviour pattern as common as the formation of herds, flocks, or schools evidently deserves attention. In the above-mentioned standard work of E. O. Wilson one can find a lot of pertinent material. The author is an entomologist, fascinated especially by the social insects, and he began to search for comparable phenomena in other animal species to understand better the mechanisms of evolution of social behaviour. His voluminous publication was a landmark in the establishment of sociobiology as a discipline in its own right.

Wilson has studied an immense amount of literature. The

3

bibliography of his main work comprises no less than 65 very large pages and contains more than 2500 references. Evidently he tried to collect as much material as possible and to arrange it in a systematic way. This alone was a very useful contribution, highly valued even by biologists who do not share all of his views. For it turns out that many questions more or less answer themselves if one merely collects all the available evidence.

The reasons for sham attacks on falcons, for instance, are more substantial than the mere inability of the predator to concentrate on one victim within a flock. Already in 1951 Nicolas Tinbergen, the Dutch ethologist who received the Nobel prize in 1973 together with Konrad Lorenz and Karl von Frisch, had given a much more precise answer. A falcon normally takes prey stooping at great speed, and only its talons are constructed for such a harsh collision. If he would try to catch his victim out of a large flock he would risk colliding with other birds and fracture his own bones. It seems that starlings 'know' about that. When above a hawk – and hence out of danger – they fly in lose formation, but they draw together into a tight flock when they are below the enemy (see also Mohr, 1960).

A further advantage of the group is that the common attention of its members is much more efficient in detecting predators than the efforts of a solitary animal. Observations of many species have shown that a predator may successfully stalk an isolated animal, but hardly ever a group (Wilson, 1975, p. 38). Even in a species as mighty as the lion which joins in groups mainly for better hunting success and for warding-off 'thieves' like jackals, hyenas or vultures from the prey, the community provides better protection for the cubs against leopards than a solitary mother could give (Schaller, 1972).

The presence of mates gives all group members the opportunity to relax a bit from their guarding against predators, and increases their efficiency in other activities. Observations of wood-pigeons have shown that the birds collect food at a lower rate when alone than when in flocks, because they spend more time looking around (Murton, 1968).

Whilst Lorenz assumes that a big herd might be easier detected by a predator than a solitary animal or a small group, Wilson holds to the contrary. According to his guess the average distance between the schools increases when the prey population coalesces into larger and larger schools; hence there is a corresponding decrease in the frequency of detection by a randomly moving predator. A problem like this can be formulated in a mathematical way. V. E. Brock and R. H. Riffenburgh (1960) using a computer model have formally proved that Wilson's assumption is correct for schools of fish as well as for flocks of birds or herds of land animals – unless one makes some additional assumptions, e.g. regular use of migratory paths known to the predators.

In any case a predator, or even a pack of predators, cannot consume at once more than a certain fixed amount of prey, and if a group consists of many more individuals their sheer numbers over-saturate the predators and provide good chances of survival for at least the vast majority of the group members. Thus, as long as the individual manages to stay amidst its mates and can avoid being isolated it is fairly safe. In this way the elementary instinctive impulse to be in the middle of the herd is easily explained.

Even the assumption – plausible at a first glance – that it must be easier for a solitary animal to find sufficient food than for a large group is not correct in many cases – especially if the food is distributed patchily or concentrated at certain places. A starling or a baboon following his group utilizes the accumulated knowledge of the most experienced group members who know where to find food in harsh times, and how to get there safely (Kummer, 1968; Hamilton and Gilbert, 1969).

The possibility of mutual grooming is another important advantage when forming groups. If one wanders about in the jungle one neccessarily collects ticks, writes the German ethologist Hubert Markl (1971). Whoever has removed the impressive collections of these irritating blood-suckers after a day spent in a tropical forest will be able to appreciate the importance of social grooming for monkeys and apes.

As for their social structure, the diverse groups of animals mentioned in this chapter are very different and in no way comparable. A fish school is what Lorenz calls an 'anonymous crowd', a conglomeration of hundreds, thousands, or even millions of individuals of approximately the same age and with no observable social organization at all. It seems to be mere chance who swims in front, and if the school changes direction the individuals formerly at the flank assume the lead (Wilson, 1975, p. 439); whereas in a herd of sheep there are certain animals, well known to the shepherd, that always are in the front row. Even more conspicuous is the strict social structure in a troop of baboons – one of the most highly organized communities within the whole animal kingdom. Yet it holds true for all these species that belonging to a group confers advantage to *all* group members.

All this, of course, does not 'prove' that Lorenz' objections against the formation of groups are completely unfounded. Actually the formation of herds, flocks or schools is *but one* of several strategies available to animals liable to be hunted by predators. Other species evolved according to other strategies (camouflage, large number of offspring, etc.) which are successful as well. Nevertheless it must be explained how an instinct manifested as strongly as the herding instinct of sheep and many other animals did *evolve*.

An animal trying hard to be in the middle of the herd has the best chances of survival; and the costs of such a behaviour are rather small compared to its benefits. One of the basic concepts of sociobiology is that such a behaviour pattern – or the ability to learn it quickly and easily – is, at least in part, *influenced by inborn (genetic) dispositions*. The individual keeping successfully its place in the centre of the herd (flock, school) evidently has a better chance to bestow this hereditary disposition on following generations than an animal not conforming to this behaviour pattern; the latter probably would soon be a victim of predators – maybe before it had any chance of procreation. Thus natural selection will favour animals with a strong inborn tendency (an instinct) to crowd in herds – or, for that matter, to perform any other successful behaviour pattern. Hence the instinct will get stronger within the species as long as there are no countervailing selective pressures, for instance increased vulnerability to epidemics in large herds.

1.2 *How does a cuckoo know it is a cuckoo?*

'Are you really sure that the herding instinct is *inborn* in sheep? Might it not be that young lambs *learn* it by imitating the adults?' The question came from a friend, a young physicist, when I told him about my intention to write this book.

'You are quite right,' I replied. 'As a rule behaviour is the result of a combination of learnt and inborn factors. However it certainly is *possible* that rather complicated behaviour patterns are inherited.'

'Inherited like blue eyes?' The question sounded rather incredulous.

'Well, not quite like blue eyes. Presumably behaviour patterns are influenced, as a rule, not just by a single gene but by the combined effect of a number of genes. Nevertheless, how does a cuckoo know that he is a cuckoo?'

'And how do you know he does?' Evidently my friend had not understood the meaning of my question.

The cuckoo, I continued, is something like an experiment of nature. It is brought up by foster parents. In its childhood it might never have seen another cuckoo, and when it hears one the call is just a background noise like the song of other birds. But when grown up it will be able to utter just that particular characteristic call though it certainly did not learn this in the nest where it was reared. The cuckoo does not 'assume' that it is a song bird like its foster parents, but mates with another cuckoo brought up like itself in the nest of another species.

As far as I could find out nobody seems to be sure of whether the cuckoo knows its characteristic call quite 'by itself' or whether it must hear the call beforehand. But at least it must be inborn to answer *just this call* and no other. And the young female cuckoo that never knew her mother and had no chance to learn something from her by imitation 'knows' by instinct that she must observe the nest of some small bird and wait for a moment when it is not guarded to put her egg with the others. A complicated repertoire of behaviour patterns must be inborn in this case.

Actually all this is not at all unique, although one might think so at the first glance. Amongst birds needing considerable parental care the cuckoo is an exception. There are however very many species of insects, fish, reptiles and other animals which just lay their eggs somewhere and leave them. The young animals never know their parents. A water turtle digs a hole with great effort in the sand of beaches, puts in a few dozen eggs, covers them with sand again and leaves the rest of the job to the sun. When the youngs are hatching they 'know' that they are not supposed to crawl subterraneously like a mole or an earthworm, but that they must get out of the sand to the surface and then into the water as quickly as possible. They 'know' more or less what they are supposed to feed on though there may be some learning processes as well. When they are grown up they find a mate of their own species and the females 'know' that they have to hide their eggs in the sand of beaches, as did their mothers they never knew.

Thus all species with no parental care – and that is the great majority of all animals – must have a certain basic repertoire of inborn behaviour patterns. But such inborn behaviour is rigid, and the possibilities to learn by experience are limited. Animals growing up with their mother or within a larger community can learn by imitation or they can purposely be *taught* by their mother and others. In this way a much larger and more flexible behavioural repertoire can be learned enabling an individual to react differently in different or changing situations. Yet, even the most intelligent species right up to man do have behaviour patterns that are carried out, as it were, instinctively, *even if they are evidently irrational.*

This again is an assertion which my young friend rejects at first. I could tell him that the description of shockingly irrational 'instinctive' behaviour of lovers has been one of the standard themes of world literature for millennia. However, since he is a scientist, I rather propose to him a simple experiment: 'Invite somebody to go with you by car and drive slowly on a path where twigs are hanging down touching the wind-screen. You will notice that the person sitting at your side - and maybe yourself too, in spite of having been told beforehand – will instinctively lower the head, close the eyes or make some evading movements when approaching a twig – in spite of the fact that both of you know very well that you are protected by the wind-screen.'

I know this from personal experience, since we must use such a path to reach our weekend house. My wife and I laughed at ourselves more than once when we made such involuntary evading movements. And once, while my wife was sitting at the wheel, I resolved that as a rational being I ought to be able to suppress this 'ridiculous' evading behaviour. I found that to do so required much more concentration and effort than I had expected. As soon as my wife started talking to me, distracting me from the self-imposed task, I noticed that I relapsed into those silly, instinctive, evading motions.

Of course one can suppress such a habit by systematic training after one has recognized it and laughed about it. Today my wife and I no longer make bows before every twig when driving to our weekend house. Instincts are not *absolute* rulers of our behaviour. Their influence can be constrained – to some extent – by reason, training, and experience.

Animals, too, can be trained – within limits – to behave in ways not corresponding to their instincts. The shepherd's dog controls my son's herd by using what might be called 'limited aggression', but he has been taught that he must not treat his sheep as prey. Other dogs without such a training do not have similar inhibitions; they will gladly kill a lamb and devour it if they have the chance.

The higher the position of an animal on the ladder of evolution the more flexible is its behaviour. It is however a basic notion of modern ethology that there are inborn *tendencies* in every animal to behave in certain ways characteristic for its species. Owing to these inborn inclinations *it can learn certain things very easily and others only with great difficulty or not at all.* There is no reason to believe that man is an exception to this general rule (Maynard Smith, 1978*a*).

As a rule inborn as well as acquired factors contribute to the individual development of behaviour, forming, as it were, a new synthesis. According to the English ethologist Patrick Bateson, director of the Department of Animal Behaviour at the University of Cambridge, behavioural development may be compared with the baking of a cake. 'The flour, the eggs, the butter, and all the rest react together to form a product that is different from the sum of the parts', he writes (1976, p.11). 'The actions of adding ingredients, preparing the mixture, and baking all contribute to the final effect. The point is, that it would be nonsensical to expect anyone to recognize each of the ingredients and each of the actions involved in cooking as separate components of the finished cake.'

But, to stick to the metaphor, this does not exclude that *when comparing two cakes* one might be able to tell that the difference in taste is mainly, or even entirely due to the presence or absence of one particular spice – or, in another case, to the difference in preparing and baking the same ingredients. Similarly when comparing behavioural development in different species one can find striking differences in how inborn and acquired factors interact

9

to form what seem to be rather similar and comparable behaviour patterns.

While animals without parental care, and also the cuckoo, need to have an inborn ability to recognize a conspecific when looking for a mating partner, others must *learn* to which species they belong. Geese and some other birds are 'imprinted'. The young gosling will follow the first moving object it sees in the first hours after hatching. As a rule this is the mother goose, but if it is a man, it will follow him on land – and in water, if the man should be swimming. Such a young goose apparently 'thinks' that it is a man itself, and later has considerable difficulty in integrating into goose society and finding a conspecific mate.

A gosling imprinted on humans will refuse to follow a goose even if it sees one later on. But immediately after hatching it will not be able to differentiate between a small slender girl and a big old man with a beard. Two days later it has learned to recognize its parents personally and, under natural conditions, will follow only them and never mistake another pair of geese for them, even if they are leading a flock of young of the same age (Lorenz, 1965, p. 57).

Genetically the goose is pre-programmed to learn something very special at a certain point in its development. Imprinting is an extreme case of such pre-programmed learning, but it is a rather general rule that an animal can learn certain things in a certain age period much easier than before or later. Pedagogues know very well that such periods of specific learning ability for certain tasks exist in man too.

Not only the cuckoo but also many birds growing up 'normally' with their parents have an inborn ability to utter their species-specific calls or songs. The chaffinch, on the other hand, must *learn* it from older conspecifics. When reared in isolation it only achieves an inarticulate stammering. However *it can only learn the song of its own species* and nothing else, whilst a parrot or a starling can imitate calls of other species and even human language. They have an inborn talent of imitation which the chaffinch has not.

What an animal can learn is not only a question of intelligence but also dependent on many other genetic (inborn) preconditions. A badger is by no means silly, but lives an extremely solitary life; and *for this reason* it cannot be trained like a dog. It is impossible to teach a badger that it must not nibble at the chair legs. If one tries to educate the animal and to punish it somehow when it does things it ought not to do, it either will react aggressively – or it will become shy and withdraw completely (Eibl-Eibesfeldt, 1950).

Only animals that under natural conditions live in a social group – or domesticated animals descended from such species – are prepared to accept a human being, as it were, as a substitute mate and to subordinate to him as to a high-ranking dominant animal of their own species. The *ability* for such a subordination is not learned and, as shown in the case of the badger, it cannot be learned by certain species. It is inborn in socially living animals.

Yet if there are inborn instinctive behaviour patterns and inborn abilities to learn certain things easily and others only with great difficulty or not at all, there must be genes triggering or influencing such behaviour. But how does such a gene work? How is it possible to hand on 'prescriptions' for certain behaviour patterns in the hereditary process?

1.3 *What indeed is a gene?*

The word gene as denomination for the smallest unit of hereditary information was coined by the Danish scientist Wilhelm Johannsen, famous for his experiments with beans which made scientific history. Beans are strict 'self-pollinators': they are fertilized by the pollen of their own blossom. Thus every bean plant is, as it were, father as well as mother of all its daughter beans. Hence all the beans harvested from one and the same plant carry the same hereditary dispositions (the same genes). Differences in size or weight of particular beans must therefore be caused exclusively by environmental influences like the position of the bean in the husk, the position of the husk on the plant, the age of the husk, the amount of solar radiation received, etc.

In his experiments carried out at the beginning of this century Johannson wanted to find out whether such differences in size caused by environmental influences could be inherited. He took some of the biggest and some of the smallest beans of several plants separately, planted them to raise new plants and repeated this for several generations. It turned out that it was *not* possible in this way to breed varieties with different bean size; or, to put it in a more general way, *acquired traits are not inherited.* The genes of all beans coming from one plant are identical. They determine a certain *bandwidth* of size within which the single beans can develop according to the environmental conditions. But *only the genes* are inherited and not the final make-up of an individual (the so-called 'phenotype') – in our case the size of the bean – which is determined by an interplay of hereditary and environmental influences.

Later scientists have deduced that the genes of the hereditary substance can code for the production of enzymes, i.e. for proteins mediating (catalysing) biochemical reactions. In the forties and fifties it was discovered that a substance called deoxyribonucleic acid (DNA) is the carrier of the hereditary information. The chemical structure of this substance has been eludicated and today it is known in which way the information encoded in it is transferred into enzymes. It turns out, however, that only about 20% of the DNA of a higher organism – the so-called 'structural genes' – contains information for the production of enzymes and a few other body proteins. The rest seem to be genes with regulatory functions, about which not much is known.

According to E. O. Wilson (1978*a*, p. 53) human hereditary information consists of about 250 000 genes of which about 50 000 are recipes for the production of enzymes. As already mentioned the vast majority of these enzymes – in fact 99% of them – and with them our biochemical make-up are identical with those of the chimpanzee (Ayala, 1980). Thus one must assume that the existing differences of certainly more than marginal importance must be due to regulatory genes.

One of the most important tasks of these is the steering of embryonic development. A fertilized egg divides into two cells which seem to be alike (otherwise there could not be identical twins). These cells divide again according to a certain 'blueprint' evidently encoded in the hereditary information, and gradually start to 'differentiate'. Some become nerve cells, others muscle, bones, skin, etc. Since every cell of an organism (with some exceptions not relevant for us here) has received the full set of hereditary information it must be the action of the regulating genes to ensure that the right recipes in the single cell are switched on and off at the right time according to the blueprint. How this is achieved is not yet known in detail in spite of a century of intensive research.

In this book we are interested mainly in genes influencing behaviour, and most of these are probably regulatory genes. The ability to produce a certain enzyme or hormone in sufficient quantities might be a necessity, but surely cannot be a sufficient condition for a particular behaviour. The inborn behaviour of the cuckoo described in the previous section or the inborn capacity of man to learn languages and to think in linguistic terms are made possible first of all by a certain kind of 'wiring' in particular regions of the central nervous system. Inheritance of behavioural tendencies is mainly the inheritance of blueprints for particular regions of the brain.

DNA, the hereditary substance, consists of very long thread-like molecules twined into a double helix by a particular kind of chemical bonding. In the process of cell division and multiplication the two strands of the double helix separate and each of them can, owing to its chemical properties, serve as a template for the formation of the complementary strand.

Usually dispersed in the cell nucleus, the DNA before cell division forms characteristic bodies called 'chromosomes' with a typical number and shape for every species. Man has 46 chromosomes, or rather 23 pairs, each pair being different in length and shape from all the other chromosome pairs. In a normal cell division all chromosomes are cleft through their whole length, with one half of every chromosome going to each of the daughter cells. The formation of germ cells is preceded by a special division process leading to the formation of egg cells or sperm cells carrying only half a set (a 'haploid' set) of chromosomes – in man, one chromosome each of the 23 pairs.

Thus an egg cell, after having been fertilized by a sperm cell, contains again a full ('diploid') set of chromosomes of which one of each pair comes from the mother, the other from the father. In normal cell divisions, creating somatic cells, every one of these chromosomes is copied and the resultant replicas go into the new cell. Before the formation of germ cells, however, maternal and paternal chromosomes of each pair come to lie in close apposition and exchange material, i.e. genes. In this way traits inherited from the two parents are shuffled like a stack of cards forming new combinations which are different in any one of the germ cells.

Children inherit exactly half of their genes from each of their parents or, to put it in another way, one half from their paternal grandparents and the other half from their maternal grandparents. Yet in the process of 'reshuffling the cards' it may happen that a certain germ cell received more genes from a grandfather and less from a grandmother or vice versa. Hence an individual might have inherited 30% of its genes from the paternal grandfather and only 20% from the paternal grandmother; whereas the individual might have received, say, 22% from the maternal grandfather and 28% from the maternal grandmother. Only when considering *an average of many grandchildren* does each one of the grandparents contribute 25% of his or her genes to the gene pool of the second following generation.

A considerable part of the genes are identical in all members of a particular species; they are a precondition for the existence of a being of that species. In man this applies to about 60% of the structural genes (enzyme recipes) and probably to a still higher percentage of regulatory genes. For the remaining 'gene-loci' there exist two or more different genes which are in competition within the species. Inherited individual differences can be due only to these genes (This paragraph is not in contradiction with the earlier statement that we share 99% of our structural genes with the chimpanzee. In many cases we have the same variable genes as the chimps.)

A few thousand of such variable genes allow more possible combinations than there are atoms in the universe (Dobzhansky, 1972, p. 62). Hence it is extremely improbable that two individuals, except identical twins, should have exactly the same hereditary dispositions. On the other hand it is equally improbable that two members of the same species, and hence the two parents of an individual, should not have at least a certain number of genes in common which are variable within the species. Disregarding this, and considering only the fact that in normal sexual propagation an individual gets half its genes from the mother and the other half from the father, one can state that two full siblings have an average of 50% of their genes in common *by descent* (with a certain amount of variation due to different effects of the 'shuffling of cards'), two half-sibs 25%, two first cousins 12.5% (one-eighth), etc. The real number of variable genes which two kin have in common is, of course, higher and all the more so the more genes the parents or grand-

14

parents had in common. In closed small populations where practically all individuals are cross-related to each other in some way (as for instance on a remote island), the number of these genes shared due to inbreeding effects is certainly higher than in a large population with considerable mixing. Children of a marriage of two cousins share many more genes with their parents and their sibs than others do.

Since there is no inheritance of acquired traits, changes giving rise to new evolutionary developments can only come about by 'chance' changes (mutations) of the DNA. I put the word 'chance' in quotation marks since mutations are infrequent but regular events subject to statistical laws of probability. They are only chance for the particular individual affected by them. The geneticist is in a similar position to the physicist who cannot predict when a *particular* atom of a radioactive substance will decay, though he can predict very exactly what percentage of the atoms of that substance will decay within a given period. In the same way one can predict with high confidence that a certain number of newborns within a certain (large) population will carry a particular mutation, though one cannot tell who will be affected.

Mutations come about as a consequence of faults in DNA copying and in other processes during cell division. Their frequency is drastically increased by the presence of certain chemicals or by the effects of radiation (ultra-violet, X-rays, radioactivity, etc.). Since every organism on earth is exposed to a certain amount of natural 'background radiation' from cosmic rays and from natural radioactive elements contained in the earth's crust this alone causes a certain mutation rate under natural conditions. By exposing an organism to increased radiation or to mutagenic substances one can increase the general mutation rate, but one cannot produce with such methods certain particular mutations at will. Techniques of genetic manipulation to introduce a particular gene into a certain organism are now being developed.

A mutation might merely change a 'word' in the recipe for an enzyme to another 'word' with the same 'meaning' without altering the gene product. Others cause insignificant changes hardly impeding the enzyme activity. There are, however, certain mutations which make an enzyme completely ineffective or strongly reduce its activity.

15

A mutation impeding the activity of a vital gene can cause death – in many cases before birth – or a grave hereditary disease. On the other hand carriers of some mutations can coexist within a species with practically equal vitality – as men with blue or with brown eyes. In between there are mutations reducing vitality a little but not decisively, and others facilitating adaptation to certain environmental conditions but causing difficulties in others.

Not much is known about how mutations affect regulatory genes. One can assume that certain mutations cause changes in inborn behaviour patterns. Such changes might have a positive or negative effect on life-expectancy, or on the chance of finding a proper mate, or of raising offspring successfully. A female cuckoo with a behavioural mutation might, for instance, survive herself but not be able to drop her eggs in the nest of another bird at the right moment and hence will have no progeny. The mutated gene is not handed over to the next generation. It dies out immediately.

Presumably not only one gene is required for the inheritance of a complicated inborn behaviour pattern but something like several dozen or even hundreds of regulatory genes, and perhaps a few structural genes too. A mutation of only one of these genes might cause only a slight change and not a complete loss of an important behaviour. Moreover, since most behaviour patterns develop from the combined effects of inborn tendencies and environmentally influenced learning processes, animals, especially higher animals, may dispose of a considerable bandwidth of individual and intraspecific variations of possible behaviour, facilitating a quick adaptation to changing environmental conditions.

1.4 *Geese after all are only human*

According to the traditional view a proper greylag goose is a strictly monogamous animal supposed to live in absolute matrimonial fidelity even beyond the death of the spouse. Yet, when Konrad Lorenz and his collaborators started observing this species under natural conditions over long periods it turned out that this supposedly 'normal case' is not at all as common as had been assumed. Young geese are sexually mature in their second year of life. If they mate at that time and provided that neither of the partners is caught by a fox, infected by worms, thrown against a telegraph wire by the wind or separated from the spouse in any other way, the two birds will in most cases indeed remain together for all their life lasting about fifty years. But the *average* life expectancy of a greylag goose is much lower. Often one of the partners is killed prematurely. The surviving spouse mourns for the lost consort for many months and a female goose sometimes never mates again – though this is *not* the rule. A widowed gander, however, never mourns longer than a year; then he looks for a new spouse. In such a second or third marriage morals are much looser, and there are often 'escapades' and 'divorces' (Lorenz, 1963/66, p. 182 *et seq.*).

To find out these facts many years of observation were required. And once, when studying observation portocols, Lorenz showed himself rather disappointed that his geese in many instances did not behave as he had expected. His collaborator Helga Fischer found this rather exasperating. 'What do you expect', she told him. 'After all, geese are only human!' (*ibid.*, p. 195).

Deviations from monogamy are found *not only* in widowed geese or ganders. Sometimes two young males form, as it were, a 'homosexual' pair, but with neither of them playing the role of the female. Each of them considers the other to be his 'wife'. This is all the more possible since male and female geese look very much alike. Copulation attempts are soon abandoned in such 'homosexual' pairs, yet the personal bond remains. Sometimes a young female is able to insinuate herself into such a male pair at the right moment and this might be the beginning of a trio – in the end it can turn out that both ganders eventually copulate and raise offspring with her.

Thus reality is much more diversified than the stereotyped picture of the strictly monogamous greylag goose. Nevertheless Lorenz considers it justifiable to call monogamy the *typical* behaviour of the species. 'By normal', he writes (*ibid.*, p. 194), 'we understand not the average taken from all the single cases observed, but rather the *type* constructed by evolution, which for obvious reasons is seldom to be found in a pure form.'

There are reasonable arguments for defining the 'typical' in this way, but when doing so it need not necessarily coincide with the 'normal'. If most greylag geese fail to reach the age of 50 years and perish long beforehand; if therefore in a normal goose population there is a considerable percentage or even a majority of animals that have lost a partner; and if such animals *generally* behave differently from those whose first marriage still survives, their behaviour too must be considered as a typical feature in the total behavioural array of the species.

That all geese do not behave in the same way in similar situations does not facilitate the work of the behavioural scientist, but it makes it all the more interesting. The comprehensive picture emerging from these observations does in no way support the idea that greylag geese can do absolutely 'anything'. Rather they have a certain repertoire of different *more or less* typical behaviour patterns, amongst them a 'typical' repeatedly observed *deviant* pattern of the 'homosexual' gander pairs which sometimes, but by no means always, develop into trios. Which of the (more or less) typical behaviour patterns is chosen by a particular animal in particular circumstances seems to depend largely on the experiences of his previous life. On the other hand one could imagine – though this has not been proved – that certain genetic dispositions as well might contribute to some behaviour patterns like those of the 'homosexual' ganders.

Diversity of possible behaviour is of course not restricted to greylag geese only. And especially the claim that a species is monogamous should be taken with a grain of salt. In most bird species so-classified, some males can be found that have two or sometimes more females at the same time, according to the ethologists Mike Baker and Peter Marler (1980). Widowed females in particular are often cared for by neighbouring males who already have wives. On the other hand 'adultery' has been proved for females of species with harem-forming males. When males of redwing blackbirds were experimentally vasectomized, nearly half of their wives had fertilized clutches nevertheless, evidently having been fathered by another male (Bray *et al.*, 1975; see also Tannenbaum, 1975, for similar experiments with bats).

Not only mating behaviour shows individual differences. In my son's herd of sheep there are *always the same* animals well known to him that are in the first row and follow him when he goes in front. There are others, but again always the same ones, that find new small paths hitherto not used by the herd.

The American ethologist Dian Fossey who first worked with the palaeo-anthropologist Louis Leakey and then, on his advice, started studying gorillas reports that she often observed a certain gorilla troop without any difficulty. They had accepted her presence without any sign of being disturbed. When the dominant male of the group died and another one took over the command, the behaviour of the whole troop changed. Now, on Fossey's approach the apes started chest beating, whacking of foliage, hiding, and showed other signs of alarm. Eventually the troop retreated into a remote area higher up in the mountains (Fossey, 1972, quoted by Wilson, 1975, p. 538).

A similarly large bandwidth of behaviour has been found in chimpanzees, by Jane Goodall in particular, who had already earned her credentials as an ethologist as a small girl when once she hid in the hen-house for hours to see how a hen laid an egg. To study wild animals in Africa had been the great dream of her youth, and when there was a chance for her to go to Kenya she resigned an interesting secretarial job and spent the summer as a waitress on the English south coast to earn her fare. In Kenya she met Leakey who immediately offered the girl without a formal scientific education a job as an assistant/secretary (Goodall, 1971, p. 17–18).

In Leakey's view the study of apes could provide new insights into the evolution of our ancestors. This had led him to direct Dian Fossey to gorillas and for the same reason he suggested to Jane Goodall that she should study chimpanzees in the field in what is now the Gombe National Park in Tanzania. For Jane this was the fulfilment of her great dream. It took months before the chimps accepted her presence, but her patience and perseverance bore ample fruits. Today the girl without a formal scientific education is a world-renowned scientist whose works we shall quote many times. Her fascinating book *In the Shadow of Man* (1971) is a veritable gold-mine of thorough observation, and throughout this work one finds examples showing that every chimp is a personality on its own with its individual traits that distinguish it from its conspecifics.

When a species is observed for hundreds or thousands of hours it becomes clear that its behaviour patterns are much more diversified than can be noted from occasional encounters. Thus former apparently contradictory reports might easily turn out to be two sides of the same coin. One and the same animal might behave differently in seemingly similar situations – for reasons not always obvious to a human observer. All the more, different individuals of

19

the same species and even the same group can have their own 'personal' traits and idiosyncrasies – and only part of such differences can be explained by different rank within the group.

Similarly, different troops of the same species often show marked differences of behaviour. 'Today we know that general statements how "the" hamadryas baboons behave are often not quite correct', Hans Kummer told me, who together with his collaborators has been studying these animals in the field since 1960. 'Rather one should say that a certain behaviour pattern was customary in a certain troop at a certain period of time.'

Looking for the typical nevertheless remains a basic job of ethology. But it must be supplemented by the notion that the most typical for all higher animals consists of variations in possible behaviour patterns with a considerable bandwidth.

1.5 *Natural selection*

The trees of a forest belonging to the same species seem to be all alike – disregarding differences of age. Yet every one of them has its own 'personality' with its individual hereditary characteristics: a combination of genes that is different from those of all other trees. As a rule these differences are insignificant and have no bearing on the survival chances of the tree. Given a fairly stable environment we can assume that nearly all the trees of a forest are well adapted to their 'ecological niche'. To be more exact: they are well adapted to the *bandwidth* of normal oscillation in environmental conditions typical for the respective region.

Every year a big tree produces many thousands of seeds. In its whole life the number may run into millions. Yet in stable conditions an average of only one of these many seeds will become a new tree. It would, however, be a mistake to consider this as an example of what is called 'the survival of the fittest'. The new tree is again a personality with its own individual traits. It has a new combination of genes which are variable within the species. Yet again this will cause only insignificant differences.

Amongst the millions of seeds perishing in a forest a small percentage probably had some disadvantageous gene combinations detrimental to survival. But the great majority of them could have become trees just as vital and well adapted to their environment

20

as those few which actually did survive. This can be seen whenever a fire, a storm, a landslide or something else destroys a part of the forest. Then many seeds of the trees in the vicinity, perhaps a few dozen or even a few hundred – and not just an average of one seed per tree – can become new trees. This, by the way, is one of the reasons why the tree produces more seeds than would 'normally' be required for maintaining the stock. The other reason is that a large number of perfectly vital seeds end up in some place where they cannot grow, are eaten by animals, or become victim of some other chance event which may have nothing to do with their hereditary dispositions.

A tree does not 'know' how many seeds it must produce in order that an average of one may survive. It can use more energy and raw materials for its own growth to be better able to compete with other trees of its own and other species – taking the risk that it might not have enough energy and raw materials left to produce enough seeds for colonizing available new land if there is a chance. Or it might invest heavily in seed production – with the risk that it might not have enough strength for direct competition with other rival trees. In real life it must achieve some sort of dynamic equilibrium: a compromise for the best possible simultaneous solution of several problems posing different and even conflicting tasks. And the species must reach a *bandwidth* of solutions successful within the bandwidth of 'normal' oscillations of environmental conditions.

A plant might reduce the number of its seeds and instead use some of its energy and raw materials to protect them with a hard or prickly shell. An animal can produce very many offspring and not care for them any further like a herring, or it can 'invest' less in the production of offspring and more in the care and protection of its brood as many birds and mammals do. But in all species, even in those with relatively few offspring and much parental care *considerably more* progeny is produced than could possibly survive under stable conditions.

Amongst the hundred millions of seeds of a certain species in a particular forest there probably will not be two with exactly the same hereditary characteristics. Assuming that a tree species has only 50 variable genes with two possibilities each – actually there are many more – there are no less than 2^{50}, i.e. about a thousand billion (10^{15}) possible combinations. Such a large variety is the precondition for natural selection to become effective as soon as environmental conditions change beyond the 'normal' bandwidth of variations.

Our forest might be situated on the slope of a mountain. Then some of the seeds will be transported to higher regions by the wind and by animals. Amongst those seeds some will be better adapted to the harsher part of the original bandwidth than others. Owing to their hereditary characteristics they will be able to thrive easier in higher regions than others. By cross-fertilization and mutation the characteristics of their progeny will change in a way which would be deleterious in the original (low) habitat but which is of advantage in the higher regions. Thus the seeds will proceed higher and higher and eventually a new alpine species or sub-species will evolve.

The same sort of process might happen when environmental conditions change on the spot of the original habitat. Some of the progeny of the original population might be selected in such a way that they can thrive under the newly prevailing conditions. Others might shift their habitat – if possible – to new regions where environmental conditions are now as they used to be in the original habitat in earlier times.

Metaphorically speaking, every organism exists on such 'mountain slopes'. There is no environment without neighbouring enviroments with slightly different conditions where individuals with slightly changed gene combinations will thrive better. Nor is there an environment that would not change sooner or later, demanding a selection of new traits better fitting the new conditions. Biologists call such processes 'adaptation', but this does not mean an intentional and directed activity of the animals or plants concerned. It is a process of *selection* of the progeny with the most appropriate genes, taking place in the course of a competition going on within the species – a competition *in which only a few can survive anyway*.

As a rule the object of selection is not a group or a family but an individual with all its inherited *and acquired* traits. But only the inherited traits can be passed on to the next generation and hence be selected. Well-trained muscles might well increase the survival chances of an animal and/or its chances of producing a large progeny. Yet these descendants will not have an inborn

22

disposition for stronger muscles than their conspecifics. They must train themselves if they want to succeed as well as their ancestors.

Genes influencing behaviour are subject to natural selection just the same as all others. If in the aforementioned example some members of a species have an inborn tendency to train their muscles particularly well already in infant play, natural selection might favour such a tendency – provided it does not bring other disadvantages. But behaviour can be selected on a non-inherited basis too, as long as an animal has a general (inborn) capacity to learn by imitation. In such cases there might be a seeming 'inheritance' of acquired traits though it really is a kind of 'cultural' transmission.

For a problem posed by a certain kind of environment there is often more than one viable solution. Thus not *all* differences among closely related species can be explained by their adaptive value in their respective environments. If there are, on an island, snails with clockwise turning shells, whereas on a neighbouring island they have shells turning anti-clockwise, this is a *chance* phenomenon having nothing to do with different survival rates for differently winding shells in different external circumstances. Similarily it is *not* due to differences in local conditions that the Indian rhino has only one horn, whereas its African counterpart has two (Lewontin, 1978). It could just as well be the other way round or both species could have the same number of horns. Even less can all variations of behaviour be interpreted as being necessarily of adaptive value. It makes sense that closely related bird species sometimes have strongly contrasting song patterns, for this is an additional barrier against inter-specific cross-breeding. But it would be absurd to assume that the melody of the one species is more adaptive for its habitat, say, a coniferous forest, than the melody of the other species which in turn would 'fit' better in a mixed forest.

There are many mutations of bodily traits and of inborn behavioural tendencies that cannot be classified in a simple way as being either 'advantageous' or 'detrimental'. In a certain environment there might be very different and even contradictory demands and there is no benefit without costs. A gene for strong muscles appears to be very advantageous at first glance, but it goes along with higher food consumption rates and might be detrimental in times of want. Very strong muscles are only 'profitable' when used often or when

23

they can drastically increase survival chances in perilous situations. The advantages of the herding instinct have been described in the first chapter – but the disadvantage, that large conglomerations enhance the spread of diseases, should not be disregarded.

Even hereditary diseases can have their advantages as shown by the example of sickle cell anemia. Caused by a mutation in the gene coding for haemoglobin, the red substance of the blood, it leads to a degeneration of the red blood corpuscles which assume sickle shape and lose much of their normal capacity to transport oxygen. One would assume that such a gene would be quickly eliminated by natural selection and hence would only appear at a frequency corresponding to the rate of new mutations. Actually sickle cell anemia is rather frequent amongst negroes and with good reason too: the gene causing the disease confers immunity against malaria. Where malaria has been eradicated the frequency of sickle cell anemia is soon reduced. Where normally malaria has not been known, sickle cell anemia is a very rare disease.

Presumably there might be similar phenomena in genes influencing behaviour (or maybe influencing behaviour *as well* as bodily traits). This is all the more likely since complicated behaviour patterns require a proper interplay of *many* genes which singly or in other combinations might have detrimental effects as well.

In a general way it is very easy to state which kind of behaviour will be favoured by natural selection: a premium will be put on any behaviour that increases the survival chances of the individual; the chances of finding a proper mate, of producing a large number of offspring; and, last but not least, the survival chances of the progeny. However, these demands might to some extent be conflicting, and every species and every individual must work out its own compromise for them.

Male courtship behaviour is intended to attract females – but it might attract predators as well. A large number of offspring seem to be advantageous – but too many of them might reduce the chance of effective parental care. Defending the brood makes sense if there is a reasonable chance to drive off the predator. If not, parents should save themselves and try to start raising a new brood rather than sacrifice themselves in vain.

That an inborn tendency for parental care has been favoured by natural selection in many species is easy to understand. Parents

24

lacking this tendency have less surviving progeny, hence genes inducing them to neglect progeny will be gradually eliminated. But why are there tendencies to behave in a seemingly unselfish way not only towards one's own offspring, but also towards other individuals as well?

Why does a worker bee sacrifice its life to defend a nest not containing its own brood? Why do young baboon males help to defend their troop though they presumably do not yet have their own progeny? Why do nursing elephant cows permit any calf of the herd to suckle from their teats and not only their own young? Why do fighting stags usually comply with the 'rules of the game' which prevent serious injury of the combatants?

All these are difficult questions for evolutionary theory. To look for answers is one of the main problems of sociobiology.

1.6 Are animals better than man?

Animals fight to gain mates, dominance rights, or the possession of a territory (needed for breeding), and all this is of vital importance to them. Nevertheless many of these combats are of the ritualized limited-fight type rather than in the style of a struggle for life or death (Maynard Smith and Price, 1973). Male rattlesnakes wrestle by intertwining their necks without using their fangs. Mantis shrimps hammer at the armoured tail segments of their opponents without harming the unprotected soft parts of their bodies (Wilson, 1975, pp. 128, 243). American honey-pot ants with their particularly vulnerable abdomens have veritable tournaments. Inhabitants of different nests march side by side in a characteristic stilting gait, drumming with their antennae on the abdomen of the adversary but without hurting it. Such tournaments might last for several days with many animals of both nests taking part. In such fights the frontiers of the respective foraging territories of the nests are fixed (Hölldobler, 1976).

In many species opponents start a conflict by a mere 'verbal dispute', supplemented by a display of imposing or threatening gestures. The end may be that one of the adversaries gives way – realizing either that he would not have much chance in a fight or that the risk would not be worthwhile. Stags seem to use roaring as a cue to the fighting ability of the opponent. To roar properly demands a lot of effort, and even the strongest stags do not manage to produce more than six bellows per minute. If one of the adversaries is markedly inferior in the roaring contest he might resign without even starting a real fight.

Tim Clutton-Brock of the University of Sussex made tape-recordings of roarings and played them back to the stags in different time intervals. Two bellows per minute did not elicit much response – after all, a stag that is not able to achieve more than that is not worth bothering about. Five per minute was considered a serious challenge. A stag hearing them threatened in the direction of the amplifyer and started rounding up his hinds. Finally, when a stag was confronted with ten roars per minute he was evidently confused and extremely worried. A challenger with such 'super-stagian' powers was indeed frightening (Cherfas, 1977).

For duels with conspecifics, males of some species have special 'fancy armaments' totally useless as real weapons. For defence against wolves or other predators a stag only uses his hooves. The antlers are reserved for competing males, and such duels have their own rules of 'fair play' which are only seldom transgressed.

In these ritualized combats there are also rules about how one of the contestants can acknowledge his defeat and withdraw without further molestation. By such submissive gestures he triggers inhibitory mechanisms in the victor, preventing further attack. Hence such intra-specific combats hardly ever lead to death or serious injury. 'Though occasionally, by some mishap a horn may penetrate an eye or a tooth an artery, we never found that the *aim* of aggression was the extermination of fellow members of the species,' writes Konrad Lorenz.

This statement, referring as it does to a particular kind of ritualized combat, has been repeatedly quoted and generalized in a misleading way. Thus many laymen have been led to believe that murder of conspecifics is a very rare event in the animal kingdom. Actually this is neither true nor is it what Lorenz really did say. In his book *On aggression* (1963/66) he quotes many examples of fish, reptiles, mammals and others violently defending their territories, chasing and even killing intruders. A rat accidentally intruding into the realm of another troop has no chance to save its life, Lorenz reports (pp. 161–2). Even a member of the native troop having been separated for a few days and having lost the troop odour is mercilessly persecuted and annihilated.

Neighbouring clans of hyenas sometimes fight pitched battles over carcasses of prey and if one of them is killed in such an encounter it might easily be eaten by conspecifics belonging to the other clan (Kruuk, 1972). Ant colonies belonging to the same species sometimes fight veritable 'wars' ending occasionally with the complete destruction of one of the colonies (Wilson, 1975, p. 244; Hölldobler, 1976). When a troop of chimpanzees divided, for unknown reasons, the males of the original troop repeatedly and violently attacked members of the secondary troop, eventually killing all the males of the secessionists (Goodall, 1979). From such and similar examples Hubert Markl (1976) deduced a general rule: species with highly co-operative social behaviour within the group are particularly apt to be very aggressive towards conspecifics that are not members of their group.

However, the victims of murder and cannibalism need not necessarily be 'strangers'. According to Kruuk, hyenas must stand guard while their cubs are feeding on a carcass in order to protect them from being eaten *by other members of their own clan!* Lion males occasionally fight about their share of the prey – which, by the way, is usually killed by the females – and sometimes such disputes end fatally (Schaller, 1972).

Among chimpanzees, which contrary to widely held beliefs are not strict vegetarians but like to improve their diet with meat, especially of young animals, cannibalism has been observed too. Males sometimes are seen to attack stranger females and to kill and partially eat their infants. In the group observed by Jane Goodall two females, mother and daughter, were seen several times to rob, kill and eat children of other females *well acquainted to them.* The mothers learned to avoid the cannibals and tried to protect their children, and if males were around they always helped the mothers. But as a rule the cannibals tried to find mothers when they were alone with their children and were eventually successful. In the course of three years only two infants of the group survived. When the mother cannibal then had a baby herself the attacks on other babies ceased (Goodall, 1979).

While such behaviour might be called 'pathological' or 'deviant', since it would lead to the extinction of the species if it became the general norm, there are examples of murder within the group or even of siblings which evidently are 'normal' and pre-programmed by nature. Bee workers regularly kill all drones in autumn when food starts to get scarce and males are not needed any more before the next summer. Newly hatched queens are sometimes killed by the workers for unknown reasons or they themselves kill the pupae of other incipient queens that could compete with them.

Pre-programmed murder of siblings is not restricted to insects either. Eagles usually lay two eggs within a time lapse of several days, and the young hatch in the same order. As soon as the second one emerges it is continuously attacked by the older sibling. The fights sometimes last several days and the parents never interfere. In the nests of the crowned eagle the younger sibling is *always* killed. In some other species of eagle there is a slight to moderate chance that both of the young might survive these first days of merciless struggle (Brown, 1970).

For the biggest eagle species, laying a second egg is just a kind of 'stand by' provision to avoid losing a whole breeding season in case one egg is accidentally destroyed. The birds are not able to raise more than one chick. Their prey are medium-sized mammals like monkeys, small antelopes or young animals which are rather thinly spread over a wide territory. To carry such a prey to the nest demands strength and dexterity. While the female is sitting on the eggs and as long as the chick is small the male is hunting alone and has to provide food for three mouths. He simply would not be able to feed a fourth one as well. The young eagle, rather poorly fed, grows very slowly. A crowned eagle is 17 months old before fledging. The birds breed only every other year (Wilson, 1975, p. 340).

Nature is cruel and there is no point in either moralizing about that or in hushing up the facts. To present animal behaviour in an idealized way – as it were, as a model for men to emulate – means drawing a romantic picture that does not correspond to reality. By no means do animals always behave in a 'chivalrous' way towards members of their species or even towards close kin. Nevertheless it is a fact that inhibitory mechanisms against killing of conspecifics do exist – and particularily in those species that possess the most dangerous weapons.

Seen in that way man is indeed in a special position, for he can produce ever more terrible weapons for which he does not possess inborn inhibitory mechanisms. A man might strangle another one with his bare hands, but such crimes are exeptional. Lorenz (1963/66, pp. 241 *et seq.*) certainly is correct when pointing out that killing men (or even animals) is much easier if one needs only to press a trigger or a button and is too far away to see the blood or to hear the cries of the victims and their begging for mercy.

Nevertheless Wilson comes to the remarkable conclusion that man does not compare badly with animals. 'Murder is far more common and hence 'normal' in many vertebrate species than in man', he writes (1975, p. 247). 'I have been impressed by how often such behaviour becomes apparent only when the observation time devoted to a species passes the thousand-hour mark. But only one murder per thousand hours per observer is still a great deal of violence by human standards. In fact, if some imaginary Martian zoologist visiting the Earth were to observe man over a long period of time as simply one more species, he might conclude that we are among the more pacific mammals as measured by serious assaults or murders per individual per unit of time, even when our episodic wars are averaged in.'

But even though murder is not uncommon amongst animals we nevertheless must deal with the question of how it was possible that ritualized fighting behaviour and inhibitory mechanisms against killing of conspecifics could evolve at all. Lorenz does not see this as a problem; it seems obvious to him that natural selection would favour behaviour patterns serving the 'benefit of the species'. Strict Darwinists, however, are not satisfied with such explanations. If 'chivalrous' behaviour towards other members of the species is inborn, as it seems to be, there must be occasional mutations, enabling an animal not to conform to the rules of 'fair play'. One would assume that such behaviour against the rules would give incremental advantage to that animal. Thus hereditary dispositions for 'playing unfair' would spread within the species, gradually replacing the genes for 'chivalry'. How can it be explained that actually the evolution of many species did *not* go this way?

1.7 'Doves', 'hawks', 'retaliators'

Though the dove is the symbol of peace it actually does not behave very peacefully towards conspecifics. The mighty gorilla is much

29

more like a 'dove' in this respect. A pigeon with a dangerous weapon like the beak of a raven would be a formidable monster, says Konrad Lorenz (1963/66).

The 'doves' we are speaking of in this section are not real pigeons. We are using the expression, as in the media, to specify an individual favouring a peaceful strategy. For the 'good of the species' it would be an advantage if such a non-aggressive – actually more gorilla-like than dove-like – strategy was the general rule. Yet for the individual, aggression against conspecifics pays. If such behaviour is due to a genetic disposition it will spread within the species in spite of being detrimental to the 'general welfare' in the long run. Thus, why do not all animals behave as 'hawks'?

Darwin was already aware that this problem required an explanation, and the founders of population genetics, R. A. Fisher, J. B. S. Haldane and others who in the twenties formed a synthesis of Darwinism and Mendelism, i.e. of evolution theory and genetics, came close to solving it. The decisive contributions however were made by scientists after World War II. One of them is the British biologist John Maynard Smith.

'As a student of Haldane's,' he reports (1978b), 'I had been taught to be distrustful of arguments that depend on "the good of the species". I thought there should be a way to explain how natural selection operates *on the individual* to promote those characteristics [i.e. ritualized fighting as described in the previous chapter]. The puzzle remained at the back of my mind until it occurred to me in 1970 that I might gain some understanding of the problem by borrowing some of the concepts of the mathematical theory of games.'

Game theory was formulated in the 1940s by John von Neumann and Oskar Morgenstern for the purpose of analysing conflicts between men and between states. It seeks to determine the optimum strategy to pursue in conflict situations. Trying to make conflicts rationally manageable it cannot but assume that the contestants themselves will behave rationally and do what is the most reasonable thing in their particular situation.

This is not the place to discuss whether such a supposition is justified for men or human governments. For animals it certainly is not. Even the most intelligent animal is constrained – much more than man – by inborn behavioural tendencies and instincts, with

30

only a small margin of 'free decision' to find for itself a successful strategy in conflict situations. But what is inborn has evolved and was favoured by natural selection because it was a successful strategy in the past. Seen in this way natural selection is quasi-'rational' and, maybe, even more rational than a human government. And game theory can help to discover strategies which under certain circumstances would be favoured by natural selection.

Maynard Smith and Price (1973) call this an 'Evolutionarily Stable Strategy' (ESS), meaning a set of behaviour patterns that will be stable under the pressures of natural selection as long as circumstances do not change. The word 'stable' must be taken with a grain of salt, since environmental conditions never remain as they are over long periods, and since animals are able to learn and their social systems are continually evolving and adapting to new circumstances. Hubert Markl (1980) therefore considers the term 'evolutionarily stable' as laden with an internal contradiction and proposes to call it an Evolutionarily Superior Strategy. 'Isn't a changing, a tracking strategy rather than a stable one apt to be superior in social animals which are able to learn?' he asked at the Dahlem Conference on Evolution of Social Behaviour.

It is however clear that certain strategies might attain at least a sort of dynamic equilibrium which cannot exist for other ones. If almost all the members of a population adopt such a strategy, occasionally occurring hereditary changes (mutations) inducing a deviating behaviour will, as a rule, be less successful and therefore will not spread within the population.

There is no need for complicated mathematical theories to see that 'dove' is not an evolutionarily stable strategy under almost all conceivable circumstances. Much more interesting, however, is the insight that pure 'hawk' behaviour is not an ESS either, except in very special situations hardly ever occurring in real life.

To apply game theory to animal conflicts one must make a sort of cost/benefit analysis of alternative strategies. The yardstick for such an evaluation is the higher or lower chance of passing on genes to future generations. Thus one must find out the amount of risk associated with an escalation of a fight and the probability ratio of such an escalation resulting in death or serious injury for one of the contestants; one must compare the costs of an injury with the benefits of victory; one must calculate the time and energy loss required

31

for a long-lasting not escalating (ritualized) fight, and find out whether such a fight is worthwhile at all, or if and when it is the most reasonable thing to give up soon.

This, in turn, depends on the value of the benefit for the victor, which may be very different under different circumstances. If there is enough room for every animal and only moderate differences in the quality of the territories to be got, victory in territorial fighting is much less important than in situations where only some of the contestants can get any territory at all; for in many species an individual without its own territory has no chance of reproduction.

For a male of a species living only for one mating period and fighting only one 'battle of his life', victory would be essential if he is to reproduce at all. In such circumstances the 'all or nothing' behaviour of the extreme 'hawk' is the only evolutionarily stable strategy. There is, however, some doubt as to whether there are any species conforming to such assumptions. Under the less extreme circumstances that pertain to the vast majority of species, a 'dove' has an *advantage* within a population consisting mainly of 'hawks'. It avoids the risk of serious injury – very widespread in such a population – and the costs of long-lasting hard fights and sooner or later will still find a chance for reproduction. Thus, if there are no alternative strategies the evolutionarily stable state will be a mixture of 'hawk' and 'dove' behaviour. This might be achieved either by aggressive and timid individuals existing side by side or by varying tactics employed by every individual – behaving sometimes as a 'hawk' and sometimes as a 'dove'.

As a rule, however, animals have more differentiated alternatives than these two extreme behaviour patterns. Assuming conditions which seem to be near reality, for many species a strategy called 'retaliator' by Maynard Smith is evolutionarily stable. Such an individual will behave like a 'dove' against 'doves', but strikes back hard when meeting a 'hawk'. This strategy can be further improved if the 'retaliator' itself sometimes escalates a bit to probe the reactions of its opponent. If the latter is a 'dove' it will withdraw. Since a real population usually has a fair amount of young, weak or disabled members who willy-nilly can only behave than as 'doves', the 'prober-retaliator' has a good chance to be an evolutionarily stable strategy, too.

Of course, values employed in such cost/benefit calculations cannot be measured in nature. They must be approximately calculated for the circumstances of different species. But then, the primary goal of Maynard Smith was not the investigation of the behaviour strategy of a *particular* species. What he wanted to find out was whether natural selection of any other behaviour than extreme 'hawks' was possible at all. His computations have shown convincingly that this may well be possible in most conceivable circumstances.

In real life conditions are of course more complicated than in the highly simplified models tested on the computer by Maynard Smith. As a rule escalation has many steps from mere threatening to ritualized and eventually to real all-out fighting. On the other hand it is perhaps not always just 'bad luck', as Lorenz assumes (see section 1·6) but maybe an *intended* escalation when a tooth hits an artery in a fight that was ritualized up to then.

Generally two contestants are not of equal strength as assumed in Maynard Smith's computer runs. Yet the stronger one need not necessarily be victorious, for there may be different degrees of 'motivation'. As a rule an animal is able to defend successfully at least the core of its territory against conspecifics, even stronger ones. In many species such fights are terminated very quickly as soon as the 'ownership rights' are clear. As a rule a healthy bird is practically invincible in the centre of its territory (Tinbergen, 1939).

1.8 *Two brothers or eight cousins*

That an animal shares many genes not only with its ancestors and its descendants but also with its siblings and other kin is well known. Yet for a long time nobody realized that this might have consequences for the evolution of behaviour. Even when the great British biologist and geneticist J. B. S. Haldane uttered this idea for the first time he apparently was not quite aware of its importance.

Maynard Smith, then a graduate student with Haldane, can well remember the moment. 'It was in the fifties in a now-demolished pub in the centre of London, called *The Orange Tree*', he told me. 'Haldane sitting there with some of his students had been calculating on the back of an envelope for some minutes. Then he announced that he would be prepared to lay down his life for two brothers or eight cousins.' (See also Maynard Smith, 1975.)

Haldane later referred to this idea in an article in *Penguin New Biology*, but he did not follow it up. It was W. D. Hamilton, a lecturer in zoology at the Imperial College in London, who took it up later, generalized it and applied it to the evolution of social insects as well. Thus a new genetic theory of social behaviour emerged which Maynard Smith called the theory of kin selection (Hamilton, 1964; Maynard Smith, 1964).

What this theory tries to explain is how inborn tendencies for unselfish behaviour towards siblings and other kin can spread within a species and hold their ground against mutations for pure egoism. This is only possible if such a behaviour does genetically 'pay'. For inborn tendencies to care for one's own brood this is easy to see. Young of parents that intensely care for them and defend them have better survival chances. Hence if such behaviour is genetically influenced it will spread. But why is it genetically profitable to lay down one's life for a brother?

The answer given by Haldane's *bon mot* and Hamilton's theory is that one shares many genes with one's kin. Hence if an animal or a human favours his kin as compared to other conspecifics, if he forms groups with his kin rather than with others and even sacrifices himself to defend such a group his genes, as it were, survive in his kin; to be more exact, genes that are identical to his own are passed on by his kin to future generations. Amongst them there will also be those genes that have furthered his tendency for unselfish behaviour towards his kin and preference of them.

Of course, such behavioural tendencies can only be spread by natural selection if they bring, genetically speaking, more benefits than costs. Since the beneficiaries of a relative who is prepared to take risks for their advantage only share a certain fraction of their genes with him, the benefits accruing to them must be considerably greater than the probable costs for him. In mathematical terms: the benefit for the recipients divided by their degree of relatedness to the benefactor must be greater than the costs accruing to the latter.

If I, according to Haldane's *bon mot*, lay down my life for two brothers (or, of course, sisters) or for eight cousins, benefits and costs according to genetical theory will just hold the balance. Only if I sacrifice myself for at least three siblings or nine cousins will I have a 'profit' in the terms of kin selection. The kin I saved will do more to propagate 'my' genes than I could have done myself. On the other hand it would be going too far – according to the standards of kin selection – if I took a more than 50% risk to save *only one* brother. If I do so, one must find another or at least an additional explanation, and cannot rely solely on the genetic theory of behaviour.

Whenever the cost/benefit ratio is unfavourable natural selection will back open selfishness rather than 'altruism'. An extreme example is the newly hatched eagles (see section 1·6). From the kin selectionist point of view their behaviour is advantageous even for the sibling that is murdered. Since the parents are not able to bring up two siblings, to murder the younger one is the only way to pass on at least indirectly 50% of his genes to the next generation whereas both of them would perish otherwise.

In real life things usually are not so dramatic, and unselfish behaviour is not necessarily a question of life and death. Costs and benefits of smaller altruistic acts are difficult to estimate in many instances. Yet, as a general rule of thumb it can be stated that whenever circumstances demand co-operation of members of a species, the formation of a community of kin will be favoured by natural selection over cooperation of non-kin (Harvey *et al.*, 1980).

A good example is a pride of lions. The main reason for them to live in groups is that they cannot run as fast as many of their prey. By hunting together and stalking the prey from several directions simultaneously they have a better chance of success than when hunting alone – and even group hunting sometimes ends in failure. Moreover a group can protect its cubs much better than a single lioness (see section 1·1). The core of the pride is a group of closely related females (mother and daughters, sisters, aunt and nieces, cousins, etc.). Admission of non-kin females into a group has never been observed. Young males leave the pride in groups before reaching maturity and try to take over a pride by chasing the resident males. Thus the males conquering a pride are close kin too (brothers, half-brothers, cousins) and all the cubs in a pride are 'double kin': children of closely related mothers and of closely related fathers (Schaller, 1972; Bertram, 1976).

Of course, nobody thinks that animals do calculate genetical costs and benefits to find the adequate 'dosage' of altruism for every case, or that they have some hidden sense to distinguish sibs from half-sibs or first from second cousins. But natural selection can, as it were, 'calculate exactly', and it can only favour those behaviour patterns that, genetically speaking, bring more benefits than costs. The evolution of the pride of lions is but one example of many for which kin selection theory provides a plausible explanation.

Elephants live in herds consisting of closely related females of several generations with their calves. The males leave the group when reaching maturity, living singly or forming loose conglomerations. Since the mothers in the herd are all kin, the calves are kin to all of them too. Hence it seems plausible that nursing females allow all the calves of the herd to suckle at their teats and that they defend them all in case of danger (Wilson, 1975, p. 494).

Chimpanzees are one of the few mammalian species of which the females and not the males leave their native group when reaching maturity and join another troop. Hence the males of a troop are close kin, whereas the females are not. This might be the reason that orphaned children are adopted by an older sibling and not by another female of the troop (Wilson, 1975, p. 125). Kin relationship of all males does not exclude fights for dominance – with brothers (i.e. sons of the same mother) helping each other against more distant kin, as would be expected according to theory. Jane Goodall (1979) tells of a male with a paralysed arm, who nevertheless was able, aided by his brother, to displace the leader of the troop and hold the first rank for seven years.

Many phenomena in bird life as well can be better understood by looking for kin relationships. *Tribonyx mortierii* is a flightless rail from Tasmania of which, for unknown reasons, there are many more males than females. Some of the females live monogamously, the others in 'trios' with two males. The stronger male of such a trio does not prevent the other one from mating with the female, though he could do so. After careful observation it turned out that the males in such trios are always brothers or half-brothers and that a trio is able to raise about 40% more young than a pair. Presumably the stronger of the males copulates more often with the female and hence fathers more than half of her young. But even assuming equal shares the trio is, calculating genetically, of advantage for the stronger brother, since his nephews and nieces, being descendants from his brother, carry 25% of his own genes. (Maynard Smith and Ridpath, 1972). Since the trio can bring up more young than a pair the costs are still smaller than the benefits in case of males which

36

are only half brothers from one mother and two fathers who were brothers – having three-eights of their genes in common.

In more than 150 bird species mature young birds sometimes remain with their parents and help them bring up younger siblings instead of founding their own family. G. E. Woolfenden has observed this phenomenon in detail in the jay species *Apheloconia coerulescens* living in Florida scrubs. About half of all breeding pairs have such baby sitters, helping to feed and defend the young. Survival rates of young are more than twice as high in nests with helpers than in nests of unaided parents (Woolfenden, 1973; Woolfenden and Fitzpatrick, 1978).

That there are similar phenomena in some mammalian species as well had not been observed before kin selection theory had been formulated and zoologists began to look for degrees of relatedness when finding unexplained unselfish behaviour. One example are black-backed jackals observed by Patricia Moehlman (1979) of the University of Wisconsin for several years in the Serengeti Plain. In many instances young animals of the previous litter remain with their parents and help them to bring up the pups of the next litter. The baby-sitters bring food to their young siblings and also regurgitate food to their mother during lactation. They guard the pups when the parents are absent and are able to drive off hyenas. They play with their siblings, groom them and help teach them to hunt.

Jackals form long-lasting pair bonds, hence the new pups probably are full siblings of the baby-sitters, i.e. they share as many genes with them as would their own young. A pair of jackals bringing up their pups unaided generally has not more than one or two young surviving to maturity; sometimes all of them perish. On the other hand three, four or even five pups survive in families with one or two baby-sitters. Hence if the pups of the new litter are really full siblings of the helpers, the latter contribute more to the (indirect) propagation of their genes than they would by trying to reproduce themselves.

An extreme example of sibling help amongst mammals is found in the East African naked mole rats. These small rodents live underground and feed on roots of certain plants; they seem to have behaviour patterns resembling some of those of social insects. So far little is known about these animals whose unusual social structures were not observed until very recently. Apparently a group consists of a single reproductive female (as it were, a 'queen') and a number of non-reproducing animals (offspring?) who forage for younger colony members and care for them as bee or ant workers would do.

'Jennifer Jarvis, Richard Alexander, and I were in Kenya recently to dig up such colonies of mole rats', Paul Sherman of the University of California told me at the Dahlem Conference on the Evolution of Social Behaviour. 'I took two colonies with me to my laboratory in Berkeley to observe them. First of all we must find out whether they really are as interesting as they seem to be. Only when we know more about them can we start looking for explanations why this species behaves in such strange, fascinating ways.'

1.9 *Who is the father?*

There are trends of fashion even in science. A new theory emerges, everybody talks about it, it becomes 'the great hit' – and is, of necessity, overtaxed. People try to explain more with its aid than it actually can explain.

One of the main tasks of the *Dahlem Workshop on Evolution of Social Behaviour: Hypotheses and Empirical Tests*, to quote its full title, was to examine whether this holds true for sociobiology as well, and especially for the theory of kin selection. Forty-four scientists from six countries, representing different disciplines, were hotly discussing this question for five days.

The answer given by the workshop can, in my view, be summarized in two main points: first, that the new ideas of sociobiology have given the whole field of ethology a great impetus; and second, that the new theoretical ideas, so far, are not very well founded on facts, and that it is now time to find out to what extent they really can contribute new insights into animal behaviour.

'A whole branch of science is full of excitement and new life,' Paul Sherman, one of the younger participants of the workshop told me. Though by no means uncritical towards these new ideas Sherman does not hesitate to admit that they are a great challenge for all biologists. 'Taking their lead from Williams, Hamilton, Trivers, and Alexander, many scientists in our field are gaining new insights into well-known old problems. There are heated discussions, competing hypotheses, a wealth of new questions to be answered. The new ideas focus attention on details hardly noticed before. Working in this field is incredibly exciting'.

Of course, the basic ideas of sociobiology have not been concocted from nothing at the desks of theorists. They are a fascinating attempt to find a solution to problems that have been puzzling biologists for a long time. But, 'theorists have advanced very fast,' said Bert Hölldobler, a German specialist on ant research, now working at Harvard University. 'The practical testing of their ideas by us field-workers lags far behind.'

The basic problem, to state it once more, is that in strict Darwinistic terms something like an evolution of *inborn* truly altruistic behaviour is simply not possible. There was nobody at the Dahlem Conference who doubted that. Everybody agreed that seemingly 'altruistic' behaviour needs to be explained; that one must find out in what way such an inborn behaviour pattern is *advantageous to the altruist himself* – directly or indirectly; or whether there are external constraints making any other kind of behaviour impossible. There was no doubt at the conference that these are real and justified questions; what the discussion centered on was whether sociobiology is capable of giving the right answers to them.

Inspired by the new ideas, some theorists in the last few years advanced bold and detailed hypotheses. As would befit an 'exact' science, they propped them up with complicated calculations. Degrees of relationship and genetic cost/benefit ratios have been worked out to the second digit behind the decimal – disregarding the fact that the data used were much too inexact for such a refined mathematical treatment. Some of them were data of other scientists collected for different purposes without special care being taken to give exact information on details relevant to the theory of kin selection. Far-reaching statistical inferences were drawn from samples that were far too small for such an exercise, and without checking whether these samples were indeed representative cross-sections of the populations examined; data scattered over a wide bandwidth were aggregated to worthless averages (see for instance, Alexander and Sherman, 1977, in a critical review of a much quoted paper by Trivers and Hare, 1976, on social insects, to which we will return later in this chapter.) All this is not convincing to a critical scientist.

One of the main difficulties for field-workers is to ascertain the

39

real degrees of relationship. '*Pater semper incertus*' (the father always is uncertain), the ancient Romans used to say; but according to Roman law the husband was to be considered as the father. For biologists trying to test the assumptions of kin selection theory such an attitude is not possible – they must know the real father. But how?

Male 'adultery' is, as we have seen, fairly common in assumedly monogamous species, female 'adultery' in species with harem-forming males. But the fact that 50% of the redwing blackbird females belonging to the harem of a sterilized male have their clutches inseminated by other males (see section 1·4) can only lead to the inference that the females of this species are not always faithful; it does not give any clue to the question how many of the young are fathered by other males if the 'husband' is not sterilized and presumably copulates much more frequently with his 'wife' than possible 'adulterers'.

In a fairly large population of rhesus monkeys brought to Cayo Santiago, (a small island off Puerto Rico) by American scientists for study under more or less natural conditions, methods of investigation used in human paternity suits were applied to get a more exact picture of real kin relationships. Surprisingly, it turned out that often up to 5% of the newborn in a troop are descendants from fathers not belonging to the troop (Sade, 1980). That rhesus females sometimes have 'affairs' with strange males was known. But presumably a female on heat copulates much more frequently with males of her own troop. Nevertheless it turns out that an occasional 'escapade' can result in fertilization.

A probability of only 5% that an offspring is the fruit of an 'illegitimate' intercourse would presumably be too small to seriously influence the evolution of paternal behaviour within a species. But to my knowledge nobody has tried as yet to find out in how many cases the male of a 'monogamous' bird species brings up young that are not his own. That, on the average, his strenuous paternal efforts result in a positive genetic cost/benefit ratio that is advantageous to him is a plausible but unproven assumption.

In the case of 'baby-sitters', too, it is not always clear whether they help to raise full siblings or half-sibs. Heinz-Ulrich Reyer of the Institute for Ethology in Seewiesen, West Germany, holds that this is not very important for *male* helpers which predominate in birds. If there is a probability of 20% that a helper contributes to the care of half-sibs with whom he shares only 25% of his genes, there would be an equal probability of 20% that when founding his own family he would be cuckolded by his wife and would rear another father's young with whom he shares no genes at all.

On the other hand many biologists think that the chance for indirect propagation of the male helper's genes via sibs or half-sibs is *not the only reason* for a young bird to remain with his parents instead of founding his own family. Baby-sitting behaviour is particularily common in species whose males must possess their own territories to get a mate; and it tends to occur mainly in saturated habitats (Krebs *et al.*, 1980). Woolfenden and Fitzpatrick (1978) suggest that in the jays they observed in Florida, helping the parents might be, as it were, the price the young birds have to pay for being allowed to stay in the parental territory; and that moreover the helpers have the chance to inherit this territory which they help to defend. The two explanations are not mutually exclusive. As a rule baby-sitters help their parents or other close kin and in this way contribute to the indirect propagation of their genes as well.

Baby-sitters not related to the parents are sometimes observed in the nests of the African pied kingfisher (*Ceryle rudis*). In this species female mortality is considerably higher than that of males and there are always surplus males in a colony trying to attach themselves to breeding pairs. According to Reyer (1980), non-kin helpers have a good chance in the next season to mate with the female they helped. Hence one would expect the 'husbands' to oppose such non-kin helpers and that is exactly what they do. As long as the parents are able to rear their young all by themselves, strange young males are attacked and driven away by the resident male. At Lake Naïvasha where a kingfisher catches a fish every six minutes on average, non-kin helpers are not tolerated. Conditions are different however at Lake Victoria. Here the water surface tends to be rough making fishing difficult for the birds; the kingfisher needs an average of thirteen minutes to catch a prey which, moreover, is often less nutritious than the fish of Lake Naivasha. In such circumstances two parents alone are not able to rear their offspring, and if there are no young of the previous clutch remaining with them as helpers, strangers are accepted.

41

An animal cannot go to the registrar to find out its degree of relatedness to another member of its troop. How then does it recognize
its kin with whom it 'should', according to kin selection theory,
preferentially co-operate? Can it recognize them at all?

Generally speaking, the answer to the second question seems
to be no. There is a considerable body of evidence that animals –
at least most of them – have no inborn traits enabling them to
recognize kin with confidence. Rather they behave towards each
other *as if* they were kin if that is probable in a certain situation.

The song-bird father 'assumes' that the young in his nest are his
own. He is not able to distinguish young begotten by 'adultery' from
his own progeny. He cares for all of them as if they were his own
children – even for a young cuckoo. Two young lion males growing
up in the same pride behave as if they were brothers, though they
might be half-brothers or 'double cousins' (children of fathers who
are brothers or half-brothers and of mothers who are sisters or close
kin).

Members of many species of higher vertebrates like apes, monkeys,
wolves or elephants know each other 'personally' and can remember
this even after long periods of separation. Wolves on 'amicable
terms' greet each other with great affection. A dog recognizes a
former human master even after years and greets him with visible
joy. Chimpanzees might embrace and kiss each other after long
separation.

American Belding's ground squirrels vigorously defend their
territories and burrows against any intruder, but a neighbouring
mother, daughter or litter-mate sister (the males leave the territory
on reaching maturity) may enter the territory, and even the burrow
in case of danger, and these close kin help each other to defend
their territory against strangers. It seems that they know and
recognize each other 'personally' even after prolonged periods of
separation (hibernation). On the other hand, non-litter-mate sisters
are only recognized as kin if they are, as it were, 'introduced' to
their elder (half-) sisters by their common mother. If the mother
dies before the young emerge above ground their older sisters treat
them like strangers (Sherman, 1980).

Rats, though very intelligent, do not seem to have 'personal' acquaintances with other members of their troop. The animals recognize each other with the aid of the common odour of the troop, which is not inborn but acquired from the environment, food, etc. Konrad Lorenz's experiments mentioned in section 6 show that a rat having lost this odour after several days of separation from the troop is treated as a stranger and mercilessly persecuted. Reversing this experiment Lorenz was able to introduce a strange rat into a troop by putting it into a safe cage within the territory of the troop until it had acquired the troop's odour.

Female lions or elephants seem to treat all females of their group as close kin. Yet if the group divides it is usually the closest kin that remain together. The same is certainly true for many species of monkey (see Chepko-Sade, 1979; Harvey *et al.*, 1980). Apes and monkeys, moreover, have all sorts of cliques and coalitions *within* the group, mostly based on kinship.

Monkeys and apes usually bear only one offspring; but it takes a long time to mature. Frequently older children are still with their mother when a new baby is born. Thus attachment ties can form between siblings of different ages which might last for life. Some rhesus males leave their group upon reaching maturity, forming bachelor bands and eventually joining another troop. One would assume that personal ties with the original native group would gradually fade out. Yet Donald Sade (1980) reports that in several instances young males that had joined another troop helped younger brothers (or half-brothers) to change over to them (see also Harvey *et al.*, 1980). This, of course is not just 'altruism' of the older brother; he gets, in this way, a valuable ally in his new surroundings.

Since in many species paternity is uncertain and brood care is mainly or exclusively the job of the mother, there are asymmetries in behaviour towards kin according to whether they are related on the maternal or paternal side. A rhesus female occupying a high rank can help her children to quickly get a 'privileged position' in the troop. A high ranking male cannot do the same since he does not seem to know who amongst the young are his children. Siblings descendant from the same mother, especially litter-mates, *know* that they are siblings – though actually they might not have the same father. Half-siblings descendant from the same father but from different mothers are in a different position. In species with harem-forming males, like hamadryas baboons, all the young originating

43

from such a harem might be assumed to be children of the same father. Though this is by no means a hundred-percent-certainty they mostly behave as if they were siblings.

A seemingly inborn mechanism for recognition of paternal half-siblings is claimed to have been observed by a team of American scientists (Wu *et al.*, 1980). Sixteen young pigtail macaques (*Macaca nemestrina*) of known genealogies were seperated from their mothers immediately after birth and reared in artificial groups of non-related individuals. When about half a year to a year old they were presented in a choice experiment with unknown individuals, among them some paternal half-siblings. It turned out that no less than thirteen of them showed a significant preference for these half-siblings as compared to other animals of the same age and sex.

When I read this my first reaction was rather sceptical. Yet when I asked scientists attending the Dahlem Conference on *Animal and Human Mind* in March 1981 for their opinions I heard a large variety of views. Some simply said that they did not believe it, but others pointed out that many reports on important new discoveries had looked just as questionable when first published. And Christian Welker of Kassel University told me that he had by chance observed a similar phenomenon in capuchin monkeys (*Cebus apella*). His experiments, he said, had *not* addressed the question of kin preference, but it had struck him that a young animal separated from its mother immediately after birth and reared apart from her, when brought back to the group, had more contact with the mother than with any other adult female. Similarly, paternal half-siblings reared in different groups, when coming later into a common group, had more contact with each other than with unknown non-kin. Welker emphasized that these were mere casual observations which he had not rigorously tested. They might be just chance phenomena in a small group or there might be other explanations, but they would deserve further investigation.

The present state of knowledge certainly does not warrant any far reaching conclusions, but it would be equally premature to reject the whole idea *a priori*. It must be checked whether the effects found by Wu's team are genuine and can be repeated by others in rigorous tests; and whether similar phenomena exist in other species.

As long as unequivocal results of such experiments are not known one can only stick to what is certain today: that most natural groups of animals do have a core of real kin and that all group members (including non-related 'immigrants') tend to behave as if they were kin – especially in the case of an outward threat by a predator or 'strangers', i.e. conspecifics not belonging to the group.

On the other hand real or presumed kin relations and/or personal acquaintance are no protection against aggression if 'higher interests' of the group are involved. The secessionist chimpanzees on which Jane Goodall reported (see section 1.6) certainly were closely related to the males of the original group and personally acquainted with them as well – and yet they were persecuted and killed by them.

In the case of insects and other invertebrates 'personal acquaintance' does not seem to be important for the recognition of kin or of nest mates. And it would, of course, be hardly conceivable that the many thousands of workers of a large bee hive or ant colony all know each other 'personally'. Yet they can distinguish nest mates from other members of the species, and they also are able to find their way back to their own nest, even if a bee-keeper places several hives in the immediate vicinity of each other.

Non-social (solitary) bees find their way by the nest odour which seems to be a combination of personal odorous substances (pheromones) of the bee and the smell of food and nest material. There are primitive bee species with dozens or hundreds of solitary individuals living side by side, every one in its own burrow or in neighbouring hollow bamboo poles. Under natural conditions every bee finds its own nest when returning from foraging. If, however, in an experiment nest material is exchanged or the nest entrance is extracted with alcohol to remove the odorous substances the bees are no longer able to find their own nest (Steinmann, 1976).

Solitary bees or wasps defend their nests against everybody and particularly against conspecifics, since brood parasitism is widespread amongst wasps. Hence according to Charles Michener, one of the grand old men of American entomology, acquisition of the ability to tolerate nest mates, and to recognize them, must have been a major early step in the evolution towards large insect societies.

Experiments with a bee species living in small groups (*Lasioglossum zephyrum*) have shown that in this species nest mates are recognized by their personal odours. The guard at the entrance to the nest recognizes mates even if nest material has been exchanged, if foreign odours such as peppermint have been introduced, or if air is continuously blown from one nest to another. On the other hand, close kin seem to have similar personal odours and 'personally unknown' bees introduced to the guard are allowed to pass easier the more closely related they are to a nest mate. In experimental mixed colonies consisting of two groups of three sisters from two unrelated inbred lines, a guard will normally accept not only her five nest mates but inbred sisters of them as well, even if they were reared in another nest and never presented to the guard before. On the other hand, in colonies formed from five inbred sisters and one 'odd' bee belonging to a different line, the latter, when acting as guard, allows sisters of her mates to pass but *not usually her own inbred sisters*, whereas each of the other nest mates, when acting as a guard, allows the entrance of sisters of the 'odd' bee.

To explain such a result one has to assume that the bees have an inborn, gentically-controlled personal odour, but that the ability to recognize the odour of the nest mate must be learned. The bees of this species do not seem to know their own odour; neither have they an inborn ability to recognize their own kin (Greenberg, 1979; Hölldobler and Michener, 1980).

In large colonies of bees or ants a personal odour of every worker evidently cannot exist. There must be a common signal for all, a nest or colony odour, which enables the animals to distinguish nest mates from strangers. One factor of this nest odour is presumably produced by the queen. On the other hand, food and nest material seem to contribute to the nest odour, too. In a classical experiment bee hives were placed on an isolated moor where only one single flowering species was available; aggressive behaviour between bees of different hives markedly declined after a while (Kalmus and Ribbands, 1952). The reverse effect of disrupting colony unity by separating groups and maintaining them on different diets was demonstrated, too – a phenomenon similar to the result of Lorenz's experiments with rats.

Larvae, pupae and newly hatched callow ant workers can be transferred into another nest of the same species and in some cases even into nests of closely related species. They are accepted by the workers in the 'foster' nest without difficulty. It is hardly likely that these animals carry no traces of the odour of their native nest. The German entomologist Bert Hölldobler, now at Harvard, favours the assumption that larvae produce a species-specific odour signal eliciting brood-tending behaviour of the workers. Pupae and callow workers seemingly still carry traces of this 'brood-care signal' whose effect overrides the signals of nest odour.

Callow workers for their part must *learn* their nest odour in the first days of their adult life – probably in a process similar to the 'imprinting' of some young birds mentioned earlier in section 1·2 They have no inborn ability to recognize kin. Workers grown from larvae or pupae kidnapped by slave-making ants later behave in a hostile manner towards their real sisters that remained in their common mother's nest (Hölldobler and Michener, 1980).

1.11 *How the improbable becomes possible*

The essence of evolutionary theory is to explain how the improbable became possible. Even the mere existence of a planet on which water could remain in a liquid state without interruption for 4500 million years is much more improbable than usually assumed. According to the American astronomer M. Hart (1979) a planet only 5% nearer to the sun than the Earth would have warmed up in a run-away greenhouse effect like Venus, whereas a planet only 1% farther away than Earth would have had a run-away glaciation like Mars.

The origin of life from inanimate matter is just as improbable as evolution from primitive micro-organisms to man. Seen in that way the evolution of altruistic traits is a relatively small improbability within a setting that is, on the whole, much more improbable.

The coming about of the improbable is based primarily on the fact that within a *very large number* of events a highly unlikely coincidence of favourable circumstances might occur just *by chance* – say a lucky combination of several infrequent, mutually-supplementing mutations. Yet, many theorists doubt that that is sufficient to explain the whole evolutionary process. The 'tree on the mountain slope' mentioned in section 1·5 and the gradual adaptation to a gradually changing environment are most probably only part of the story.

In the course of evolution it occurred many times that a species well adapted to a certain ecological niche, and still existing in that niche, gave rise to the formation of another species well adapted to another ecological niche. But such an evolution cannot have happened in just one jump. There must have been intermediate stages not well adapted to either of these niches. How could such intermediates survive long enough, until further mutations and further selection achieved the adaptation to the new niche? Or, to use a metaphor of population geneticists: how could the valley between two adaptive peaks be crossed?

This question has been addressed mainly by the famous American scientist Sewall Wright (1931, 1945, 1969), and the core of his answer, put simply, is that *chance* changes with no immediate adaptive value were much more important in evolution than previously assumed, and that chance processes might become effective not only in large but *also in small numbers*. Populations, says Wright, are in many cases divided into smaller units that are not completely isolated from each other, but have only sparse contact. And in just such small groups chance events become important. Some genes present in the total population might be missing in one or the other of many small sub-groups. Within a small group extravagant and even slightly disadvantageous combinations of genes might persist for some time, because competing genes are by chance not present in that particular group; and just for that reason such a group might, in favourable circumstances, cross an 'evolutionary valley'. Once the 'ascending slope' to a new adaptive peak is reached, the process will go on by itself; and as soon as adaptation to the new ecological niche is accomplished the new successful combination of genes can be spread by emigrants colonizing free habitats.

The first to consider that such processes of 'group selection' might have been involved in the evolution of altruistic traits, at least in certain circumstances, was Haldane in a book published in 1932. Wright (1945) and others further developed these ideas. In a large population an inborn behaviour pattern serving the general welfare, but having more detrimental than positive effects for the altruist himself will of necessity be superseded by mutations for more egoistic behaviour. In a small group such mutations towards egoism might be absent or be eliminated by chance. Hence, an altruistic trait might be stabilized within the group and *exactly for that reason* such a group might master certain difficulties in a way that other groups are not able to do. Emigrants carrying the genes for that particular altruistic trait might later intrude into territories where other groups had perished just because of their egoistic behaviour. Similarly it is conceivable that only the descendants of the altruists are able to colonize a new harsh environment where survival is only

48

possible for a very co-operative group, whereas any mutations towards a more egoistic behaviour will be mercilessly eliminated by natural selection. Maybe the highly organized troops of hamadryas baboons are an example of this.

Opinions diverge as to whether and to what extent such processes of group selection actually might have been instrumental in the evolution of altruistic behavioural tendencies (see Wynne-Edwards, 1962; Wilson, 1975, p. 113; Maynard Smith, 1978a). Very detailed calculations of population geneticists (Uyenoyama and Feldman, 1980) show that evolution of altruistic traits is considerably more difficult by kin selection as well as by group selection than one would assume when merely verbally stating the idea, but that in certain circumstances, especially those envisaged by Wright, it is possible in both ways.

The chances for the evolution of unselfish behaviour, in any way possible, are best when the costs of such behaviour to the 'altruist' are small as compared to the benefit to be gained by the recipient. A good example might be the general tendency for kind behaviour towards all small children of a troop, irrespective of kin ties, observed in many social species, in particular in monkeys and apes, and the willingness to help children when they are in danger. The advantage of such a behavioural tendency for the 'altruist' is that his own children and grandchildren will profit from it, too.

Great benefit at small cost is also a good precondition for the evolution of mutual aid behaviour. That it is worthwhile not to 'cheat' but to reciprocate 'obliging' behaviour and that such a tendency for 'reciprocal altruism' might hence be favoured by natural selection under certain conditions was shown by the American zoologist Robert Trivers (1971). Cheating will not pay if both partners of such a mutual relationship often need each other's help, because the cheater himself soon would lose the benefits of mutuality.

The ability to form long-lasting personal bonds with other members of the troop enhances another form of reciprocal altruism common in monkeys and chimpanzees: the formation of coalitions and cliques within the troop. C. Packer of the University of Sussex repeatedly observed this behaviour in anubis baboons living at Gombe National Park in Tanzania. A male tries to enlist another by glances and movements of the head to help him against a third. Frequently the object of the quarrel is access to a female on heat.

The two males fight together against the third that is consorting with the female. The one that has asked for help takes over the female, while the helper continues to fight her original consort. Packer's observations (1977) have shown convincingly that such aid is indeed based on mutualism. The male that asked for help will himself help the ally on other occasions. Apparently there are, within the troop, pairs or cliques of males co-operating against other males – but without disrupting troop cohesiveness against other dangers.

Anubis males leave their native troop at maturity and join another troop. The life history of some of the males observed by Packer is known. Thus it is an established fact, at least in some cases, that males helping each other originate from different troops and most probably are *not* close kin. This, of course, does not exclude the possibility of mutual aid between animals that are kin.

Female rhesus monkeys form cliques of individuals mutually helping each other. In most cases these females are kin, but occasionally allies were observed that certainly were *not* closely related (Sade 1980).

Presumably reciprocal altruism evolved from a behaviour pattern of mutual aid between kin which was later extended to 'friends' that were not kin. Such mutual aid as a rule produces a personal bond preventing the partners from 'cheating' each other.

A curious combination of 'baby-sitting' and reciprocity has been observed by the American ornithologist Stephen T. Emlen (1981) in the highly gregarious white-fronted bee-eater (*Merops bullockides*) in Kenya. Whereas in most other species helpers are mainly young animals that have not yet started breeding on their own, role reversals from helping to breeding *and vice versa* are commonplace among bee-eaters. Often an individual that acted as helper in one breeding season is in turn assisted by one of those whom he had helped when he or she starts breeding in a following season. Within a limited observation period Emlen was not yet able to ascertain whether the helpers are always kin to the breeders, but he did find not only children helping their parents but also a case of a father helping one of his children. Individuals who lost their brood, e.g. by flooding of their nesting burrow, often return to their parents as helpers and then start breeding again in the next season, usually with the same mate.

1.12 *Slime moulds and siphonophores – organisms or societies?*

When you and I are talking about an organism we know what we are talking about – or do we? If we call a bee hive a 'social organism' we know that we use the word in a metaphorical way. A bee hive or any other society consists of many individuals whereas an organism is just one individual. The difference seems to be evident, and thus it may strike one as pedantic to ask where you would draw the border-line between an organism and a society.

In this chapter we are going to deal with animals for which such a question is fully justified – and hard to answer on the face of it. They belong to a fair number of unicellular and multicellular species, and their common characteristic is such a close physical unity of single 'individuals' that they can hardly be distinguished from multicellular organisms. Such pseudo-organisms exist in many different, not closely related groups of invertebrates. Evolution evidently went this way independently several times. Some of these species forming 'colonial' super-organisms are closely related to species with a lower degree of social co-operation, enabling scientists to follow in great detail the evolution of intermediate stages.

All these pseudo-organisms typically consist of a number of individuals that have partly or totally surrendered their 'personality' to become organ-like parts of a larger entity. On the part of the individuals this is, as it were, an extremely 'altruistic' behaviour – though it sounds a bit strange to talk of the 'unselfishness' of an unicellular amoeba, or of such a primitive animal as a coral.

Amongst single-celled organisms, slime moulds (Acrasiales) have reached the highest degree of such 'unselfish' co-operation. The individuals are amoebae, which cannot be seen without a microscope and which live on the soil, in leaf litter, or in rotting wood. They feed on bacteria, and as long as there is enough food they live like proper amoebae, propagating themselves by frequent cell division. When food grows scarce, however, a dramatic change occurs. Many thousands of amoebae stream together from all sides to coalesce into a sausage-shaped body of about 0.5 to 2 millimetres in length. This newly formed body, easily visible to the naked eye, now behaves like a primitive multicellular organism. It has distinct front and hind ends, and creeps in the direction of heat and light. After about one or two weeks it transforms into a fruiting body, with some of the amoebae forming the base and the stalk whereas others become spore-bearing spheres at the tip rising a few millimetres above the base. The spores are eventually shed to form new amoebae as soon as environmental conditions permit (Bonner, 1967; Wilson, 1975, p. 388).

A biologist not informed about the existence of slime moulds and seeing such a pseudo-plasmodium or a fruiting body, would, no doubt, assume that this were a primitive multicellular organism. And the contrary cannot be 'proved', unless one has previously agreed on a definition of an organism based on its *development*. You and I, my son's dog, the tree in front of your window, and other 'normal' multicellular organisms developed from a single mother cell by cell division and not by aggregation of many similar cells which had existed in a single-celled state for many generations. Fertilization, uniting two highly specialized and extremely different cells, cannot in any way be compared with the formation of a pseudo-plasmodium. But even fertilization is not a necessary condition for the formation of a multicellular organism. A tree can be grown from a cutting as well as from a seed. And for many lower animals which we are going to mention in this chapter asexual reproduction is a normal mode of propagation. Hence the life cycle of the slime moulds certainly is not an example of the 'normal' way of evolution from single-celled to multicellular organisms.

For the 'benefit of the species' the form of propagation of slime moulds certainly is advantageous. The fruiting body is many thousand times bigger than a single amoeba and can spread the spores much farther. The chances that at least some of them will end up in favourable environmental conditions are much greater than for a single amoeba forming spores by itself. But the aggregation into a pseudo-plasmodium and a fruiting body entails that those amoebae forming the base and the stalk do not have progeny. As long as the cells forming spores and those not reproducing are all descendants from the same mother-amoeba, they can be considered as 'identical twins'. They all have the same genes, and forming the fruiting body is a method of spreading those genes (and individuals carrying them) as far as possible. However, in the laboratory the fruiting body can be formed from amoeba with different genetic properties – as long as those differences are not too extensive. Whether, and how frequently, amoebae of different descent actually do coalesce into a common fruiting body under natural conditions is not known. One

52

can merely speculate that as a rule the pseudo-plasmodium might be formed mainly by amoebae belonging to one or two 'sibships'. Hence every cell (or at least most cells) not involved in reproduction itself has a good chance that some of its genetically identical siblings will form spores. Striking the balance, the advantages of this solution seem to outweigh the disadvantage even for those cells that do not reproduce themselves.

Amongst the multicellular organisms there are many colony-forming invertebrates living in the sea, like sponges, bryozozoans, corals, and other coelenterates. Individuals of these colonies more or less fuse into a larger super-organism. Most of these species are sessile, i.e. fixed to the substratum like plants. They are capable of sexual as well as asexual reproduction. Mating is not known; reproductive cells are just shed into the water, as many plants shed their pollen into the air. Fertilized reproductive cells develop into larvae which eventually take a foot-hold on the sea bed and found new colonies.

Asexual reproduction in these animals is mainly in the form of 'budding'. Somewhere on the body of the mother organism – in many species it is not just at one particular place – a bud arises and develops into a new individual. In the fresh-water polyps and other sessile but non-colonial species, this daughter organism develops into a floating medusa similar to a jellyfish which after a certain time alights on the bottom, becomes sessile, and forms a new polyp. In colonial invertebrates, budding new individuals generally do not completely separate from the mother organism; they remain connected to it, and hence to the whole colony, by a common digestive canal. Thus all members of the colony contribute to the communal feeding and every one of them can get its share as soon as one of them is lucky enough to catch a prey.

The next level of social organisation is division of labour among the colony members. Some specialize in catching or digesting prey, others in defence, others in the production of sexual cells. Since all colony members are descendants grown by budding from one mother individual, not propagating and leaving that job to other members of the colony does not entail any disadvantage for the spreading of the genes of all of them.

The highest level of social division of labour has been attained by the siphonophores. These animals form free-floating colonies, e.g. the Portuguese man-of-war. At first glance they look like true jellyfish which are single individuals, and in German they are called '*Staatsquallen*' (state jellyfish). A colony of the species *Nanomia cara* consists of one individual at the top specialized to form a gas-filled float and carrying the whole colony. Underneath there are 'nectophores' working like little jet motors. They squirt out jets of water, driving the colony in the opposite direction, and by altering the shape of their openings they are able to alter the direction of the jets and hence the path followed by the colony. Through their action the colony can move rather quickly in any direction and at any angle and can even execute looping curves. Every one of the nectophores is a single individual with its own nervous system, but possesses nerve strands connecting it to the other nectophores and co-ordinating their actions.

Further down on the stem with the common digestive canal are: gastrozoids with long branching tentacles specialized to get and distribute food, medusa-like individuals specialized in the production of sex cells, and scale-like individuals protecting the stem with no other function. New individuals arise by budding in two specialized regions, one above and one underneath the nectophores (Mackie, 1973; Wilson 1975, p. 383). Other siphonophores are similarly organized though differing in certain details.

A siphonophore colony arises from one fertilized egg which develops into a larva. New individuals (zooides) are formed by budding from the larva but without separating from it, and develop their specialized functions as pseudo-organs. That it is really *a colony* with social division of labour and not an organism – at least not what is usually called an organism in biology – can only be shown by following the development of the individual pseudo-organs of this super-organism. They arise not from a group of cells in an embryo gradually differentiating into an organ, but from a 'bud' giving rise initially to a primitive coelenterate individual, which remains in contact with the colony and later specializes in a certain duty within the social division of labour.

The border line between an organism and a society (colony) is drawn rather arbitrarily in zoology. Should somebody maintain that a siphonophore is indeed an organism whose organs are developing in another way from that which is usual in a 'normal' multicellular organism, it would be difficult to contradict. One could merely state

54

that this super-organism arises from a colony in its individual development as well as in the course of its evolution.

1.13 *How can there be social insects?*

Three-quarters of all known animal species – about 800 000 – are insects. Though they are all small their total biomass per unit area exceeds that of all vertebrates in most terrestrial habitats (Wilson, 1975, p. 397). There are more species of ant in one square kilometre of Brazilian forest than all the species of monkeys and apes in the whole world.

Insects, presumably, were among the first animals that came to colonize land about 400 million years ago. They found a new world with gradually evolving plant life and hardly any animal competitors. They used the opportunity and entered a very large number of ecological niches. Hence their immense number of species spreading all over the world.

Especially successful were the different groups of social insects: ants, bees, wasps and termites. Ants in particular can be found all over the globe except in extreme polar regions. According to Wilson (1975, p. 421) their total world population might be in the order of a thousand billion (10^{15}) individuals.

Societies with sterile castes caring for the brood of other individuals are known only in social insects. Evolution went this way at least twelve times independently: once in termites, once or twice in ants, at least twice in wasps, and eight or even more times in bees. Except for the termites, all social insects belong to the one group of hymenoptera.

Why is it only insects that form societies with sterile castes? And why are nearly all of them hymenoptera? As a first answer Wilson advances a statistical argument: in a group of animals comprising 800 000 species there is simply a higher probability that evolution would create, by mere chance, a sub-group especially likely to produce forms of high sociality than there would be amongst annelid worms with their 7000 species or amongst starfish with their 5300 species.

The facts beg the question of whether hymenoptera and termites, though not closely related, have some common traits pre-adapting them for high forms of social life – but the answer seems to be no.

Termites, which might be called social cockroaches, are a special case. The starting point of their social evolution seems to be their need for particular symbionts. They feed on wood or cellulose which they cannot digest unless aided by certain micro-organisms – single-celled flagellates – living in a chamber of their guts in a similar way to cellulose digesting micro-organisms which live in the stomachs of ruminants. The main problem for these wood feeders is how to obtain their symbionts, for without them they starve. To survive they must feed on excrement of conspecifics containing such flagellates. Newly hatched larvae get this dainty morsel and since the chamber of the guts containing the flagellates is lost with every moulting they must eat some excrement again after each moult. The symbionts of wood-feeding cockroaches – close relatives of termites – are only transferable at the time when the larva is moulting. Hence only animals still moulting, i.e. older larvae and not grown-ups can provide the flagellates for the newly hatching progeny (Markl, 1971). Assuming a similar mode of symbiont transfer for the ancestors of the termites this might have been one important prime mover for the evolution of their social system.

Termite colonies are founded by a *pair* of king and queen who take some transferable symbionts with them to feed to the newly hatching larvae. The male helps care for the first brood; he stays with the queen and fertilizes her at intervals. The larvae do not develop into pupae but become 'nymphs' in their penultimate developmental stage, i.e. animals not very different from the grown-ups. Higher larval stages, particularly nymphs and adult but not reproducing females *and* males form the castes of workers and warriors. On the other hand *only females* become sterile workers or warriors in all social hymenoptera (ants, bees, wasps). Though there are at least eleven independent lines of evolution to society-forming species in hymenoptera, males always became only 'drones' with no social function except fertilizing the females.

Honey-bee males die when mating; part of their genital organ remains in the female – and those that did not succeed in the mating competition and hence serve no useful purpose are killed in autumn by their sisters. In some ant species 'useless' males are literally starved to death by the workers – and the males do not seem to be able to get food for themselves. In all social hymenoptera studied so far, males do not participate in any way in social life. Even if they can survive the mating act they die soon afterwards. They never help found new colonies; this is only done by one or several already-fertilized females.

Why are all hymenopteran colonies 'women's societies'? Why has evolution never resulted in hymenopteran males participating in the social division of labour? To answer these questions Hamilton (1964) referred to the idea of what is now called kin selection.

Hymenoptera have a special system of sex determination, leading to asymmetrical kin relations. In most sexually reproducing animals, and in man as well, one of the sexes has one 'pair' of unlike chromosomes for sex determination (see section 1.3), whereas the other sex has two sex chromosomes that are alike. Male humans have 22 pairs of chromosomes that are alike and one pair consisting of a fairly big so-called X-chromosome and a much smaller Y-chromosome, whilst women have two X-chromosomes of equal length and shape. The egg cells produced by women each contain only half a set of chromosomes, one from every pair, amongst them one X-chromosome. The sperm cells produced by the males each contain half a set with either an X-chromosome or a Y-chromosome. Depending on which kind of sperm fertilizes an egg, the child becomes either a boy or a girl.

In other mammals, sex determination is similar to man; in birds it is the other way round, i.e. males have two sex chromosomes that are alike and females have two that are different. The sex of the offspring depends in this case on which kind of egg cell is fertilized. In certain species of bug one sex has one chromosome more than the other.

In hymenoptera (and a few other invertebrates) males arise from unfertilized eggs – they have no father – and females from fertilized ones. At copulation the sperm gets into a special sperm storage chamber which the female can open or close when laying eggs. Thus the mother can determine the sex of her offspring at will. Wilson (1978a, p. 12) assumes that this system originated in primitive parasitic wasps that lay their eggs into killed or paralysed prey intended to serve as food for the larvae. By being able to determine the sex of the offspring at will the mother could reserve large prey for daughters which are bigger and need more protein, whereas unfertilized eggs giving rise to smaller males would be laid into smaller prey.

This system promotes female predominance in hymenopteran societies on two accounts. First, it enables the mother to produce males only when they are needed, i.e. before the mating season. In temperate climates many bee and ant societies consist of females only in winter time – or they dissolve in autumn with only fertilized females overwintering to found new colonies next spring. On the other hand, this kind of sex determination entails that sisters are more closely related to one another (share more genes) than to their brothers.

Males arising from unfertilized eggs have only half a set (a haploid set) of chromosomes and hence only half as many genes as females. As in other species they inherit 50% of the genes of their mother, but for the haploid males themselves these are 100% of their own genes, since they have no father. A male shares on the average 50% of *his* genes with a sister. However, since the brother has no father and they have only a common mother, he is like a half-brother to her; the sister shares only 25% of *her* genes with him.

Since the males are haploid, there can be no 'reshuffling of the stack' (compare section 1.3) when producing their sex cells. They produce only one kind of sperm containing all their own genes which are passed on to all their daughters – sons they cannot have. As a consequence full sisters with the same mother and the same father are more closely related than in a species with a 'normal' system of sex determination. They share all the genes of their father and on the average half the genes of their mother, in total about 75% of their own genes.

Therefore one would expect especially close co-operation between sisters in a hymenopteran society – and so it is. The brothers are pushed onto the fringe of the society; they become 'useless' drones. According to Hamilton this is a plausible explanation of why all the hymenopteran societies are 'women's societies', whereas in termite colonies with their 'normal' symmetric kin relations, females *and* males can become sterile castes of workers or warriors.

A further consequence of the kin system in hymenoptera is that sisters, sharing about 75% of their genes, *are more closely related than mother and daughter*, which have only 50% of their genes in common. According to genetical cost/benefit calculations hymenopteran females hence ought to be more interested in rearing younger reproducing sisters than to produce their own daughters. It is no

58

sacrifice on the part of the worker if she does not produce her own daughters. She does *more* for passing on her genes to future generations if she brings up sisters.

At first glance this idea of Hamilton's looks very fascinating. A problem hovering over evolutionary theory since Darwin's days is solved in an elegant and very simple way. The Oxford zoologist Richard Dawkins (1976, p. 187) calls this 'one of the most spectacular triumphs of the selfish-gene theory'. According to the German ethologists Wolfgang Wickler and Uta Seibt (1977) the question, so far not answered, of how selection, counting offspring, could bring about sterility of individuals gets a satisfactory solution.

Actually, however, Hamilton's idea so far is no more than a startling hypothesis. Whether it really can explain the observed facts remains to be proved. For the genetic cost/benefit calculations lead to satisfactory results only in case of workers rearing *full* sisters with whom they share 75% of their genes. Yet queens of many hymenopteran species must copulate with several males on their nuptial flight – a honey-bee queen up to twelve times – to get enough sperms for all the eggs they are going to lay in the course of their lives. Hence workers very often rear *half* sisters with whom they share only 25% of their genes – whereas they would pass on 50% of their genes through their own daughters.

Protagonists of Hamilton's thesis (as Trivers and Hare, 1976), sometimes suggest that the sperms of the males are clumping in the queen's sperm chamber and are used up, as it were, parcel by parcel. If that were true, the workers in a bee or ant society would, at a given moment, indeed be mainly full sisters. According to the scientists gathered at the Dahlem Conference on the Evolution of Social Behaviour there is, however, very little evidence for a marked sperm clumping effect (Harvey *et al.*, 1980). Genetical investigations in diverse species of ants and bees show that workers are in many cases not full sisters. Their average degree of relatedness is nearly always considerably lower than 75%, frequently below 50% (Crozier, 1980).

Considering these observations, kin selection theory is not sufficient to fully explain the facts. Either there have been other additional – or predominant – factors promoting the evolution of insect societies all the way; or the first hymenopteran societies were indeed founded by females mating with only one male and everything else is later adaptations of ancestral societies with sterile castes that proved to be highly successful.

The second possibility cannot be ruled out – all the more so, since not all of the evolutionary lines, at least eleven of them, leading to the formation of hymenopteran societies, can be traced back. In particular one does not know any living species as closely related to the ants as cockroaches are to termites. One can only speculate about the ancestors of the ants, not to mention their social behaviour. There are, however, thousands of wasp and bee species living either alone (solitary) or in small primitive societies. Observing them one can see at least two possible ways leading to the formation of a sophisticated insect colony. One is via co-operation of sisters, the other one via co-operation of mother and daughters. The second one conforms better to Hamilton's ideas, but even in this case it is as yet a rather unresolved question whether the prime mover of evolution was indeed the genetic (seemingly 'altruistic') 'desire' of the daughters to raise sisters instead of own daughters or alternatively the individual ('egoistic') interest of the mother to have helpers caring for her brood.

1.14 *Who manipulates whom?*

The ancestors of the hymenoptera who 'invented' sex determination with haploid males were, according to Wilson, most probably primitive parasitic wasps. Certainly they were animals that left some provisions for their larvae – a prey or a pollen-nectar mixture – as solitarily living hymenopteran species do today. Such provisions attract predators much more than the tiny larvae themselves. In particular, evolution of hymenoptera created many types of brood parasites laying 'cuckoo's eggs' in the provisions of others. The evolutionary history of this group of animals seems to have been a continuous struggle between species that invented ever newer methods to protect their brood and others that invented ever more sophisticated methods of brood parasitism. The selection pressure exerted by the brood parasites must have been enormous, writes Hubert Markl (1971).

One line of defence is guarding the nest with the brood and the provisions for the offspring. Another one is reducing the number of offspring and feeding them as they grow up, as many birds do, without storing food that attracts predators. Both, especially the guarding, can be done much more efficiently if two or more mothers co-operate in building and guarding a common nest, so that at least one of the adults is always present.

An interesting example is found among paper wasps (*Polistes*) that build their well-known nests from chewed plant material which looks like thin cardboard. Every spring such nests are founded by overwintered inseminated females. Frequently, but not always, other females join the foundress. Most probably they are individuals who, for some reason, did not manage to start a nest of their own. When they have a choice the wasps prefer to join a sister rather than an unrelated female.

Later on dominance quarrels can be observed. The foundress lays most of the eggs and tries to prevent her associates from egg laying; she even eats or destroys their eggs. She spends most of the time in the nest caring for the brood, whereas the other females have to do most of the dangerous food-gathering for a brood containing only few of their own offspring. Nevertheless even the subordinate females gain indirectly by helping to rear nieces with whom they share, on average, three-eighths of their genes, and directly if they succeed in sneaking in at least a few of their own eggs, as compared to *Polistes* females trying to set up a new colony all by themselves. For such solitary females are frequently unsuccessful and their whole brood perishes (Metcalf, 1980; Harvey *et al.*, 1980; Krebs *et al.*, 1980).

It is questionable whether the behaviour of the subordinate females might be called 'altruistic'. It rather represents a low level of personal success – they have no other choice. And there is the chance that one of them might become queen, if the foundress perishes by some mishap. On the other hand, they sometimes are chased away by the foundress after the first daughter brood has hatched.

These daughters of the first brood are relatively small, probably due to insufficient nourishment. Their ovaries are underdeveloped; they cannot reproduce and all become workers caring for a new brood of reproductive siblings of both sexes. Hatching of this second brood in late summer heralds the disruption of the colony. The males are chased away by the workers in mid-August. They cluster

61

on old nests or on other suitable places. Later they are joined by females. Mating takes place on sunlit structures or in caves destined to serve for overwintering females. The males die with the onset of the winter.

In many other species of more or less primitively social wasps and bees aggressive behaviour of the 'queen' against other females has been observed, too. The objective of such behaviour is presumably to reduce the other females to 'workers'. Daughters moreover might be manipulated in their larval stages by being fed in such a way that they become infertile. In highly evolved societies with many thousands of individuals such behaviour patterns of the queen would be futile. She could not possibly supervise all the workers. Hence aggression is replaced by more subtle forms of control. A honey-bee queen emits a special sterilizing substance from her mandibular glands which is eagerly taken up by the workers, when exchanging food with the queen, and spread all over the population of the hive. Replacing the queen by a filter paper soaked in this substance has the same effect. It is as if 'the pill' had become an addictive drug!

Seen in this way, the prime mover in the evolution of wasp and bee societies would seem to be the *efforts of the queen* to make other females, and in particular her own daughters, into baby-sitters for her brood which is threatened by many foes. According to Charles Michener, natural selection promoted the evolution of queens able to manipulate their daughters in this way. In support of his view he refers to the fact that queens in the primitively social bee species *Lasioglossum zephyrum* differ more from females of closely related non-social species than workers do. This suggests that most of the evolution has been by queens, evolving to control their offspring, rather than by workers evolving as 'altruists'.

Colonies are founded in this species by overwintered females, and as long as the foundress survives, her daughters (the 'workers') actively reject mating attempts by males. They do so in spite of the fact that they are fully functional females able to reproduce; indeed, one of them becomes the new queen when the foundress dies, usually in June, and then accepts mating, often within a day. Thus it seems that the queen is able to inhibit mating of the workers.

The behaviour of *Lasioglossum zephyrum* cannot be explained by kin selection theory, since the queen frequently copulates with several males and hence the workers care for half-sisters as well as for sisters. After the death of the old queen they help the new queen (their sister or half-sister) rearing nieces or 'half-nieces' (see also Michener, 1974).

Another possible mechanism of evolution has been suggested by Eric Charnov of the University of Utah (1978). A mother putting her eggs in her daughter's nest has an advantage, since children are more closely related to her than grandchildren. On the other hand, according to genetical cost/benefit calculations, it is no disadvantage for the daughter if it is a full sibling and hence mechanisms to avoid maternal brood parasitism would not be selected for.

This statement is generally valid for all organisms with sexual reproduction, but in hymenopteran species the daughters have a special chance to turn such maternal acts to their advantage, if they themselves lay unfertilized eggs producing males whilst caring for fertilized eggs of their mother to rear sisters with whom they share more genes than with their own daughters. Actually there are many species of ants, bees and wasps with such a mode of propagation most closely approaching Hamilton's ideas. In some of these species there is strife between the queen 'wanting' to lay all the eggs herself and trying to eat or destroy the unfertilized eggs of her daughters, and the workers trying to hide their own eggs before the queen can destroy them. In other species the queen seemingly puts up with the fact that the workers produce most of the unfertilized eggs. In some species of bumble-bee, stingless bees (meliponines) and ants up to 95% of the males are offspring of the workers (Wilson, 1975, p. 416).

On the other hand, there are species like the honey bee that have solved the conflict in the other way; the queen lays all the eggs. How it is possible in such species to prevent the appearance of mutations making workers immune to the sterilizing hormone of the queen and enabling them at least to lay unfertilized eggs, is one of the great mysteries in the evolution of social insects that cannot be explained convincingly by kin selection theory.

According to the American zoologist Robert Trivers the conflict between queen and workers might be shifted onto another plane as well. In the aforementioned much-quoted paper, which he wrote together with Hope Hare (1976), it is claimed that the queen is interested to 'invest' equally in male and (fertile) female progeny (for more about the notion of 'parental investment' see section 3.2); workers, on the other hand, should be expected to invest three times as much in sisters than in brothers. This argument, based on the asymmetrical relationships in hymenoptera, is not as obvious as it looks at first glance and needs a sophisticated exposition which we will skip over here. Moreover, it can only be applied if the workers do not lay unfertilized eggs and if they do indeed rear *full* siblings, i.e. if the queen mates only with one male – which cannot be stated with certainty for many of the species mentioned by Trivers and Hare.

As long as males and reproductive females are about equal in size the ratio of investment into the two categories equals the numerical ratio of these animals; if there are large size differences the total weight ratio of all males to all reproductive females should be compared. According to Trivers and Hare this ratio of 'investment' would be expected to be near 1:1 if the queen manipulates the workers as Michener and others assume, whereas it should be near 3:1 if the workers manipulate the queen as Trivers and Hare assume according to Hamilton's theory. In slave-making ants, however, the ratio of 'investment' should be expected to be near 1:1, since the brood is cared for by workers of another species.

Trivers and Hare then searched the literature on 21 ant species for pertinent information and published a table which, they claim, 'confirms' their expectations. However, if one does not confine oneself to the text but looks closely at their statistics it turns out that the bandwidth of variation of the sex ratio reaches from 3 males to 1 female at one extreme to 8 females to 1 male at the other. Hence the bandwidth goes *for beyond* the expected range *in both directions.*

When checking the original papers that Trivers and Hare used to work out their average figures for different ant species, one can find even larger deviations. In one of the species mentioned, M. Talbot (1943, cited by Alexander and Sherman, 1977) investigated twenty nests. Eight of them did not contain any sex animals at all, one only males, one only females, one a large female majority (nearly 3:1), nine contained large male majorities ranging from 2:1 to 21:1. One must ask whether there is any point at all in working out an 'average' from scarce data with such a wide scatter. To me, at least, it seems fairly evident that there must be *other factors* as well as those implied by Trivers and Hare causing such staggering differences in the sex ratio of different nests.

Actually, such factors have been found, at least for a species living in central European forests (*Formica polytena*). Small nests in cool locations produce only males, whereas large nests in warm locations produce predominantly or exclusively female reproductives (Gösswald, 1951; Gösswald and Bier, 1954, cited by Dumpert, 1978). To avoid misunderstandings it might be repeated here that both types of nests produce, of course, workers, i.e. infertile females that are not counted in the calculations of Trivers and Hare.

In a honey-bee hive many hundreds of drones are produced every year, but, as a rule, only one surviving new queen. Trivers and Hare argue that one must take account of the workers accompanying the swarming queen in this case. But then, of course, the ratio is much more than 3 females to 1 male.

Considering all these objections it is hard for me to see why this paper got so much attention and how it could be quoted by so many authors without reservations (see for instance Dawkins, 1976; Wickler and Seibt, 1977; Dumpert, 1978). Yet Bert Hölldobler has an explanation: 'The paper of Trivers and Hare,' he says, 'fills a gap in Hamilton's theory. The biological data are insufficient, and much is not correct in detail. Nevertheless it is a brilliant work that has given many a valuable impetus to the scientists working in the field.' In a similar vein one of the Dahlem documents (Oster *et al.*, 1980) calls the paper of Trivers and Hare an ambitious and heroic effort, which, however, 'failed unanimously to convince the scientific community'.

Stated as a generalized rule like 'If you have to co-operate then do so preferably with kin' the theory of kin selection can certainly be applied to social insects, too. This is confirmed by the fact that, according to Hölldobler, the hundreds or thousands of queens living side-by-side without competition in the multi-nest supercolonies of some ant species are supposed to be sisters or other close kin. There is, however, much less agreement as to whether Hamilton's initial pivotal idea is correct: the idea that the evolution of hymenopteran colonies with non-fertile female workers was possible mainly because females, in hymenoptera, are more closely related to their sisters than to their daughters.

65

1.15 The four pinnacles of social evolution

In one of the most impressive chapters of his main work Wilson (1975, pp. 379 *et seq.*) deals with what he calls 'the four pinnacles of social evolution'. Social systems, he says, have originated repeatedly in many major groups of organisms, achieving widely differing degrees of specialization and complexity. Four groups, however, have climbed to peaks of social evolution high above all others: the colonial invertebrates dealt with in section 1.12; the social insects; the non-human mammals; and man.

In his view the colonial invertebrates like siphonophores, corals or bryozoans 'have come close to producing perfect societies'. They have reached 'the highest social grade ever attained in three billion years of evolution' (p. 383). Division of labour, specialization and socialization have gone so far that the most highly developed colonies might just as well be called organisms.

Compared with these colonies the societies of social insects like termites, ants or bees are, according to Wilson, much less perfect. The bodies of single insects are much more sophisticated than the bodies of coelenterates and other primitive invertebrates; thus they cannot be transformed into quasi-organs of a larger community. A physical reunion in a colony resembling a large organism is impossible, and individual mobility of single members of the society is indeed one of the preconditions for the success of the social insects; it enables the colony to send out scouts to look for food and 'labour forces' to gather it if the scouts are successful.

All social insects have a high degree of division of labour and specialisation and also a high degree of altruism manifesting itself in all-embracing food sharing and suicidal defence of the nest. The single individual of an insect society is 'cheap' and easily expendable. It is programmed to sacrifice itself as well as others without hesitation. The altruism is inborn and completely impersonal and it goes side-by-side with pre-programmed murder of siblings for which there is no use. If an ant could think, writes Wilson (1978a, p. 199), it would consider any striving for self-realization or for personal reproductive success as biologically unsound and the very concept of individual freedom as intrinsically evil.

Actually an ant's brain is several orders of magnitude smaller than the smallest mammalian brains. Most of its nerve connections are permanently wired. Its social behaviour is rigid and fixed by instinct, its learning ability is very limited. 'Individual relations' seem to be unknown in the large colonies of ants, bees, and termites with their many thousands of individuals. Members of such states can distinguish castes but not individual nest mates. According to Wilson their societies are based on 'impersonal intimacy'. This is facilitated by the fact that an insect state is actually a giant family.

As for the vertebrates and especially the mammals occupying the third of Wilson's four pinnacles, none of them has societies as highly developed as those of the social insects, but taken as a whole they are more social, in the special sense that a larger percentage of species has achieved some level of sociality. Thus there seems to be a strong impelling force driving vertebrates continually a few steps along the road of social evolution and this force, according to Wilson, is their intelligence. Mammals in particular have a much higher learning ability than even the most highly developed insects; they have much better means of communication, using olfactory, accoustical and optical signals, and a much larger repertoire of diversified behaviour patterns. They are able to recognize conspecifics *as individuals* and maintain with them personalized relationships that they can remember for long periods. Thus dominance hierarchies within a group of vertebrates usually are established once and for all – or at least for long periods of time – with only a few encounters, the results of which seem to be remembered by all concerned.

But this tendency for social co-operation is opposed by a countervailing force preventing the evolution of societies comparable with the insect societies. In Wilson's view this counterforce is a different sort of genetic relationship. With a few exceptions, like the (all-female) herds of elephants, mammalian societies do not consist of kin only. There are no sterile castes either. Members of a vertebrate society are in continual competition for maximum reproductive success. While natural selection has programmed social insects to give priority to the general welfare of the colony before looking after their own selfish interests, social mammals are continually striving for the most profitable compromise between their personal interests and the advantages accruing to them by belonging to a group.

The typical vertebrate abilities of improved communications, personal recognition and increased behavioural modification enable some mammals to form selfish sub-groups within society. In many cases such groups consist of clusters of close kin, but in some species even individuals that are neither sexual mates nor genetically related may form cliques. The existence of such sub-groups limits co-operation within the larger community. Thus, according to Wilson, a typical vertebrate society favours the striving after self-preservation and protection of the closest kin at the expense of the social cohesion of the group.

Human societies, in Wilson's view, are essentially vertebrate in their structure but on a higher level of complexity. Man has broken old vertebrate constraints not by reducing selfishness, but rather by more intelligence and his ability to establish long-remembered contracts for mutual benefit, which might last for generations. Without renouncing individual reproduction human society has reached a degree of division of labour and social co-operation at least comparable to those of social insects. In his abilities of communication man surpasses all other organisms.

Comparing the species occupying the four pinnacles Wilson finds a paradox: the oldest and unquestionably most primitive species have achieved a higher degree of social cohesiveness and altruism than the younger and more highly developed forms. 'It seems as though social evolution has slowed as the body plan of the individual organism became more elaborate.'

To explain this paradox Wilson uses arguments of kin selection: siphonophores, corals and other primitive invertebrates are able to form colonies resembling a large organism because they are colonies of genetically identical individuals 'born' by budding. 'Absolute genetic identity makes possible the evolution of unlimited altruism.' Social insect colonies are giant families of close kin, and in hymenopteran nests workers share 75% of their genes if they are full siblings. Mammalian siblings, on the other hand, (with the exception of identical twins) share only half their genes and so do parents and children. Amongst other kin the amount of common gene is still lower and, moreover, a mammalian society consists, as a rule, not only of kin. Thus, Wilson thinks that one could not expect mammals to achieve the same level of social co-operation as social insects do. What seems astonishing to him is the fact that man was able to transcend this limit and 'reverse the downward trend in social evolution that prevailed over a billion years of the previous history of life'. Exactly how man has been able to cross to his fourth and highest pinnacle remains 'the culminating mystery of all biology'. Seen in this way, however, 'it perhaps seems less surprising that the human form of social organisation has arisen only once, whereas the other peaks of [social] evolution have been scaled repeatedly by independently evolving lines of animals'.

It is indeed fascinating to read this and to see how Wilson draws an all-embracing picture from the slime moulds up to man, trying to explain all social evolution in the light of one unifying theory. Unfortunately, however, the theory has a flaw: it is not true. Or rather, it is not quite true. There are exceptions for each of the first three pinnacles which do not fit into the general picture. And Wilson is much too serious a scientist as to let himself be carried away by the momentum of his own ideas and to gloss over or conceal such facts.

Amongst the slime moulds it seems to be possible for genetically not quite identical amoebae to coalesce into a fruiting body. In colonial tunicates (far ancestors of vertebrates) colonies sometimes merge that have only part of their genes in common (H. Oka in Burnet, 1971). Amongst social insects termites have the same genetical relations as most other animals including mammals and yet are able to form colonies like ants or bees with their special hymenopteran kin ties. Moreover ant and bee workers are in many cases only half-sibs sharing only 25% of their genes with each other and with future queens. Amongst some mammals there are cases of close cooperation between non-kin mentioned in section 1.11 which cannot be explained by kin selection.

All this does not mean to imply that Wilson's great unifying theory is simply wrong. There are only a few exceptions, and in the great majority of cases the genetical explanation is plausible. But it seems that there are other factors *as well* as kinship relations which can enhance the emergence of highly organized social co-operation.

Much more important in my view, however, is the question of whether Wilson's thesis of a downward trend in social evolution lasting more than a billion years is correct at all and whether he uses an appropriate scale of values in this respect. Certainly, for an 'ant able to think' the mere idea of individual self-realization would be an unsocial abstrusity, a typical vertebrate whim. But sometimes I wonder whether Wilson himself as an entomologist is not approaching too much the position of his 'thinking ant' by judging the evolutionary level of a society *only* by the degree of division of labour and social co-operation *without asking for the degree of personal freedom accorded to the individual within society.*

When trying to judge the achievement of a society from the viewpoint of a typical vertebrate, and hence also in a really humane – and human – way, we might ask how well it solves the task of *combining* the promotion of general welfare within the community with the chances of self-realization for the individual. Applying such a value scale there is no downward trend in social evolution, but rather an *increasing* perfection of societies in newly evolving species. For even an ant or a bee has not only a more highly developed body than a single zooid of a siphonophore or a coral colony, it also *has retained much more of its own individuality* within a highly organized society than the members of a colony of primitive invertebrates forming organs of a pseudo-organism. This applies even more so to the members of highly developed societies of birds or mammals.

Seen in this way social insects have scaled a higher pinnacle than siphonophores, and socially living birds and mammals a higher one than insects. Man, in this view, does not occupy a separate fourth pinnacle but the highest peak of the third, high above the other mammals. For as imperfect and amenable to improvement existing human societies might be, they still constitute *the best compromise so far achieved* in evolution between promotion of general welfare by highly developed social division of labour and maximal chances for the personal realization of the individual within society. It might even be added that the quality of this compromise gradually improved in the course of prehistoric and historic development of human societies. Today we have achieved a higher level of specialisation and division of labour as well as greater chances of individual self-realization than in the stone age.

70

2

Can one extrapolate from animals to man?

2.1 *The new synthesis*

Charles Darwin did not know of the existence of his contemporary Gregor Mendel; the scientific establishment of that epoch never really took notice of the research work of the Augustinian monk of Brno. The time was not yet ripe for the idea that biological phenomena could be defined in mathematical formulae. One did not realize yet that the chance of heredity in the individual is subject to the laws of statistical probability establishing order on a higher level.

The three botanists who rediscovered Mendel's laws in 1900 – and other early Mendelians for that matter – were not Darwinists. Thus it was not before the twenties that scientists like R. A. Fisher and J. B. S. Haldane tried to combine the achievements of Darwin and Mendel. They laid the foundation of what in theoretical biology is usually called the Modern Synthesis. The core of this synthesis is population genetics dealing with heredity phenomena within 'populations' – i.e. the members of a species living together within a limited territory. Within the last decades the Modern Synthesis has fundamentally reshaped many branches of biology, as for instance taxonomy which form a mere discipline systematically ordering species became a science establishing their evolutionary relationships.

Darwin already had realized that behaviour too – and especially the evolution of unselfish behaviour patterns – needs to be explained in the light of his theory, and Haldane, as mentioned in section 1·8 suggested an important idea for such an explanation. Yet, comparative ethology, the science of studying behaviour, developed initially outside or, at best, on the fringe of the Modern Synthesis. Actually

71

Konrad Lorenz recognized very early that there *is* an evolution of behaviour. In his work on ducks he did show that similar behaviour patterns may acquire a different – as it were, a 'metaphorical' – meaning in different but closely related species (see also Lorenz, 1963). But Lorenz is not a Darwinist in the strict sense. Occasionally he satisfied himself with explanations that behaviour patterns evolved because they contributed to 'the benefit of the species'. An attempt to explain behaviour phenomena in a way that was really consistent with evolutionary theory was not made until recently by the works of Hamilton, Maynard Smith and others mentioned in chapter 1 of this book.

Although the explanation of unselfish behaviour is, according to Wilson, 'the central theoretical problem of sociobiology', the scope of this new branch of science would be severely limited if it were confined solely to this question. It is defined rather as 'the systematic study of the biological basis of all social behaviour' (Wilson, 1975, pp. 3–4).

Wilson's main scientific achievement is that he tried to combine with the Modern Synthesis a multitude of knowledge created in the last decades in different branches of science, and thus to formulate a neo-Darwinist even more comprehensive 'New Synthesis'. His book, he says (p. 4), 'makes an attempt to codify sociobiology into a branch of evolutionary biology and particularly of modern population biology'. In the past, the development of sociobiology had been slowed by too close an identification with ethology. Wilson wants closer connections with ecology, defining relationships of organisms with their environment; with demography, giving vital information concerning growth and age structure of populations; and with population genetics, telling about the distribution of genes within populations and the co-efficients of relationships within societies.

To what extent Wilson succeeded in the formulation of his New Synthesis at the first attempt is, in my view, of only minor importance for the evaluation of his scientific achievement. The main importance is in *posing the task*. Already it can be recognized that sociobiology has given valuable impetus to many branches of biology. It has drawn attention to a host of new and interesting problems which must now be investigated in detail. Certainly the contents of sociobiology will develop and change in the course of such research work – as is the case in any thriving science. But the task of achieving the New

Synthesis will persist. Biology needs a homogeneous theoretical basis, free of internal contradictions and embracing *all* its branches. Much more dispute is raised by the question of whether and to what extent sociobiological reasoning can be applied to man. In dealing with such problems Wilson is very cautious over details, much more so than Konrad Lorenz (1963), Desmond Morris (1967) or Robert Ardrey (1970). But in principle he goes much farther than any of them – or, at least, he formulates his basic idea with much more precision. To put it in a simple way his thesis is like this: *men are living beings, hence all scientific disciplines dealing with man and his activities ought to be considered as branches of biology.*

For the present, he says, sociobiology focuses on animal societies, but in principle it is also concerned with the social behaviour of man and his ancestors and with an investigation of adaptive features in the social organisation of people living still under more or less primeval conditions. Human sociology still stands apart from sociobiology because, in his view, it confines itself mainly to an empirical investigation of human social behaviour without asking for evolutionary explanations. It is most successful when working in a similar way to taxonomy and ecology in former times, when they confined themselves to the detailed description of particular phenomena and simple first-order correlations. Those two branches of science, however, have been reshaped in the last decades by their integration into the neo-Darwinistic Modern Synthesis. Each phenomenon is now weighed for its adaptive significance and then related to the basic principles of population genetics. Human sociology and the other human and social sciences are, in Wilson's words, the last branches of biology waiting to be included in Darwinistic evolutionary theory. 'One of the functions of sociobiology, then, is to reformulate the foundations of the social sciences in a way that draws these subjects into the Modern Synthesis' (p. 4).

Still more pointedly Robert Trivers (1977) wrote in the magazine *Time*: 'Sooner or later, political science, law, economics, psychology, psychiatry, and anthropology will all be branches of sociobiology'. And Wilson himself declares (1975, p. 562): 'Scientists and humanists should consider together the possibility that the time has come for ethics to be removed temporarily from the hands of philosophers and biologicized'.

It is hardly surprising that such ideas did not find much approval amongst workers in the fields of human and social sciences.

Speaking at a symposium at San Francisco State University Wilson later said that he was surprised by the initial reactions to his book. He had not expected much response from the social scientists. He had taken it for granted that man is subject to sociobiological analysis no less than to genetic or endocrinological investigation. His intention had been to describe principles and methods of sociobiology, to offer them as tools which some social or human scientists might pick up and try out. But now he realized that he had underestimated the tradition of autonomy existing in the social sciences (Wilson, 1978b).

To me, all this does not sound very convincing. Being professor at one of the leading American universities Wilson at least must have known that scientists – to put it in 'sociobiological' terms – are a 'species' with a very conspicuous territorial behaviour; that scholars of all disciplines zealously watch over the integrity of their scientific 'hunting grounds'; hence that harsh reactions were to be expected when he, as an outsider, knowing (in their view) nothing about their work came along and claimed that their disciplines should be placed under the tutelage of another branch of science.

At the aforementioned symposium Wilson declared that he had wanted to contribute to bridging the gap between the 'two cultures' (i.e. natural and human sciences). But to establish a *collaboration* between different branches of science provoking the other side with extreme theses certainly is not the best way.

The main bone of contention, however, is not just a matter of style. Some of the things Wilson and Trivers say are not merely undiplomatic; they are simply and squarely wrong – and this was clearly spelled out by many biologists. To quote but one example: John Maynard Smith (1975) defined his objections in a very simple comparison when reviewing Wilson's book. Knowledge of biochemistry, he wrote, is essential to an understanding of evolution, but evolution theory does not hence become a branch of biochemistry. Similarly the study of animal societies probably can give important clues to understanding human societies and their origins, but this does not mean that sociology and the other social sciences could be incorporated into the Modern Synthesis. For evolutionary changes are ultimately changes in the frequencies of

74

genes in populations, whereas in human societies – as Wilson himself emphazises – drastic and continuous changes can take place without being driven by genetic change; neo-Darwinistic theory therefore is not apt to explain such phenomena. Cultural evolution has its own laws.

Even graver still are the objections against Wilson's demand for 'biologicizing' ethics. For, as Maynard Smith does not omit to emphasize, a behaviour that is 'natural' need not be right. Yet, ethics is not confined to the task of *explaining* how and why certain value judgements evolved in certain groups of men. It has primarily a *normative* task. It must judge values according to certain scales and it must be able to explain and give reasons for such judgements. Sociobiology might contribute to exposing roots of the evolution of certain moral notions – though even that is doubted by many a human or social scientist. But it certainly cannot contribute to the normative task of ethics, for nature has not set a goal to human evolution from which one might deduce value scales or value judgements for particular situations.

To give an example: animal species with a high social structure are co-operative *within* their group but, as a rule, aggressive against conspecifics not belonging to their group (see section 1·6). One can take it for granted that such a behaviour pattern existed in our animal ancestors, whilst on the other hand corresponding tendencies of sharp delimitation and aggression against neighbouring tribes or peoples can be found in nearly all peoples living in primeval conditions. Though many human and social scientists reject such analogies I cannot quite see why they might not be used as *working hypotheses*. It might well be worthwhile to investigate whether hostile behaviour against strangers is perhaps partly *inborn* in man and not just a product of education. Pedagogues studying this problem might find that – owing in part to inborn behaviour tendencies – it is quite easy to imbue young people with the idea that some 'others' – members of a neighbouring nation, of another race or religion – are inherently their foes. Should such an inborn tendency of hostility against strangers really exist, educating in a way reinforcing or directing this tendency might, in fact, be much easier than educating in the spirit of seeing brothers – or children of God – in *all* men.

Thus sociobiology might give many a valuable impetus to disciplines such as anthropology, sociology, pedagogics or psychology.

It might alert these sciences to problems which, maybe, are not only of purely academic interest. But for investigating such problems one cannot use the techniques appropriate for research of animal societies. The study of man requires its own methods adapted to the special character of our species.

As for drawing practical conclusions from the results of such investigations, sociobiology is certainly *not* the discipline apt to do this. Actually one can find different views – and practices – concerned with whether people *ought* to be educated in a chauvinistic or in an internationalist spirit. Such views can be supported with a whole array of political, ethical or religious arguments, but hardly with sociobiological theses. Assuming it to be true that there is in human nature an inborn tendency for hostility towards strangers, this might be accepted as a fact with satisfaction or with some resignation; yet it is equally possible to conclude that under such circumstances one must make special efforts to *counteract* such inborn tendencies, because in the nuclear age we cannot afford any longer the assiduous cultivation of enemy images.

I, for my part, hold to the latter view. And I can even support it with the quasi-sociobiological argument that a nuclear world war would be detrimental to the benefit of our species as well as to the reproductive success of any of its members. But it would seem catastrophic to me to discuss ways and means how to avoid the holocaust of such a war as a special problem of applying sociobiological knowledge to human society as one might be inclined to do if one strictly adhered to Trivers' thesis.

Of course, Trivers will object that he evidently did not mean it that way. But his own highly exaggerated claim actually begs for such imputations. Political and economic sciences, law and ethics never will become mere branches of biology. And that's just as well too.

2.2 *Human nature and the mutual relations among sciences*

One of the most prominent critics of sociobiology is Marshall Sahlins, professor of anthropology at the University of Chicago and author of a booklet on *The Use and Abuse of Biology* (1976). There Wilson is quoted as disclaiming any attempt to account biologically for the whole of human social life; perhaps only 10% could be laid to biology.

76

'This retreat, if it is one, is not enough,' says Sahlins. For, in a sense, biology – but also physics or chemistry –account for 100% of human social life: all cultural life must, of course, conform to natural laws. But these laws, according to Sahlins, only set limits for culture; they cannot explain cultural phenomena happening, as it were, on a higher plane. Relations between culture and nature are *hierarchical*; the wisdom of cultural processes consists in putting natural systems to the service of its own intentions (Sahlins, 1976, pp. 65–7).

Metaphorically speaking one could say that a man falling from a window is as much subject to gravity as a stone. But such a trival statement does not disclose anything about the essence of being human. What discerns man from all other species is that he can fly without having natural wings. He can do so thanks to his culture – not by ignoring natural laws, but by thoughtfully applying them and putting them to his service.

To describe the mutual relations between anthropology and physics such a metaphor is probably sufficient. But is it really true that the essence of the hierarchical relations between biology and the sciences of human behaviour does consist only of the trivial fact that natural laws set limits to culture?

In his book *On Human Nature* published in 1978 Wilson makes a new – and in my view much more successful – attempt to define the mutual relations between sociobiology and the human and social sciences. Sociobiologists, he says, consider man as though seen through the front end of a telescope. Thus they see him diminished in size and at greater-than-usual distance in order to view him simultaneously with other species, or, to use Wilson's phrase, simultaneously with an array of other social experiments (p. 17).

In his view the relation of biology to the human and social sciences is similar to the relations of physics to chemistry, chemistry to molecular biology, or molecular biology to physiology. A scientist with a broad view, he says, must be well acquainted not only with his own discipline but also, on the one hand, with the more general discipline which provides foundations for his own science and, on the other hand, with the more specialized discipline using the results of his own branch of science. Thus a scholar of chemistry ought to study certain branches of physics and molecular biology. In essence Wilson says something very similar to Sahlins who speaks of the hierarchical relations of science. Yet in Wilson's view the mutual relations

77

between the more general and the more specialized discipline are much closer – and there are many examples in the history of natural sciences supporting this view.

The new ideas of modern physics on the structure of the atom and the forces acting between atoms and groups of atoms have indeed reformulated the foundations of chemistry. Today it is possible to *explain* many phenomena (for instance, valency) which old chemistry could only describe. Progress in physics was the pre-condition for developing ideas on the spatial (stereochemical) structure of complicated organic molecules enabling scientists to infer their biochemical properties.

A very interesting example of an effect reaching over several hierarchical levels is the elucidation of the molecular structure of the hereditary substance. The first model idea of the structure of that substance was formulated not by a geneticist or molecular biologist but by one of the great men of modern theoretical physics. The Austrian Nobel laureate Erwin Schrödinger, after having left his country to avoid living under Hitler's rule, held a series of lectures at the University of Dublin in February 1943 examining biological phenomena in the light of physical quantum theory. In these lectures he explained the idea that the substance carrying the hereditary information must have the properties of an aperiodic crystal.

At the first sight this seems a contradiction in itself. The very essence of a crystal is, after all, its regular, periodic structure – a certain configuration of atoms repeating itself again and again. But Schrödinger knew very well what he meant. A single gene, he said, must be a rather small structure, consisting of not more than a few thousand atoms at the most. How, did he ask, could such a small structure have such stability that it can be passed on through many generations without appreciable change? How is it possible that rather large amounts of energy are required to induce a mutation, i.e. a change of hereditary information – as can be shown by inducing mutations by radiation? All this, he said, could only be explained if the atoms in the hereditary substance were connected in a very stable structure, as in a crystal. Yet, at the same time, they must be arranged in some aperiodic manner for otherwise they could not have an information content. In the following year O. T. Avery, an American bacteriologist, discovered that the hereditary substance which must have such properties was not the protein in the chromosomes as had been hitherto assumed but DNA (deoxyribonucleic acid).

Schrödinger's lectures, published later as a small booklet (1944), were of seminal importance for many young scientists returning after the war to civil life and looking for new tasks. Two of the three scientists who later got the Nobel prize for elucidating the structure of DNA were put on the right track by reading this booklet (see M. Wilkins, Nobel lecture, 1963; J. D. Watson, 1968, p. 13, referring to F. Crick). And both of them were working with the tools of physics to solve a problem of molecular biology: Wilkins with X-ray-crystallographic methods; Crick and Watson with theoretical stereochemical deliberations, and with spatial model building of the DNA molecule. What they found out in the event was a striking confirmation of Schrödinger's ideas: the DNA double-helix has indeed the physical properties of a crystal, but inside the helix there are several kinds of pairs of nitrogenous bases which (as pairs) are all of equal size. Hence the structure can be stable like that of a crystal. But the base pairs follow each other in an aperiodic sequence. They are like letters of an alphabet containing the hereditary information.

I have dealt with this example at such length because I think that it gives a very good idea of how one discipline can influence another one. Schrödinger never claimed that the essence of life could be defined exclusively in terms of quantum physics. Yet it was just his very deep insight into his own discipline that enabled him to see biology as probably no biologist of his days would have been able to do. Thus he was able to develop a new kind of model idea – and this idea was, as it were, a 'hit'. It was the impetus for a number of brilliant young scientists to approach a crucial problem of biology in a new way.

For Wilson, apparently, relations between sociobiology and human and social sciences should be of a similar kind. Biology, he suggests, 'is the key to human nature'. Perhaps it would be more correct to say one of the keys. Anyway, social scientists should not just ignore this key. However, Wilson expressly emphasizes that 'social sciences are potentially far richer in content' (1978a, p. 13). Thus they cannot simply be replaced by biology.

The main difference between Wilson and Schrödinger is that the latter presented deliberations concerning another branch of *natural* sciences whereas Wilson wants to bridge the gap between the 'two cultures'. And many human scientists believe that methods and ideas of natural science cannot be applied to the investigation of human behaviour since human consciousness is different *in principle* from that of all animals.

'Starting a little before agriculture, there was a rapid change in technology which spread across the world in a very few thousand years,' declared S. L. Washburn, professor of anthropology at the University of California, Berkeley, at the aforementioned symposium at San Francisco State University (1978*a*, p. 13). 'The conditions that had dominated human evolution for some millions of years changed, and the nature of the change, the speed of the change and the rate of diffusion all show that the changes were the result of learning, not biological evolution ... The conditions that dominated the evolution of *Homo sapiens* no longer exist, and a theory of evolution cannot be indiscriminately applied as if the contemporary situation were similar to that of thousands of years ago ... Most human behaviour has no close counterpart in any non-human animal, and this is the most important conclusion of the study of human evolution.'

In what follows we shall see that there are changes as a result of learning which might be called an incipient culture in animals, too – and not only in the most highly developed ones, for that matter. It is true that the speed of such changes and the rate of diffusion are much quicker than the tempo of biological evolution – *but this applies to animals just as well as to man*. Though culture certainly is more important for human behaviour than for animal behaviour, there probably was not an abrupt change of conditions, but a gradual transition.

But even granting that human evolution has its own laws, different from those valid for other organisms, human behaviour nevertheless must have *evolved* from animal behaviour. Thus there is a good argument for assuming that we probably will be better able to understand the man of our times if we know how, from an animal, he *became* what he is today.

When I wrote down this sentence for the first draft of the preface of this book I thought that it was self-evident and did not need to be proved. Only later when studying further literature on this topic did I find that this idea is disputed. According to Washburn, 'a strong case can be made that the founders of social science would have been far better off if they had never heard of biology or evolution.'

Washburn takes this position though he himself in many enlightening papers (see, 1978b; or Washburn and Lancaster, 1968) has used very interesting comparisons between apes or monkeys and man. To support his claim he uses two main arguments. First, that there are many examples of an abuse of biologic theories in dealing with human relations. Well-known examples are: the so-called 'Social Darwinism' justifying the exploitation and the scandalous conditions of early capitalism with quasi-Darwinistic slogans like 'struggle for existence' and 'survival of the fittest'; and the pseudo-scientific 'race theory' of Hitler in Germany.

In my view this argument of Washburn's is not convincing. Power politics uses everything at hand to justify its crimes and to indoctrinate people – human as well as natural sciences, philosophy, arts and religion. The philosophy of Hegel can be called a justification of the Prussian authoritarian state – but should one therefore reject, in principle, the application of philosophical ideas to the investigation of human problems? The inquisition claimed to be operating in the spirit of Christ; Stalin claimed to be a Marxist. There is no doctrine that cannot be abused.

Certainly sociobiology has ideas apt to be abused and sociobiologists ought to take note of this. But are there no such ideas in theories of proper human and social sciences? Can it be denied that Freud's psychoanalysis or Skinner's behaviourism might be abused? Of course, the danger of abuse of scientific theories is a grave problem – *but it is not a special problem of applying ideas of natural sciences to the behaviour of man.*

Washburn's second main argument is that much more is known about human behaviour than about the behaviour of apes or other animals. In principle he admits that experiments on apes and monkeys may alert human scientists to certain problems. But alerting is not proof, he says, and the problems confronting human sciences can, in his view, not be usefully framed by starting with animal behaviour.

At the same symposium Kenneth E. Boulding, the well-known economist and sociologist (who, on the whole, has a much more balanced view about sociobiology than Washburn) stated that human social systems are complicated and must be treated for what they are. Human beings, he says, have consciousness, have images of the future, have very complex systems of values, and there is a danger of over-simplification when comparing human societies with animal societies. They demand their own description and their own evaluations.

This, however, is not denied by serious sociobiologists, though there is hardly one of them who does not occasionally slip into ill-founded and superficial comparisons between animals and man. Yet the value of an incipient branch of science cannot be measured by the number of its errors, but only asking whether it has produced new ideas that might be valuable for the progress of science.

2.3 *What is a human being?*

Man is a descendant of ape-like ancestors, but according to biological taxonomists he is *not a naked ape*, i.e. not a species of apes with certain peculiarities (Simpson, 1972). Rather he is considered to be the only surviving species of a special genus (*Homo*) and even a special taxonomic 'family' (Hominidae) which together with other families of apes and monkeys belongs to the 'suborder' of Anthropoidea and to the order of Primates.

With the modesty so typical of us, we have called our species *Homo sapiens sapiens* – the doubly wise man. *All* men living today belong to this one species. An anthropologist can define the special characteristics of the body of an eskimo or of a Hottentot, and one need not be an expert to be able to distinguish between them, but if chance brought together a male of the one race with a female of the other they would be able to have viable and *fertile* children and not only infertile hybirds. Conquerors of all races and colours have performed such experiments a million-fold in human history by mixing with subjugated peoples.

That there are well-defined bodily differences among different races and peoples is not just an invention of 'racists' though in most cases there are gradual transitions and no sharp delimitations between their habitats. Single genes, as for instance those for blood groups, can as a rule be found in all races and peoples, but with different frequencies. Our ability to recognize an individual as belonging to a particular race is based on the fact that there are many genes with different frequencies in different populations (Dobzhansky, 1972). There is not the slightest scientific foundation for the specious claim that negroes, coloured people or some other races are genetically more closely related to our animal ancestors than the metropolitan white 'master race'.

Looking back into the past, there is, of course, no clear frontier between animal and man. Present human beings evolved in the course of millions of years from ape to man, passing through several intermediate stages. Bones of such intermediate forms have been found. These creatures had bigger brains than apes and smaller ones than man and many other characteristics which are 'in between'. It is hardly possible to define a particular point in this evolution from whence our ancestors were 'more man than animal'.

One will never be able to study the behaviour of our animal and semi-human ancestors by direct observation. What can be found in the caves of pre-humans only yields sparse and certainly incomplete evidence on their diet. Tools must have reached a certain degree of sophistication before we could recognize them as such after hundreds of thousands of years. From direct observation we know that chimps use sticks, twigs, leaves and stones as 'tools' and that sometimes they prepare them for the intended use, but if such a 'tool' were found later one could hardly recognize that it had been used by an animal. Thus, if we want to speculate about the behaviour of our pre-human ancestors we have to rely mainly on indirect methods.

Sociobiology can contribute to such deliberations much more than by mere superficial analogies that might be correct or not. It has several methods of evaluating the *probability* of whether an inference might be justified.

The first method is the comparison with *all* closely related species. Thus family structure is very different in different species of apes (more about that in chapter 3) and hence does not allow inferences on the family structure of our ancestors. On the other hand a close and long-lasting bond between mother and child and a pronounced phase of socialisation is typical for *all* apes and monkeys; hence it is very likely that our ancestors behaved in just the same way – all the more so since present men do so as well (Wilson, 1975, p. 551).

The second method is the comparison with species living in *similar environmental conditions*. Today it is generally assumed that our *animal* ancestors had already left the forest and became inhabitants of the steppe. To be more exact, it was probably the forest that left them. Apparently they lived in a region where forest gradually transformed into steppe due to climatic changes. They had to adapt to life in the steppe like baboons and geladas, and this certainly had its effects on their social structure. Baboons and geladas are the only species of primates with stable family units that join into larger well-organized troops (Kummer, 1968). Possibly our ancestors had some similar kind of organization.

The third method is the application of *general* sociobiological rules to man and his ancestors. This is the way to arrive at the supposition that there might be an inborn behavioural tendency of hostility against strangers in man (see. section 2·1). Similarly incest taboos, which can be found in nearly all peoples, might be assumed to be a cultural superstructure based on inborn behavioural tendencies inherited from our pre-human ancestors; for most socially living animals have behaviour patterns working in a way that makes incest unlikely or impossible (for more, see section 3·15).

The fourth method, last but not least, is *direct sociobiological analysis* of behaviour of peoples living under more or less primeval conditions. Of course, one must be careful not to over-simplify human behaviour, but if there are comparable adaptation processes in comparable circumstances there is at least good reason for the assumption that similar mechanisms might be at work in both cases.

When studying man, sociobiology need not confine itself to 'universals' – i.e. to behaviour patterns found in *all* (or nearly all) men which probably are, at least in part, genetically influenced. Even animals not particularly high on the ladder of evolution often have a repertoire of *different* behaviour patterns enabling them to react differently to varying environmental conditions. Sociobiology can plausibly explain why an animal as simple as a male wren which is, as a rule, monogamous can become a 'bigamist' in certain circumstances. Man is a much more complicated being than a wren, and he adapts to different circumstances mainly on a cultural level. Nevertheless the combination of ethology and ecology demanded by Wilson for the study of animal societies might just as well be applied to tribal peoples.

Some of the peculiarities of man, things that actually distinguish him from all other species, can be seen in very clear relief when comparing him with those animals that long before the evolution of man already had societies with the character of city-states with a sophisticated division of labour: the ants. These most successful of all social insects have spread in the course of hundreds of millions of years all over the globe except the extreme polar regions. They have occupied a very large number of ecological niches – but in doing so they split up into more than 12 000 different species, each adapted to its special circumstances; species which, as a rule, cannot interbreed.

Man also spread all over the globe, he intruded into the most diverse habitats wholly or partly displacing other species from their ecological niches. But he adapted to all these different ecosystems mainly *culturally* and not genetically and hence many laws of natural evolution do not fully apply to him. There is no animal on earth able to exist in so many different habitats without having adapted to them by splitting into different species. Man has preserved the unity of his species. And just because he adapted *culturally* he could spread into all sorts of ecological niches much quicker than any other group of animals could have done.

Only two million years ago our ancestors were beings in between animal and man, only able to exist in tropical conditions. Half a million years ago, maybe even earlier, members of the genus *homo* – though not yet of our species – were living already in many regions of the temperate zone of the Old World. They had learnt to use fire and to cover themselves with animal furs. Thus they were able to survive harsh winters in spite of the fact that *biologically* they were not well adapted to the climatic conditions of the temperate zone (Simpson, 1966; Campbell, 1972).

Environmental manipulation for protection against climate or predators is practised by many species. The mere building of nests is a rudimentary form of such an activity. Beavers can change the character of a whole landscape by their constructions. Ants have a leading position in this respect, too. They are similar to man in adapting to different circumstances mainly by behavioural and not by bodily modifications. And they evolved the ability to carry out certain 'crafts'. Many ant species 'milk' aphids to get the sweet honey dew excreted by them. Some ants are even proper 'dairy farmers', fetching aphids into their nests, constructing 'stables' for them where they feed and milk them. South American leaf-cutting ants have a sort of horticulture. They cultivate fungi on a mixture of chewed leaves and faeces and harvest them. Some of these fungi are, as it were, 'cultivated plants' that can only thrive in the 'gardens' of the ants which remove the 'weeds' competing with the fungi.

'Could such phenomena be called culture?' I asked Bert Hölldobler at the Dahlem Conference on the Evolution of Social Behaviour.

'As a rule the term culture is applied to abilities that are *learned* and passed on by instruction, hence the answer must be no,' he replied. 'A young leaf-cutter queen carries a bit of the fungus with her on her nuptial flight and starts cultivating it, when founding a new nest. Later the newly hatching workers take over the "garden" and care for it without being taught by the queen. Their behaviour is inborn.'

The ability to carry out 'horticulture' or 'dairy farming' is genetically pre-programmed in certain ant species. Members of a particular species are able to master *just one* of these crafts and only in the particular way for which they are programmed. They cannot learn the crafts of other ant species. Man, on the other had, can grow crops *and* raise cattle; he can learn many different crafts and is able to pass them on non-genetically by teaching other men. But are we really unique in this capability?

2.4 *Do animals have culture?*

Biologists talking about 'culture' use the term in a slightly different sense than that used in everyday language. 'By culture we mean those behaviours that are transmitted from one individual to another by teaching and learning', writes John Tyler Bonner of Princeton University (1979). The behaviour itself, transmitted in such a non-genetical way, might be much more primitive than the sophisticated horticultural activity of the leaf-cutter ants. But the ants' behaviour is *inborn*, permanently wired into their nervous systems and therefore rigid and fixed, whereas learned behaviour is much more flexible.

'Culture' in this sense requires an inborn ability to learn, and is enhanced by an ability to imitate as can be found in apes. Its genetical basis is an inherited blueprint, a wiring of the brain that makes learning possible. Within limits an insect can learn, but the brain of even the most highly developed insect is so much smaller than a vertebrate brain that its learning ability is rather small. 'Culture' is mainly a phenomenon of higher vertebrates.

Its main advantage is that it enables an individual to adapt quickly to different environmental conditions by using different (learned) behaviours. Hence a species can *simultaneously* intrude into several ecological niches and can do so much quicker than by genetic adaptation. Man, as mentioned in the previous chapter, has achieved a particularily high perfection in this strategy, but he is by no means unique in this achievement.

Even a simple bird, common on European shores and not distinguished by a high degree of social evolution, the oystercatcher (*Haemotopus ostralegus*), has done the same trick – of course in a more modest way. This black and white pigeon-sized bird with a red beak and long red legs feeds either on worms *or* on mussels but never on both. Put another way, it feeds on worms where there is an adequate supply of them; but once upon a time members of this species invented two methods that enabled them to intrude into a new habitat where there was not enough worms and to live on mussels.

The first invention, still relatively simple, is to peck hard at the mussels when they are closed at low tide until their shells break. The second, much more sophisticated innovation, is to quickly insert the bill into the mussel when it is open at high tide and cut the muscle that closes the shell, thereby making the prey defenceless.

It seems that one bird cannot learn more than one of these techniques, and evidently it needs considerable training – taxing, as it were, its mental abilities to the limit. Worm-eating young oystercatchers are independent at the age of 6 or 7 weeks, whereas mussel-eaters do not master their craft before they are 18 to 26 weeks old. There is, however, no genetic disposition for the ability to learn either one craft or the other. When the English scientist Norton-Griffiths (1969) swapped eggs of the birds with three different feeding modes, the young learnt the technique of their foster-parents without any recognizable tendency to revert to the way of life of their real parents.

There is a big difference, therefore, between the oystercatcher and man. The bird can learn *but one* craft, whereas man can master a number of techniques at the same time. Nevertheless, the bird had already found out that one can make inventions that open the way into a new habitat.

Other birds are inventive, too. A finch species observed by Darwin on the Galapagos Islands invented the *use of tools*. Holding thorns or cactus stings in its bill the bird stabs insects living in tree bark and gets them out. In this way he can intrude into the ecological niche occupied on the continent by the woodpeckers, which do not inhabit those islands. Competing with a woodpecker the finch probably would lose the contest. But the invention has enabled it to make the best of an existing opportunity and to do so much quicker than by biological adaptation, i.e. by the evolution of a long and pointed bill.

Titmice in Britain only recently invented the trick of piercing the aluminium foils covering milk bottles placed on the doorstep, and thus getting at the cream. This new avian sub-culture is spreading quickly.

An animal that never knew its mother, like a turtle or a cuckoo, must have an inborn programme telling it what to eat and *what not*. It must have inbuilt inhibitory mechanisms to avoid unhealthy or poisonous food. Such a programme is rigid; it cannot cope with environmental changes in the food supply. Even for a predator fairly high up on the evolutionary ladder such an inborn prey recognition programme will do. What carnivores teach their young is primarily *techniques* of hunting rather than recognition cf prey. Cats, wolves and others sometimes bring living prey to their young and let them practise. Of course, even a dog or cat reared by man has a hunting instinct. But the animal will be a more efficient hunter if taught the relevant techniques by its mother.

For omnivores like rats, inborn programmes evidently will not be sufficient. They cannot possibly have an instinctive knowledge of all the food items they might eat and still less of all the poisons they ought to avoid – all the more so since they are able to avoid new poisons synthesized by man that did not exist before. Obviously they must be able to learn what to eat and what not.

Rats are very shy when presented with a new food, and try it at first in very small amounts. If they have any intestinal or visceral trouble within 12 hours after ingesting the new food, they associate it – as a rule correctly – with the smell and taste of this food which they will avoid in future (Rozin, 1976). By experimental manipulation rats can be made so suspicious of any new food that they would rather starve to death than try it (Richter, 1953, quoted by Rozin). For an animal which man has unsuccessfully been trying to poison and eradicate for thousands of years such a behaviour, on the border of paranoia, makes sense and is consistent with its reality, writes the American psychologist Paul Rozin (1976).

Monkeys *learn* from their mothers and from other members of their social group what they should eat. Mothers of some species pass on chewed food to their infants. Young baboons sometimes sniff at the mouth of their mother when she is feeding – presumably to learn what food she selects (Kummer, 1971, p. 27).

Unknown food is initially avoided by monkeys. In captivity baboons eat bananas with delight. Free living baboons that have never known bananas dare not touch them at first. When the fruits are offered repeatedly, a few enterprising young animals will eventually start trying them, whilst the old animals are very 'conservative' and reject any innovations (*ibid.*, p. 126).

Evidently *both* kinds of behaviour pattern are valuable for the group, complementing each other in a very useful way. The enterprising and inquisitive behaviour of the juveniles makes new sources of food or, maybe, new tools accessible. Yet the rigid conservativism of the old ones is a very necessary safety reserve which will survive a new behaviour or a new food for at least ten years and guarantee the further existence of the group, even if there is a snag in the new 'culture' that is not apparent at once (Kummer, 1971, p. 129).

Knowledge about their foes seems to be inborn in some species but must be learned by others, and hence is part of their 'culture'. According to Konrad Lorenz (1963/66, p. 45) old and experienced jackdaws hardly take any notice if a young bird shows fright at some meaningless stimulus. 'But if the same sort of alarm proceeds from one of the old males all the jackdaws within sight and earshot immediately take flight. Since, in jackdaws, recognition of enemies is not innate ... it is probably of considerable importance that great store is set by the 'opinion' of old, high-ranking, and experienced birds.'

Whereas the benefits of being able to learn and the greater flexibility of behaviour achieved in such a way are obvious, the 'costs' of intelligence are much more difficult to recognize. They include expenses for the construction and maintenance of a more sophisticated central nervous system, such as the need to have a bigger head and a higher metabolic rate in the brain and also the costs of learning itself. Thus, not knowing a predator by instinct might mean death to an individual that has not yet learnt to recognize it (M. E. Dawkins *et al.*, 1981).

A remarkable repertory of tool use has been observed in chimpanzees. They brandish, wave and throw sticks to intimidate others; use them as a pokers to get out honey from a hive of wild bees, and as levers to open boxes. They use leaves to wipe dirt from their bodies and indeed, as it were, as 'toilet paper' and to dab at wounds (Goodall, 1971, p. 218). Infants watch the adults as they use tools, pick them up and play with them, imitating the adults' behaviour. When two-year-old chimps in captivity are denied the opportunity to play with sticks their ability to solve problems with the aid of sticks at a later age is reduced (Wilson, 1978a, p. 30).

Even tool *making* behaviour is no special prerogative of man. Chimpanzees strip off leaves from twigs to prepare them for use in 'fishing' termites. At the time of the termites' nuptial flights, when their mounds are open, the chimps insert such a twig or plant stem into the tunnels. Termite warriors bite into the supposed intruder, and when withdrawing the twig the 'fisherman' ape can collect them (Goodall, 1971, p. 42–45).

An even greater achievement is the preparation of 'sponges' from chewed leaves to lift water from tree holes not directly accessible to the mouth. The chewed leaves are dipped into the hole and then sucked out. In this activity the 'tool' is prepared from a 'raw material' that has to be considerably changed for use (Goodall, 1971, p. 97).

Very interesting examples of invention were observed by Japanese scientists in macaques, a species closely related to the rhesus monkeys (Imanishi, 1963; Kawai, 1965). On the small island of Koshima the scientists regularly put sweet potatoes onto the beach to attract a troop of monkeys they wanted to observe. One macaque girl started to wash the tubers in the water of a streamlet and soon a few animals of her age group imitated this behaviour. Within five years nearly 80% of the troop's younger animals were washing the potatoes, whereas only 18% of the older ones did – all of them females that had learnt the behaviour from their children.

The place of washing gradually was shifted from the streamlet to the sea. Mothers, when washing their tubers, took their babies with them who, in this way, got acquainted with the wet environment at a very early age. They not only learnt washing from their mothers and started to dip the potatoes into the sea water before every bite – presumably to salt them – they also got used to moving about in the water which had been avoided by earlier generations. Bathing and splashing became a favourite pastime for the children on hot days. Young monkeys learnt swimming and diving, some of them started to collect seaweeds and tried to eat them, one young animal swam to a neighbouring island. A large new habitat had been opened for the macaques.

Later on the observing scientists put wheat on the sand of the beaches, and the girl that had invented the potato washing, by that time an adolescent of four years, invented something new and even more interesting: she threw the wheat-sand mixture into the water – the sand sank, the wheat floated on the surface and could be easily collected. This behaviour, too, was imitated.

What the Japanese scientists observed at Koshima is the emergence of a new 'culture' gradually becoming a 'tradition' of the group. Presumably similar things can happen under natural conditions as well, but there is hardly a chance to witness such a rare event by mere field studies in an unmanipulated environment. Only the experiment of presenting the food on the beach created the challenge for these 'inventions'.

That old animals are a most valuable store of experiences and 'traditions' is obvious. The coexistence of several generations within a group facilitates the passing on of such 'traditions', not only from parents to children but also among other individuals. In times of drought an old baboon might remember that once upon a time, when he himself was still an adolescent, the herd was led by an old male to a water hole outside the normal territory used by the troop. This stored experience might save the troop from perishing, and simultaneously the young animals would learn that 'tradition' and pass it on to later generations (Kummer, 1971, p. 126).

Reading such reports one can see very clearly that what we call human culture today has roots reaching back far beyond the origin of a special human evolution; to ancestors that certainly were animals and not yet men or even mere 'half-men'. There is no need to elaborate that even the most 'primitive' human culture is much more sophisticated than all incipient 'culture' in non-human animals. But as Darwin already discussed in some detail, it is the *complexity* rather than the mere existence of human culture that is peculiar to man (see also Simpson, 1972).

2.5 *Baboon democracy*

When hamadryas baboons wake up in the morning they leave their sleeping places in the rocks and sit down in the sun to warm up. Mothers nurse their babies, children play, adults groom each other, a male copulates with a female. After an hour or two the moving about in the group becomes more frequent. Young adult males get up with their families and move – in various directions – beyond the area hitherto occupied by the troop. Then they sit down again to see how and if the others respond to their movement. This to-and-fro business might last for an hour or more until, at last, the whole troop departs (Kummer, 1971, p. 17 *et seq.*,).

The herd Hans Kummer observed when he started his studies of hamadryas baboons in the sixties in Ethiopia usually moved off as one group in closed formation. Alexander Stolba, a graduate student of Kummer's, who had chosen decision processes in hama- dryas baboon groups as the theme for his doctoral thesis (1979), found another behaviour pattern in a neighbouring larger herd. Departure here was as a rule in three sub-groups which he called bands. These were stable units within the herd consisting always of the same individuals.

The family of a hamadryas baboon is a harem group of one male, several females and their children. Several such groups form a 'clan' to which belong also old males that have lost their harem and sub-adult males that have no females yet or are just laying the foundations of their future harems by assembling some immature girls around them. The band consists of several clans. Presumably all the males of a clan are close kin, and the degree of relatedness among the males of a whole band seems to be closer than to the other males of the herd.

For hamadryas baboons the decision of where to go is vital. In a day they march something like 8 to 13 kilometres, sometimes even 20 km. If there is not enough food or water at their destination it might be fatal for some of the weaker animals. But how does the decision about where to go come about?

Neither the clans nor the bands, and even less the whole herd, have a 'leader' like the 'matriarch' in a herd of elephants. According to Kummer (1968) the first advances of the young males with their families might be considered as 'proposals' for diverse directions of departure. But *who decides* which one of these proposals is eventually accepted?

After twenty months of intense observation, Stolba has come to the conclusion that in hamadryas baboon groups such decisions are taken in a 'democratic' way. All participants cast their 'votes' as it were, for one or other of the 'proposals'. The main voters seem to be the adult and sub-adult males, but probably there are subtle contributions of females and young animals as well.

Before departure in the morning and also during the day when decisions about the direction to be taken are required males have more contact with each other than at other times. As a rule an adult hamadryas male is surrounded by his females and children; other adult males, do not approach them too closely, indicating that they respect him as possessor of his harem. Yet as soon as decisions about the route to be taken are imminent one often can observe that a male approaches another one with a 'contact grunt', exchanges glances, than turns round and presents his red buttocks (a friendly gesture in baboons) and departs indicating a certain direction.

In the morning, before departure, males observe each other with much more attention than at other times. A young male suggesting a certain direction moves a few metres with his family, then sits down and waits for the reaction of the others. Agreement is shown by others moving in the same direction. To mark non-agreement males remain sitting and look down to earth as if they were still half asleep – though, actually they had been wide awake before and had attentively registered the movements of others. To catch the attention of others, a male might stand in a characteristic pose, stiff on all four legs, for several minutes before he moves in a certain direction.

It seems that in the morning agreement on the direction to be taken is first of all established in the individual clans. To warm up, the baboons sit on the sunny side of the rock or on the side protected from wind. But when they start moving off, an intended direction is clearly visible; thus they might go to the cold north-western side of the rock if they want to depart in that direction. Agreement among the clans of a band usually is established during further moves down the rock before final departure. As a rule the vote of the males of medium age who have the largest harem groups is decisive. Those whose 'proposals' have not been accepted join the general departure.

Only a few times did Stolba observe that the clans had not yet finally agreed on the route to be taken when they were leaving their sleeping rock. In such exceptional circumstances he could recognize the influence of the oldest and most experienced males – usually hardly noticeable. These males are the only ones that are able to hold up a column already on the march by sitting down on an exposed elevated place visible to all, looking down to the earth to register their non-agreement. Their high potential to influence decisions seems to arise when the younger ones who usually decide seem not to be quite sure what to do, says Stolba. In such a situation one of the old males might temporarily take over the lead of the clan.

When departing from the sleeping rock the baboons always use one of a number of well defined paths. Each of them points in the direction of a certain territory where there are sizeable feeding places and at least one water-hole. That these places are well known to the animals can be inferred by the fact that they start running about 500 metres before reaching their destination, even if it cannot yet be seen.

Only the first stretch of a route is bound to a certain path; using this path indicates the intention to spend the noon-time rest at a certain water-hole. On the way the animals of a band might divide up into clans or even smaller units to forage more effectively. Groups belonging to the same clan try not to lose sight of each other, or try to keep contact by their characteristic 'bahoo' calls. On the other hand the distance between the foraging clans might become so large that they lose contact. Nevertheless all the clans of a band usually arrive at the same water-hole at noon, as if they had 'agreed upon' that in the morning.

This agreement, however, is executed in a flexible way. The route indicated by the path taken at the departure in the morning might be changed later if food supply is insufficient, or if there are predators or humans in the region of the intended goal. If all the clans of a group are in contact with each other when changing the route they all arrive at noon at the new goal, i.e. at a water-hole other than that indicated by their path of departure in the morning. If, on the other hand, they lose contact when one or the other clan has decided to change the original plan for some reasons, the clans spend their noon time at different water-holes. According to Stolba this is a rather rare occurrence.

On the way back the band might again divide up into smaller sub-groups. Again the baboons forage blossoms, fruits and shoots of acacia trees, roots and berries. As a rule they return to the same sleeping rock from whence they departed in the morning; there are, however, some bands that change their sleeping place more frequently than others.

Decisions about the details of the route to be taken while on the way are arrived at in the individual clans in the same 'democratic' manner as the main decision in the morning which primarly refers to the water-hole where the group is to rest at noon time.

2.6 *Animal and human language*

Observing a baboon troop, one can clearly see that the animanls have a large repertory of signals for communication. There are alarming and alluring calls, threatening, submissive and many other kinds of glances, gestures and sounds. Baboons can 'speak' to each other and every one of them can understand what is said.

When writing his book on primate societies published in 1971, Hans Kummer still believed that such baboon communication is limited to the here and now. 'Hamadryas males preparing for departure are able to signal the direction in which they are ready to go,' he wrote, 'but probably they cannot indicate the particular food source that attracts them. . .[They] cannot designate a time and a place for meeting again after they have separated.' (Kummer, 1971, p. 31).

In view of the observations described in the last section this view must now be corrected. Baboons seem to be able to communicate about a distant goal, *provided it is known to all of them*. This, however, really seems to be the limit of their communication. An old male might *know* how to go to a perennial water-hole lying outside the usual tracks of the troop; he can lead the others there, but he cannot *tell* them where to go.

Man can do that. He can *name* things, even if they are far away. And in all human languages, even in those of people living in very natural 'primitive' conditions, one can form abstract notions and discuss opinions. 'Tales of tribal natives who cannot count beyond 4 and who have vocabularies of only two or three hundred words betray the shortcomings of gullible travellers, not of the natives,' writes George Simpson (1966).

Human language, too, has its interjections, expressing moods or emotional states in a similar way to animals. We might say 'Ouch!' having hurt ourselves, though nobody is present to hear it. But even a dog can do much more than simply yelp when somebody treads on his tail. A dog with a hurting paw, if unable to help himself, goes to his master and puts the paw on his knee, and a man with only a little experience of dogs will soon realize, owing to the whole behaviour of the animal, that this gesture is not in this instance an invitation to play but a request for help. Still, the master must find the thorn which the dog has in his aching paw; the dog cannot tell him exactly where it is. You realize the differences between human language and 'dog's language' very clearly when you have to communicate by gestures with somebody who does not understand your language, or when you have hurt your tongue, or cannot use your mouth for some other reason.

Yet human language is not only a means of communication, that is much more complex and sophisticated than any animal 'language'. It does not only convey information, it is an instrument to *generate meaning*, helping us to think in a logical way. The organization of the human brain enabling us to learn languages and to think in verbal terms is, according to most scientists, one of the most important differences between man and animal. The blueprints for such an organization of our central nervous system are encoded in our genes. The ability to speak and to think in words is inborn to all normal men. The precondition is not only a special language centre in the brain, but the general mode of wiring in our whole thinking apparatus which evidently is much more complex than in any animal.

Language, according to S. L. Washburn (1978a), is 'unique to man, a product of singularly human evolution, a behaviour not found in any other animal. . . Without language, human behaviour might be interpreted along rules similar to those governing the behaviour of other animals. With language, the rules change, and human social behaviours cease to be under genetic control.'

The last clause of this quote is questionable, and not only because the wiring of our brain enabling us to speak is genetically transmitted. However, it is certainly true that 'the rules change' with the evolution of language. Inborn dispositions now influence social behaviour of man and its further evolution *in another way*, though they do not simply cease to have any effect at all. It is also true that there is no animal able to speak in a similar way to man. Nevertheless, research work done in the last two decades has shown that even in this respect we are not quite as unique as was previously assumed.

Observations of vervets (*Ceropithecus aethiops*) have led to the conclusion that they have at least three different kinds of alarm call with evidently different 'meanings'. Barking is the leopard alarm and monkeys on the ground respond by climbing the nearest tree, whereas those in the trees do not take much notice. A call sounding like 'rraup' means 'eagle in sight' and the vervets hide in dense bushes. Chattering refers to a python and often the monkeys respond by looking down, converging on and mobbing the snake, as small birds mob an owl (Struhsaker, 1967).

Studying these behaviours in detail Dorothy Cheney and Robert Seyfarth of Rockefeller University found that adult vervets know their foes exactly and that they only cry alarm when there is real danger. Thus they are able to distinguish a martial eagle (*Pollomactus bellicosus*) that does indeed prey on vervets from other eagle species that do not. Young vervets must learn this exact knowledge. They sometimes give a false leopard alarm at the approach of a hyena or a warthog, or an eagle alarm when seeing a heron, a stork or even a falling leaf, but they do know at least the categories of 'predator approaching on the ground' and 'danger from the air' and do not mix them up. When they hear alarm calls they look at their mothers and imitate their behaviour (Cherfas, 1980; see also Seyfarth, Cheney and Marler, 1980). That the alarm calls are indeed not merely 'exclamations' but intended *to convey information to others* is shown by the fact that bachelors who have left their group and wander about alone before joining another one never utter alarm calls when they see predators.

Communications in young chimpanzees in quasi-natural conditions was studied by Emil Menzel (1975). Six to eight young wild-born apes were kept living together in a large outdoor enclosure for a year. In this time they formed a very compatible and stable social unit. They tended to remain a group and did not want to be separated. Their communication was mainly by gestures and glances, which, as a rule, are intelligible for a human observer even without formal training.

97

In his experiments Menzel locked the apes in a small cage at the border of the enclosure, took one of them out and showed him several places where food was hidden. Then the chimp was returned to the group and soon after all of them were released from the cage. Every member of the group in turn was shown around and new hiding places were used in every new round. As expected, every one of the animals was able to lead his comrades to the hidden food.

The memory of the chimps for the hiding places was excellent – 'better than my own', Menzel comments. Hardly ever did they search in wrong places. One of the chimps remembered eighteen hiding places correctly, others fourteen to sixteen of them. As a rule the apes did not follow the trail used by the experimenters when showing them the hiding places, but took their own routes, which were very efficient.

The informed animal led the others by going a few steps ahead, then glancing back to see whether they followed him. If not, he beckoned with a wave of the hand or a nod of the head, or he tapped a preferred companion on the shoulder. If the others did not want to follow, the informed ape whimpered or tried to pull one of his comrades by the hand or leg. In most cases such long preliminaries were, however, not required. The informed animal could lead his comrades to the goal quickly. He did not necessarily have to go in front of the troop. As soon as the direction was clear, some others might run ahead, glancing back periodically to ask, as it were, whether they were still on the right track –much as human children would do when running ahead of their parents.

The 'team spirit' is very strong among such young chimps. An adult ape often tries to keep a tasty mossel just for himself; he might try to deceive others and lead competitors away, in particular a superior animal that could oust him. The young animals tested by Menzel, however, behaved differently. When the informed chimp alone was let loose and allowed to move about in the enclosure while the others were kept in the cage he did not go to collect the food all for himself but stopped near the cage whimpering and trying to open the cage door. For similar reasons it was not possible to test whether the informed chimp could *tell* the others where to go, if he himself was put in the cage while the others were turned loose. They remained near the cage trying to liberate their whimpering comrade and went nowhere.

In some of the experiments one of the chimps was shown hidden food with a snake nearby. When the troop approached such a place later it was evident that not only the leader but the others too had some idea of what to expect. At a distance of about 10 metres the informed chimp stopped and then hooted or barked alarm. Thereupon sometimes one of the other apes would pick up a stick, approach the hiding place of the snake and club it. If Menzel removed the snake after showing it to the informed chimp but before letting the others loose, the apes mobbed the assumed hiding place, started beating at it, then climbed trees to look around and see where the snake had moved to. If, on the other hand, the informed chimp had been shown food without a snake the whole troop would approach the hiding place without any precautions.

In other experiments two chimps were shown different hiding places, one with a small amount of food and the other with a large amount of food. It was evident that they could inform each other about the relative size of what they had seen. The majority or even all animals followed the chimp that had seen the larger food depot – irrespective of personal allegiances.

'Chimpanzees perceive the world and interpret each other's behaviour in ways that are not ridiculously different from the ways we ourselves use,' writes Menzel. 'Whether or not untrained chimpanzees have real language as a linguist would define it, they possess information processing systems, predominantly visually based ones, which are to a considerable degree of the same form as our own verbal language and serve the same biological functions.'

2.7 Apes at the computer console

Experiments to teach chimpanzees human language by bringing them up together with human infants were unsuccessful (see Hayes, 1951). The animals never managed to speak more than a very few words and even these were hardly recognizable. The main reason probably is that they lack a nervous system controlling the fine tuning of movements of the lips, the tongue and the larynx as required for articulation. On the other hand the difficulty does not seem to be a lack of intelligence. This has been shown in experiments to teach ape children non-acoustical languages. Most of these projects worked with young chimps and these experiments are the best documented, but there was also one project with a young gorilla and one is going on with an orang-utan.

One approach pioneered by R. A. and B. Gardner, and followed later by several other workers, is to teach the apes the sign language used by American deaf-mutes (see for example, Gardner and Gardner, 1978; Terrace, 1979*a*). David Premack (1976) uses as 'words' magnetic plastic symbols which have to be fastened to a table. The Rumbaughs have geometrical signs fixed to a computer key board which are to be used as 'words' by the apes (see Rumbaugh, 1977). The last approach has the advantage that all utterances of the apes remain on record whereas a trainer might overlook some of them or simply might not have the time to record them all.

All these optical languages use abstract symbols. Many of the hand signs of the deaf-mute are not just intensified gestures: similarly the plastic symbols or the signs on the computer key board are not just simplified pictures of the things to be named. The meaning of these 'words' cannot be guessed by some similarity with the object they name. It must be learned. The Rumbaughs moreover took the precaution to change repeatedly the position of the signs on the key board in order to make sure that the chimps really learned the symbol and not just the position of the key to be pressed.

Summarizing the reports available at that time Wilson (1978*a*, pp. 25–6) concluded that the brightest apes 'can learn vocabularies of two-hundred English words and elementary rules of syntax' and that they even sometimes invent new word combinations on their own as, for example, 'water bird' for a duck. In recent years however some doubts have been raised whether all these achievements were indeed real and not just over-interpretations on the part of the human experimenters (for a summary see Risteau and Robbins, 1981).

As mentioned in the last section, chimps in natural conditions use very expressive gestures. According to photographs presented by Savage-Rumbaugh *et al.* (1980*a*) a young chimp who was never taught sign language made gestures that could easily be interpreted as words of this language – and the 'words' (i.e. the gestures) even fit well in the context of the situation.

Word combinations like 'water bird' might just as well indicate that the chimp sees water (a pond) and a bird (a duck). There is no evidence that the ape really wanted to express the idea of a 'bird inhabiting water' (Terrace *et al.*, 1979). Moreover, young apes like human children often playfully produce nonsense combinations of words. If some of these combinations seem to have a meaning for a human observer this does not prove that they are more than pure chance on the part of the ape.

Some critics even go further and ask whether the apes do not merely respond to inadvertent cues given to them by their trainers. According to this view the chimps read not so much the words but the behaviour of their trainer who, without realizing it, gives them cues as to when they are about to give a correct answer – for which they get a reward (see for example, Sebeok and Umiker-Sebeok, 1979). How well the chimps do observe their trainers is shown by an example given by David Premack (1971, footnote 2): 'In the beginning Sarah [a chimp girl] was taught with the verb in the terminal position, but this rule was violated so often by her English-speaking trainers that we had to accept the normal English verb position. The two forms are now generally used interchangeably. However with the one trainer who has insisted on the terminal verb position, Sarah uses the terminal position; with all the other trainers she uses both forms.'

While there certainly is good reason to be careful of inadvertent cues, critics trying to explain *all* ape language work in this way obviously seem to be far off the beam. Apes solving problems in the absence of any human, or in the presence of a 'blind' teacher who did not know the proper answer meanwhile, have convincingly shown that they are able to learn much more than merely to observe their teachers. But do they really learn the use of *words*? Or, as Terrace puts it in the title of one of his papers (1979*b*): 'Is problem-solving language?'

One can train a pigeon to peck red keys for food and green keys for water and to distinguish properly the colours of the keys in such a task, but, as a rule, one does not say of such an experiment that the pigeon has learned the *words* for food and water (see Savage-Rumbaugh *et al.*, 1980*a*). Does the superiority of the chimp over the dove simply lie in the fact that it can learn to press one or two dozens of different keys in order to get different things?

An ape might be able to use a fairly large number of signs immediately after a training lesson when the teacher showed them to it, but without further training the ape will forget most of them. If one counts only those signs that the ape is able to use spontaneously in at least one proper context and without prodding or being shown by the teacher the 'vocabulary' is not nearly as much as two hundred words but hardly more than a few dozen. Yet even that is an impressive feat.

At the present state of the art many scientists think that it is premature to ask whether an ape can master a rudimentary syntax (see Seyfarth *et al.*, 1981; amongst them are Savage-Rumbaugh and Terrace, in a group report of the Dahlem workshop on animal and human mind, 1981). An ape can ask in short, correct, but ever-similar sentences for certain things or for actions like tickling or hugging – one chimp girl trained by the Rumbaughs even typed. into the computer the linguistically correct but unfulfillable request: 'Please machine tickle Lana period.' But is he or she able to understand the meaning of a word in *different* contexts, even if the object referred to is neither present nor wanted?

To answer such questions with confidence one often would need very strict and exactly controlled experimental conditions, but this creates new sorts of problems. For, as the English philosopher Mary Midgley points out (1978/80, p. 230), 'experimenting' is a notion that cannot be explained to the chimp children who, quite naturally, turn to their human tutors for help when confronted with a difficult situation. 'What they do here is by no means stupid,' she writes, 'and they might well think of the unresponsive humans as stupid or mulish... When everything is geared to experimental purity, what is going on is bound to become unintelligible to the animal, which is expecting a normal personal approach, and has grounds for doing so, since it is in general treated with friendship. The fact that it is puzzled and flounders when this friendship suddenly gives way to something mysterious does not show stupidity – rather the opposite. A child would do the same... I cannot help feeling that this fact brings an element of falsity into the chimp experiments. We are waiting to see how far they can respond like people while [using them as experimental objects and] treating them in a way in which people could not possibly be treated.'

In recent years the Rumbaughs tried to overcome these difficulties in experiments with two chimp boys that were trained to communicate via the computer. In one set of these experiments one of the chimps was led into an adjacent room and shown how food was hidden in a container. Then he was brought back to the key board and asked about the container's contents. The other chimp could see the answer on the computer screen and then ask for the food on his key board. Only if both of them were correct were they given the food for sharing. Soon they were able to perform very well in these tests with more than 90% correct solutions (Savage-Rumbaugh *et al.*, 1978). In another set of similar experiments one of the chimps had to ask the other for a specific tool he needed to open a container. Only if the tool was handed over in correct fashion were both of them allowed to share the container's contents.

That the test results are influenced not only by the command of words came out very clearly when one of the chimp boys was given a tray with a variety of food items, the other one watching this through a window of the neighbouring room. Spontaneously the observing chimp used the key board asking the other one to give him some of the food. With encouragement by the tutors, as would probably be necessary for human children as well, the one having access to the food handed the required item through the window. The younger one never made a mistake in this procedure. The older one, however, sometimes 'did not understand' properly, giving, for example, chow instead of chocolate. Since he knew very well the word for chocolate when he himself was asking for it, it can be inferred that such 'errors' were not due to lack of linguistic abilities.

In a recent series of experiments the Rumbaughs taught their chimps to distinguish 'foods' from 'tools' (inedible things). After being taught these two categories with three items each (orange, bread and beancake; key, coins and stick) the apes were able to label correctly other items as belonging to one or other of the categories. Even in their mistakes they showed some logic. Thus, one of them classified the cutting board, which they often lick after use, as food. Next they learned to label photographs of things, and finally the chimps were shown the signs (the 'words') for different items and asked to put them in one of two boxes, one bearing the sign for 'food' and the other the sign for 'tools'. In 16 trials, one of the chimp boys correctly categorized all the 17 signs presented to him, while the other one made but one mistake. With these experiments the Rumbaughs claim to have unequivocally proved for the first time that chimps really do understand the meaning of the symbols they use (Savage-Rumbaugh *et al.*, 1980*b*).

This, of course, does not answer the question of whether the languages taught to the chimps by man open for them a new dimension of communication, as it were, enabling them to tell each other significantly more than they could do with their natural communication system. Emil Menzel whose experiments were described in the preceding section is rather doubtful. In a letter to me he writes:

'I have never said that chimpanzees can communicate *all* they know or wish to say under any conceivable situation that might be devised for them. (Obviously they can't – and neither can humans.) What I intended to say is that adult chimps (like any species for that matter) already have a communication system that suffices very well for the situations they encounter naturally, and that it has yet to be demonstrated that language-trained chimps can communicate any more effectively with each other than wild chimps can. Further, the language training experiments rest on a highly anthropocentric conceptualization of communication and I am not sure what these studies really tell us either about natural chimp communication or about human language.'

Menzel then suggests an experiment to compare the social organization of two groups of chimps in more or less natural conditions: one group of 'language-trained' animals and one natural, wild-born social unit. Preferably the study ought to span at least two generations and should not involve any further human interference after the initial training. 'If one generation after the training had terminated the offspring of the language-trained individuals had formed a unique type of organization for chimps and were doing things with their human-instilled system that went beyond anything the control group could accomplish, that would be something to really get excited about. Rumbaugh's experiment is, in my opinion, very interesting and provocative, but it does not settle the question it addresses. What it shows is that the "natural communication system" of *Sherman and Austin* [i.e. the two chimp boys used in the experiment] did not suffice for them in a situation in which they had already been trained to be completely dependent on people and a computer keyboard. What it tells us about the inherent limits of the communication system of chimpanzees in general, or about the superiority of alternative systems, is a completely open question.' (See also Menzel, 1978a).

2.8 *Why are apes so intelligent?*

Chimp children brought into an enclosure unknown to them start exploring it very cautiously. First they go in just a few metres, returning quickly to their original position; eventually they go further and further afield until at last they have investigated the whole area. In principle their behaviour is not very much different from that of a mouse exploring a new habitat.

An adult chimpanzee behaves in another way. 'When visiting Emil Menzel I had the chance to see that,' Hans Kummer told me. 'The chimp introduced into the enclosure sat down near the entrance for about a quarter of an hour just scanning the territory with his eyes. Then he rose and without a moment's hesitation went straight to the most suitable sleeping tree, climbed up and built a nest. It was indeed impressive to see how the animal was master of the situation. It had deliberated beforehand and then knew exactly what it wanted to do.' (See also Menzel, 1978b).

No less impressive were experiments of the American psychologist Gordon Gallup. He put mirrors in front of chimpanzees' cages and watched their behaviour. To start with, the chimps believed that they saw other animals and tried to communicate with them. After two or three days, however, they seemed to realize that they saw themselves. They began using the mirror to look at parts of their bodies normally invisible to them; they made faces and looked into the mirror while removing bits of food from between their teeth (Gallup, 1970).

Did they indeed know that they saw their own images? To test this Gallup did a further experiment. Chimps acquainted with mirrors were anaesthetized and had red patches painted onto their faces while unconscious. A dye was used that cannot be smelled or felt. When returning to consciousness the animals, every one of which was kept in a separate cage, did not show any sign of noticing the colour patches. Yet, as soon as the mirrors were put up again, they immediately saw the change, spent a long time looking into the mirrors, touching the patches and examining the fingers afterwards by eye and nose.

Similar experiments with rhesus monkeys and macaques were unsuccessful. The monkeys did not come to realize that they saw their own images, and gibbons did not do any better (see Wilson, 1978a, p. 26). In a recent experiment gorillas too failed to recognize their mirror images. They did not pay any attention to coloured patches painted onto their faces that were visible only in the mirror, while they frantically groomed similar patches painted on their wrists (Suarez and Gallup, 1981).

Thus we can see on many different occasions that chimpanzees – and in most cases gorillas and orang-utans as well – have much higher mental abilities than monkeys, and looking back at evolutionary history with hindsight it does not seem to be very surprising that the species most closely related to us show the highest degree of intelligence. If there had not been good preconditions in the *common* ancestors of man, chimpanzee and gorilla to start with, human mental abilities probably could not have evolved as quickly as they did. But *why* is it just the great apes that are especially clever? What was the special challenge, the special selectionary pressure causing just the ancestors of these species to evolve an intelligence far surpassing that of any monkey or indeed of any other animal?

Observing chimps or gorillas in their natural habitats one might be inclined to think that they possess more intelligence than they might ever be able to use under natural conditions. The well known German zoologist Bernhard Rensch even maintained (1965) that brains of higher animals are generally able to reach a much higher performance than what is normally required under natural conditions.

But what is the meaning of the word 'normally' in such a context? According to Hans Kummer (1971, p. 147) it is reasonable to assume that some of the most highly developed faculties of a monkey or ape do not manifest themselves except in critical situations. And such situations are far too rare to be observed my mere chance by a scientist doing field studies. Only by confronting an animal with extraordinary situations in an experiment can one delineate a behavioural repertoire that comes close to the animal's full capacities.

What is found out in such experiments is not whether an animal actually uses this or that particular behaviour pattern in natural conditions but whether it has the intellectual capacity required for such a behaviour. If such mental abilities enable an animal *only once* to survive in a very dangerous situation, or to mate successfully and oust a competitor, natural selection will favour such cleverness.

There are quite a number of good reasons why primates in general should be intelligent. Tree-dwelling animals must be able to judge distances exactly and to know beforehand whether a branch of a tree will be able to carry them (Wilson, 1975, p. 515). 'They escape their

106

predators by fleeing to heights where the latter cannot follow them, and this requires a high degree of sensomotoric co-ordination', writes Hubert Markl (1971). 'When fleeing at breath-taking speed from tree to tree, the animal, as it were, must test the route in his imagination before starting, to avoid blind alleys.' This necessity to judge spatial relations correctly and to choose the best of several possibilities might be one of the roots of primates' intelligence.

Another one is the necessity of continual correct judgement of the 'social space'. In many societies of monkeys and apes cliques and coalitions *within the group* are a very prominent feature. To be successful the individual must move very cleverly in a rapidly fluctuating 'social field'. There is either no seasonal rhythm at all for alternating social activities or it is only faintly developed. Tropical monkeys and apes as a rule have no definite mating and breeding seasons to compare with the rutting time of stags. Babies are born all the year round though there are certain peaks of increased sexual or birth activity. Hence the social structure does not change regularly with the seasons; there are no general seasonal variations in the activity of endocrine glands and hence no general changes in mood and motivation. A group of socially living primates must perform all its activities within one unchanging social structure. The individual ape or monkey must monitor multiple signals in the behaviour of many of his group mates simultaneously and continually adjust his own behaviour to the changing mood of others who themselves are adjusting their behaviour in the same way. 'Such a society requires two qualities in its members: a highly developed capacity for releasing or surpressing their own motivations according to what the situation permits or forbids; and an ability to evaluate complex social situations, that is, to respond not to specific social stimuli but to a socail field.' (Kummer, 1971, p. 36).

According to the British ethologist Michael Chance (see for instance, Chance and Jolly, 1970), primate males are exposed to sexual stimuli most of the year. Access to females, however, is only allowed to a few high-ranking males in some species, whereas in other, more 'liberal', societies young and subordinate males are tolerated and allowed to copulate with females at the beginning and end of the oestrous period when they are already or still sexually active, but not at the peak of the oestrus when there are the highest chances of fertilization. Hence what is permitted and what not depends on many circumstances, not least on who is present and sees what happens.

Females, on their part, seem to have their preferences, too, (see for instance, Bachmann and Kummer, 1980). Apparently they are not always particularly keen on being the sexual objects of influential older gentlemen, to put it in a human way. The dominant males, on the other hand, evidently are not able to exercise a perfect control over the females in heat. This is clearly shown by the fact that males not even belonging to the group father 5% of the offspring in rhesus monkeys (see section 1.9; Sade, 1980). How many offspring are sired by subordinate males of their own group utilizing a favourable situation is not known. But merely to find such an opportunity requires a lot of intelligence. Thus the mental ability to see the opportunity for a sneaking copulation and to utilize it without exposing oneself to excessive risk often will lead to immediate reproductive success and hence will be favoured by natural selection.

All this, however, is just as valid for macaques and baboons as for chimpanzees and gorillas. It shows a lot of good reasons for the intelligence of higher primates, but it does not explain the special mental abilities of the great apes. The question of why the African apes have intellectual capacities that they can never or hardly ever use in their jungle habitat cannot be answered.

To our ancestors, however, who from forest dwellers had become inhabitants of the steppe, these abilities certainly must have been of great advantage. For an ape, living in the open land is much more dangerous than living in the jungle. He cannot flee to a safe tree to escape a predator. Food sometimes is rather scarce. A sufficient supply of water, posing no problem in the rain forest, can become a question of life or death. For solving all these problems the ability to quickly adjust to unknown and unexpected situations must be of very high survival value.

Maybe it is wrong to say that forest dwelling apes *never* make use of their full intellectual potential. But certainly these abilities must be used much more frequently in the steppe. This seems to be a plausibel explanation of why a being with human intelligence evolved from apes living in open land.

Having dealt at length with the impressive mental abilities of apes

108

and monkeys, it might be apt to refer to their limitations as well. Surprisingly they lack certain sets of behaviour patterns found in other much more primitive animals.

Quite a number of monkey species are at home in regions with marked seasonal changes of rainy and dry periods and with concomitant fluctuations of food supply – yet none of them ever collects or stores food for lean days as a squirrel or a hamster would do (Kummer, 1971, p. 146). Monkeys never build nests or dens where a mother could give birth to her young or where a sick or wounded animal could find refuge for a few days. In this respect, too, primitive rodents are clearly superior – not to mention the highly sophisticated dwellings of a beaver or a fox.

Overhanging rocks or trees are sometimes used as protection against rain or hail by apes and monkeys – but only if the refuge is very near. Only the big apes build sleeping nests and these, according to Kummer (1971, p. 36, 146), 'are poor, roofless constructions built for only one night... Hundreds of bird species build nests a hundred times more elaborate than the chimp nest, which is the highest achievement of primate building activity'.

Of course, in rodents the 'crafts' of storing food or building nests are inborn, whereas primates would have to *invent* such behaviours. But considering their many other inventions (see section 2.4) their lack of initiative in this respect seems rather surprising. Only once did Jane Goodall (1968) observe a chimpanzee building a nest with a roof to which it returned repeatedly on rainy days in the following weeks. But this invention *was not imitated*, unlike the sweet-potato washing of the macaques. It was not the starting point of a new cultural tradition but rather was forgotten.

'When inspecting known primate technology one can only be unimpressed,' Kummer wrote in 1971 (p. 145). 'Their lack of elaborate technical skills compares unfavourably with those of many so-called lower vertebrates and many invertebrates... Although primates have prehensile hands their use of tools is modest.'

'Do you still hold this view today?' I asked Kummer, when I visited him in 1980.

'As for apes this must, of course, be revised,' he replied. 'There are many new observations meanwhile, in particular on chimps, that show extensive use of tools. But for monkeys, what I wrote is still valid.'

Monkeys, he continued, are very cunning in their social relations. A male Barbary macaque takes a baby on his arm when approaching an animal of superior rank to appease him. A female baboon threatens against another one whilst at the same time presenting her rear to a male whose support she wants to solicit. 'Thus we are seeing acts of using con-specifics as "tools", as it were,' he said. 'But in twenty years of work I never saw a baboon taking a stick and using it as a tool or tearing out a tuft of grass to put it underneath his bottom when resting on hard rock. I cannot understand this limitation of their tool-use to the social field only.'

2.9 The genetics of apes

Of todays apes, chimpanzee and gorilla are at home in central Africa, orang-utan, gibbon and siamang in south-east Asia. The Asiatic species live on trees, the African apes spend a considerable part of their time on the ground.

That there are no apes in comparable habitats of South America is not surprising. The tectonic plates carrying the African and the South American continent separated long before the onset of a special lineage leading to today's apes. What the taxonomists call the 'superfamily' of New World monkeys (Ceboidea) is clearly distinct from the Old World monkeys (Ceropithecoidea) and the apes. There is no species or genus of monkey that can be found on both sides of the Atlantic, not even closely related genera.

What is much more surprising is that there are no apes in the jungles of the Indian sub-continent though there is a land bridge to south-east Asia today, and the plate carrying India was connected to Africa in the fairly recent past, according to geological time scales. There are many closely related species living both in India and in Africa such as elephants or rhinos. Fossils of ape ancestors have been found on the Indian sub-continent. Where are their descendants?

One rather extravagant answer to this question is that the Indian apes did by no means become extinct—but that they are the ancestors of man (see for instance, Washburn, 1978b). However, there are, so far, no hard facts to support this idea, whereas there is a considerable amount of circumstantial evidence indicating that our ancestors lived where our nearest relatives, chimpanzee and gorilla, are still living today: in tropical Africa.

The first group to branch off from the common evolutionary tree of apes some 30 million years ago were the Hylobatides (gibbon and siamang). Whilst this would appear to be beyond dispute the mutual relationships and the descent of the other apes and of man are far from clear. Different methods of investigation lead to widely different results.

A bone or a tooth of a chimpanzee or gorilla can be recognized by an expert at first glance as not belonging to a human skeleton. The comparison can be extended to the presumed common ancestors, several ape-like species of the group of Dryopithecidae that were fairly common in jungles of the Old World about 15 to 25 million years ago. Today's apes are much more similar to these ancestors than man. The ape skeleton has hardly changed within the last 15 million years, except in getting bigger, whereas that of our ancestors underwent a radical evolution.

The main changes of the human skeleton, which occured over a very short time span according to evolutionary scales, are: increase of the cranium volume (brain size) with accompanying changes in the face; changes literally from head to toe resulting from the transition to upright posture and bipedal motion, such as changed place of connection between head and spinal column, alterations in the curvature of the spinal column, changes in the construction of pelvis, legs and feet; a large and strongly opposable thumb; changes in the teeth, in particular reduction in the size of male canines. Moreover, there are further alterations in morphological traits not visible in the skeleton, but undoubtedly encoded in the genes: more complex *organisation* of the brain which is even more important than the mere increase in size; changes in mouth and pharynx and respective nerves enabling articulate speech; the loss of a fur coat; the large size of the female breasts outside the lactation period; and others as well.

In summary, the differences of anatomy are considerable and justify the scientists in putting man into his own taxonomic 'family' separated from the apes. Judging by morphological criteria it was assumed that the main lineage leading to the apes split into three branches simultaneously: one leading to man with very strong and rapid changes, one leading to the orang-utan, and the third one leading to the African apes, with a later split into the gorilla and chimpanzee lineages.

A rather different picture emerges when trying to ascertain the mutual relationships of man and apes with biochemical methods, mainly developed in the last decades. The most exact but also the most laborious and expensive of these methods is the detailed chemical analysis of certain enzymes or of the appropriate genes in the DNA (for experts: the amino acid sequence and the nucleotide sequence, respectively). Other methods, not quite as exact but cheaper and easier to handle, are: the comparison of the number, shape, and fine structure (banding) of the chromosomes; the comparison of mutual immune reactions of the serum of different species and of its distribution in an electrical field (electrophoresis), and finally DNA-hybridization, i.e. checking to what extent DNA of different species can form double helices – an indication of identical or very similar genes.

Except for immune tests all of these methods are fairly new and probably still liable to be improved. Yet, as a rule their results are compatible with each other as well as with traditional evolutionary systematics based on morphological traits. Using the new methods, a number of open questions of taxonomic and evolutionary relationships have been answered convincingly. But just when applying biochemical analysis to apes the results show considerable scatter, in particular concerning the ancestral relations of the orang-utan. On the other hand all of them give convincing indications that chimpanzee, gorilla and man are three very closely related species (Simpson, 1972; King and Wilson, 1975; Ayala, 1980).

Considering all the evidence together and judging it according to its weight Francisco Ayala, a Spanish geneticist working at the University of California, comes to the conclusion that the lineage leading to the orang-utan branched off earlier from the African ape lineage than the branch leading to man. Biochemically, man is as closely related to both the African apes as the gorilla is to the chimpanzee, whereas the relationship of both of them (and of man) to the orang-utan is not just as close.

Conventional taxonomy, which considers all apes, including gibbon and siamang, as one 'family' whilst putting man and his ancestors in another one, does not conform to the biochemical facts. Biochemical differences between man and apes are very small. As mentioned in section 1.3 man and chimpanzee share more than 99% of their structural genes. Such a value, as a rule, indicates two closely related species belonging to the same genus; in any case it is much smaller than the 'genetical distance' expected of genera belonging to the same family not to mention genera which, according to conventional taxonomy, belong to different families, such as man and apes. The genetic distance between man and gibbon is larger than the usual distance between species of the same genus, but still considerably smaller than the ordinary distance among genera of the same family (Ayala, 1980).

Thus, the biochemical evidence certainly supports the assumption of a rather late branching-off of man from the ape lineage. 'Presumably about 10 million years ago,' Ayala told me. 'Or, rather, between 8 and 15 million years ago.' Washburn (1978b) sets the likely date even later still – probably between 5 and 10 million years ago.

The biochemistry of the common ancestors of man and ape is, of course, not well known. The investigation of the species existing today leads to the conclusion that all of them, man as well as apes, did *not* have any significant biochemical evolution within the last 15 million years, but only some random changes of no importance. This is in striking contrast to the anatomical evolution which was insignificant in apes but very rapid and extensive in man.

The existing and clearly visible differences between apes and man are in all probability due to evolutionary changes in the steering genes (see section 1.3), but Ayala emphasizes that this is a plausible hypothesis only, so far not supported by any factual evidence.

2.10 *Our animal ancestors*

The oldest ancestors that we probably do not share with any other living species were apes. In the essence they were no more human-like than today's chimpanzees or gorillas. But considering all the facts mentioned in the last chapters the intellectual potential of such animals should not be underrated.

Most probably our animal ancestors were living in an area where dense forest gradually transformed into open land. About 14 to 9 million years ago there was a general cooling trend in several tropical regions coupled with tectonic and mountain-building activity. Thus large forest habitats were fragmented and quite a number of species were compelled to adapt to new conditions. From inhabitants of dense large forests they became inhabitants of woodland, forest-border regions or of gallery forests lining the streams (Kennedy, 1978).

In geological deposits of these times dug out in Kenya and in

Pakistan, bones and teeth of several ape species were found that apparently were 'inhabitants of two worlds', collecting food in the forest as well as in the savannah (Kolata, 1977). One genus of these 'woodland apes' called *Ramapithecus* that existed in Africa as well as on the Indian sub-continent is supposed by many scientists to be a direct ancestor of man.

For the time between 8 and 4 million years ago the fossil record of human ancestors is very scarce. One can only guess that the descendants of some apes living on the forest fringe gradually became inhabitants of the steppe, similar to the baboons and geladas. Life in the steppe being harder for an ape than life in the forest it is hardly likely that such a shift of habitat was voluntary. Rather these animals probably *had to become* inhabitants of the steppe because the character of their territory changed and they either were separated from the forests by some natural barrier or could not withdraw there because the woods were fully occupied.

No traces have been found so far of these hypothetical 'steppe apes'. The next fossils are about 4 to 5 million years old and belong to several species of the genus *Australopithecus* living in African savannahs and steppes. 'Australopithecus' means 'southern ape', but whether it still had a thick fur coat as modern apes do is not known. In any case these creatures were bipeds, moving in a fairly human-like manner. They had human-like hands with highly opposable thumbs, a denture hardly different from that of modern man, *and a cranium volume no larger than that of a chimpanzee!*

If we consider that the essence of humanity is our intellectual capacity and not our upright posture, then at least the early specimens of the 'southern ape' were indeed apes, or in any case non-human animals and not semi-humans. They were *bipeds with an ape's brain*, much more similar to man in their outward appearance than a chimp, but hardly more intelligent than a modern ape. The explosive evolution of the human brain only started about 2.5 to 3 million years ago and was finished about 100 000 years ago. Within this period the brain volume of our ancestors trebled.

Nothing is known about the behaviour of the putative 'steppe apes' assumed to have existed about 7 million years ago, forming the link between the *Ramapithecus* and the 'southern apes' (the Australopithecides). Nevertheless it is possible to make some fairly well-founded inferences about their probable way of life. The hard environmental conditions in the steppe must have required adaptations in social structure. Inhabitants of the steppe, like hamadryas baboons and geladas, are the only species of monkey having a social organisation with several levels: families integrated into larger well-organized troops. Equally, chimpanzees living in open woodland bordering savannahs have a much tighter social structure than those inhabitating dense forest (Itani and Suzuki, 1967; Crook, 1972).

Geladas, as far as is known, are strict vegetarians; baboons have occasionally been seen hunting; chimpanzees, on the other hand, are true hunters – about 5% of their diet consists of animal protein. Presumably the putative 'steppe apes' were hunters as well and for the 'southern apes' the fossil record shows clearly that all sorts of animals – reptiles, birds and even mammals as large as elephants – were a regular component of their diet.

'Why do chimpanzees hunt', I asked Richard Wrangham of Cambridge University. 'Is a pure vegetarian diet not sufficient to feed them well?'

'One cannot say that,' was the answer. 'If you feed chimps with plant products only there are no nutritional deficiencies. But animal protein is a very high quality food.'

'And why do gorillas not hunt just as well?'

'They can't. They are too slow.'

Chimpanzees have a very remarkable hunting behaviour. Their preferred prey are young animals like warthog piglets, little bush-bucks and, in particular, young monkeys. Even human babies are reported to have been attacked by them. Nearly always they hunt in pairs or larger groups. Often they approach their prey from several sides simultaneously, cutting off all routes of escape. Usually very noisy, chimps when hunting become quiet and tense, communicating with quick glances and movements of the head. Sometimes they mix among groups of monkeys, seemingly quite peacefully and then suddenly attack a young animal (Goodall, 1971).

Geza Teleki, a Hungarian scientist living in the USA describes a scene of a group of chimpanzees and baboons, altogether twelve animals, sitting together, apparently quite relaxed. Suddenly several chimps pounce on one of the baboons, grab an infant he is holding and immediately begin to tear it apart as they huddle in a tight cluster. The baboon barks furiously at the chimps and pushes with his hands at the back of one of them but with no apparent avail. The

115

baboon infant is soon halved, the chimps climb nearby trees and start consuming their prey (Teleki, 1973).

A prey animal is usually killed by either breaking its neck with the hands or by grabbing one of its legs and hitting its head against a tree or a stone. Usually the prey is shared between the hunters; other chimps approaching and holding out a hand with a begging gesture might get a piece of meat too.

Our ancestral 'steppe apes' probably did hunt in a similar way, gradually attacking larger prey and increasing the meat component of their diet. In their new habitat they must have learnt to stand their ground against carnivores for whom they were competitors as well as prey. Thus the apes must have been able to fend off attacks of predators and to defend a prey against being robbed by carnivores; on the other hand they probably soon learned to scavenge prey hunted by others. Since our ancestors probably did not have such impressive teeth as male baboons or chimpanzees, one might assume that they used sticks and stones to fight carnivores – perhaps even before they used such tools for hunting. In experiments chimpanzees have been seen to use sticks against stuffed leopards.

2.11 Stone age or bone age?

Everybody uses the term 'stone age', although it is basically misleading. Of course, scientists looking for relics of pre-human and early human culture must stick to what they can find, and that is mainly stones that do not decompose even in the course of millions of years. Yet, to shape stones with stones is a very toilsome job indeed. Thus, what we call stone age certainly was much more a 'wood age' and a 'bone age'. One only needs to break a dry branch over the knee to get a point or a sharp edge. One only needs to break bones with a stone to get at the marrow and one will have bone splinters of different shapes, some of them probably very apt for use as the point of a spear.

Tribes living in the 'stone age' – i.e. not knowing how to produce metals – did exist up to our century. Studying such peoples, ethnographers could see how all sorts of raw materials – leaves, lianas, mussel shells, horns, tendons, feathers, etc. – are used to make tools. Yet only observation of chimpanzees in the field finally made clear that the 'stone age' must have begun long before the existence of *Homo sapiens*.

'Old incredulity dies hard,' writes Sherwood L. Washburn (1978*b*). 'When Peking man [now called *Homo errectus*, a semi-human living about 500 000 years ago] was first found, he was declared to be far too primitive to have made the stone tools found in association with his remains. The next unjustified victim of incredulity was *Australopithecus*; surely, the consensus had it, no one with such a small brain could have made tools... Chimpanzees behavior is therefore enlightening: it shows that a typical ape is able to use objects in far greater variety and with greater effectiveness than anyone had suspected.'

In the course of evolution towards man our ancestors had to re-invent many behaviour patterns that are inborn in many other species but do not belong to the normal repertory of apes (see section 2.8). Observation of rodents might have helped them to realize that creating stores for lean times is a good idea. But merely realizing this was not enough. There are only a few food items, like nuts or seeds, that in a tropical climate can be stored in their natural state for long periods. Even in our times more than half of the harvest is lost to store pests in many Third World countries. To be able to store food effectively our ancestors had to invent techniques of preservation like cooling, drying, or salting, which go much further than any methods of storage used by animals.

A very important invention was gathering of small food objects like seeds, fruits, berries, nuts, eggs, mushrooms, etc. – not for the personal use of the gatherer but for other members of the group. The foraging and exchange of food is one of the pillars of social behaviour of ants and bees, and there are mammals too, like wolves and jackals, that regurgitate pieces of meat in the den to feed a lactating mother and the pups. The human stomach is not adapted for such a form of transport, and in the hands one cannot carry much small food. To be able to forage 'like the bees' our ancestors had first to invent containers for the transport of small food items.

Two very important inventions of pre-humans, which we share with no other species, were the use of fire and the use of furs for clothing and for making tents. Both of these inventions are attributed to *Homo errectus*. Together with gathering and making stores they probably were the preconditions for an advance into the temperate zones of our planet. Fire-places about half a million years old have been found in China, France, Hungary and elsewhere.

The first great complex of inventions of *Homo sapiens* was again

117

an acquisition of behaviour patterns well known to many terrestrial mammals: the conquest of water as an important living space. Bears, for example, do very well at swimming and fishing, but in the archaeological evidence about pre-humans there is a remarkable absence of remains of fish or shellfish. 'Since the consumption of shellfish in particular leaves huge middens, the negative evidence is impressive', write Washburn and Lancaster (1968, p. 294).

For our ancestors up to about 40 000 years ago, water must have been a hostile element, they claim. A macaque starts running in water and thus can swim like a dog. When getting used to water as happened at Koshima (see section 2.4) the monkeys need not learn swimming itself. They are able to do it by a transformation of their inborn motor patterns. An ape, on the other hand, starts climbing in water and therefore cannot swim. The same is true of a human who cannot swim *by nature* – unlike a dog, a bear, or a macaque, – but must *learn* it. For a gorilla even a shallow, narrow stream seems to be an insurmountable barrier (Schaller, 1963). So it probably was for our ancestors up to the Neanderthaler.

It can be assumed that water lost this air of being an hostile element for *Homo sapiens* only after he had learnt to swim. Then he started to collect shellfish, to build boats and kayaks, to fish and eventually even to hunt large acquatic mammals. Human diet was considerably enriched by this development; consumption of fish rich in vitamin D probably was a precondition for colonizing regions of the Far North. Simultaneously water was transformed from a barrier to a connecting way. Inland waterways are often easier to use than jungle paths; by crossing lakes or sea bays distances can be considerably shortened, and finally man went onto the open sea.

In Australia unequivocal evidence of human occupation goes back for more than 30 000 years. But even at the two peaks of glaciation in the last ice age, about 50 000 and 20 000 years ago, when sea level is supposed to have been 200 metres lower than at present, there presumably was no land bridge from Asia to Australia. The main water barrier is believed to have been at least 80 kilometres wide – and even wider about 40 000 to 35 000 years ago when there was less glaciation and the sea level was higher. If these assumptions are all correct marine technology of early *Homo sapiens* must have been much more elaborate than most prehistorians imagine. For to found the population of a continent a *whole group* of people must have travelled or accidentally drifted across the water barrier – and, strangely, no Australian tribe known today would be able to build a craft required for such a task (see also White and O'Connell, 1979).

The last great complex of inventions of the 'stone age' was made about 10 000 years ago: agriculture and cattle farming. These, too, are techniques known to ants for a long time (see section 2.3), but only man united them into an integrated system of agricultural production.

Certainly, men before the invention of agriculture were not semi-animals. There is no biological difference between us and humans belonging to the gatherer and hunter peoples, and in the view of Claude Lévi-Strauss (1968), one of the grand old men of anthropology, all human societies, even the most 'primitive' ones, are much more complex and sophisticated than any kind of animal society. Be that as it may, there certainly cannot be any doubt that large-scale transformation of the environment by humans, far exceeding anything that beavers or ants can do, did not start before the invention of agriculture.

2.12 *Productivity of labour, exploitation, and slavery in animals and man*

According to widely held views the introduction of agriculture led to a rising productivity of labour and thus created the preconditions for 'modern' forms of social division of labour. There must have been surplus agricultural yields, it is claimed, before there could exist of caste of priests not active in immediate productive life but occupied solely with 'higher' tasks, among them sorcery and medicine, astrology, astronomy and calendar making, or geometry, architecture and the proper construction of irrigation channels.

Marxist basic ideas about the advent of exploitation are based on similar concepts. The primeval gatherers and hunters are assumed to have been unable to exploit others, since productivity of labour generally was too low. According to the picture presented by Friedrich Engels, the friend and collaborator of Karl Marx, in his famous book *The Origin of the Family, of Private Property and the State* (1884, chapter 2) human labour at that stage did not yet yield any significant surplus above what was needed for maintenance;

119

only with the advent of cattle breeding, weaving, the use of metals and eventually agriculture did conditions change.

As we shall see, Engels, according to the state of knowledge of his time, probably underrated the productivity of peoples living in a primeval state. Yet, certainly, sheer logical consideration shows that a certain level of productivity of labour is an essential – though not necessarily a sufficient – precondition for the advent of exploitation and slavery. Hence one could ask about the productivity of labour of animals and whether there are amongst them any phenomena comparable to exploitation.

The productivity of a pied kingfisher at Lake Victoria (see section 1.9) is so low that the birds are not able to rear their young without the aid of a 'baby-sitter'. This, of course, is an extreme example, but generally a song bird has to 'work' hard all day to get enough food for itself and its young. The 'productivity' of these and many other animals depends to a large extent on environmental conditions which they cannot influence.

The 'working time' of monkeys has been considered by Hans Kummer (1976). According to him a baboon spends about 6 hours a day wandering about looking for food, and another 3 hours for intense social contacts like mutual grooming and play. The rest of the time is devoted to rest. The animals cannot prolong the daylight period and sleep most of the tropical night which lasts 11 hours. The daily search for food requires at most 1 hour of hard work, like climbing or digging. The other 'work' is just walking and picking food. Monkeys in the field usually can depend on ample food reserves which, as a rule, they do not fully utilize. There are only a few regions where there are regular famines every few years. In general baboons do not 'work' to exhaustion, and if there is need they can double their daily performance. They are, however, visibly tired after an unusually long daily march and go to sleep earlier on such days.

A pride of lions spend a large part of the day lazily resting without doing any 'work'. A successful hunting raid does not take more than perhaps half an hour and provides enough food for the whole day. Thus 'productivity of labour' is high and there are good preconditions for exploitation – which indeed are utilized. Males that have conquered a pride (see section 1.8) do not hunt themselves, but appropriate part of the prey hunted by the females. The males,

120

however, are not quite without any useful function. Being taller and stronger than the females they can drive away more easily all those scavengers that try to steal some of the prey. Nevertheless it is a fact that the females provide for the males of their pride.

A special form of exploitation is so-called 'slavery' in ants. As mentioned in section 1.10 some ant species rob larvae and pupae from other nests of the same species or from nests of closely related species. After hatching, the robbed ants behave as if they were in their own nest and work for the kidnappers. When in the nest of another species they are something in between a domestic animal and a slave, though there is not much difference between the slave-makers and the exploited species.

The degree of dependence on 'slaves' varies over a wide range in different slave-making species. Some only occasionally have 'slaves' that do the same work as the slave-makers – though, of course, not for their own kin but for the offspring of their kidnappers. At the other end of the spectrum there are species like *Polyergus rufescens* whose mandibles have been transformed so much that they can only be used for fighting. Ants of these species can neither feed themselves without the aid of 'slaves' nor care for their own brood (Dumpert, 1978, p. 148 *et seq.*; Wilson, 1975, p. 368 *et seq.*).

It is tempting to compare the societies of the ant species mentioned first with human societies at the onset of slavery, when slaves and their masters basically still did the same sort of work as among the Indians on the Northwest Pacific coast (see below). Societies of species like *Polyergus rufescens*, on the other hand, might be compared with highly developed slave societies like those which existed in ancient Egypt, Greece or Rome. Though it is true that these human societies could not have continued to exist without the labour of slaves, the differences must not be neglected. 'Slave-making' in ants is an inborn (genetically pre-programmed) behaviour as is horticulture in leaf-cutting ants or 'dairy farming' of aphids by other ant species. Slavery in man is part of human 'culture' and so is human agriculture. The *economic system* of the states of antiquity was dependent on slavery, and the slave masters had no need to learn how to do all the sorts of work that were performed by slaves, but they did not have bodily deformations making them unable to work as *Polyergus rufescens* ants have. What human slave-holders in antiquity probably did have were psychic deformations which

121

made them consider productive work as below the dignity of a free man.

Productivity of those humans still living as gatherers and hunters under primeval conditions seems to have been underrated for a long time. Only recently has it been realized that these people as a rule do not just carry on at the fringe of starvation. At an international conference on *Man the Hunter* held at the University of Chicago in 1966 (see Lee and DeVore, 1968) the nutritional state of the gatherers and hunters was considered to be in most cases better than that of Third World agricultural peoples.

Nearly all gatherers and hunters are nomads, and since they have no domestic animals to carry loads they must carry all their possessions themselves – including infants – when changing their place of residence. Hence their possibilities to possess things or store food are rather limited. Generally they live on a mixed diet: the women gather seeds, nuts, fruits, mushrooms, edible roots, eggs, shellfish, edible insects, honey, etc; the men hunt and fish. The menu is rich and balanced and when one food item becomes scarce there is nearly always a chance to switch over to something else. Vegetable food collected by the women constitutes for most of these peoples the bulk of their diet, but meat is the most highly valued food. Larger pieces of prey are, as a rule, divided up among all the inhabitants of a camp. Archaeology and ethnography alike show that humans, like chimpanzees, preferentially hunt young or sub-adult mammals (Laughlin, 1968).

A Bushman woman in the South African Kalahari steppe can without much effort collect in one day enough mongongo nuts and/or other vegetable products to feed her family for three days (Lee, 1968, p. 37). Hunting returns are, of course, not as regular and partly a matter of luck, yet as a rule men do not go hunting more often than every second or third day. A similar 'productivity of labour' is reported from many other peoples living in primeval conditions. Excluding the inhabitants of the Far North, famine seems to be less frequent amongst gatherers and hunters than amongst peoples practising agriculture – and actually some of the latter take refuge in gathering and hunting in times of drought. At the end of the season, before new ones get ripe, there are still old mongongo nuts to be found in the Kalahari even in lean years.

122

Among the peoples not practising agriculture, the Indians on the Pacific Northwest coast of North America had permanent houses in villages numbering more than a thousand people, even before contact with the white man (Suttles, 1968, p. 56). They lived by fishing, hunting, and gathering shellfish and berries. There was abundance of food in the migration seasons of halibut and salmon, but supply was unevenly distributed throughout the year and food had to be preserved and stored, which was women's business. Storing food to sell to others in times of shortage was a recognized and widely practised method of acquiring wealth (ibid, p. 60). When somebody had used up all his stores and could not get credit any more he had to sell one of his daughters or himself as a slave; in some tribes prisoners of war and their descendants were made to slave as well. Tribal chiefs had up to twenty slaves (ibid., p. 66). They had monopolies over the trade with inland tribes, collected tributes and redistributed them in their villages (ibid., pp. 65, 67).

Thus it seems that high productivity of labour which can be attained even without agriculture is by itself not sufficient for the advent of slavery. For men, hunting is not just labour that might be done by slaves but enjoyment as well and an activity that brings prestige. Only when there are permanent settlements and well-developed methods of preserving food does *accumulation of wealth* become possible: only then does slavery become worthwhile.

The way of life of today's tribal peoples does not necessarily give a correct idea of the state of mankind before the invention of agriculture. Within the last 10 000 years there presumably has been technical progress in gathering and hunting too. Even primeval peoples without contact with Europeans might have had some trade with cultures knowing the use of metals, and in this way might have got, for example, metal points for arrows. On the other hand, gatherers and hunters today live in regions considered as marginal, at least from the agriculturalist's point of view. In the more fertile regions which they inhabited before the advent of agriculture they could probably find plenty of food even with the more primitive techniques of former times. Thus one might ask why agriculture has been invented at all.

'Why should we plant, when there are so many mongongo nuts in the world?' Bushmen ask today (see Lee, 1968, p. 33). What was it that caused men all over the world to leave such a paradisical state, to bend their backs in hard toil and to eat their bread with sweat of their brows?

2.13 *When did the population explosion start?*

Many seeds of plants cannot be digested by man in their natural state. They must be soaked, boiled, ground or prepared in some other way, and for doing so one needs implements. Seeds cannot be roasted on a barbecue like a piece of game. To boil them one needs vessels that withstand fire; and pottery is younger than agriculture. Grinding stones, however, already appeared in pre-agricultural times (Washburn and Lancaster, 1968, p. 295). Perhaps a pulp of ground seeds was baked to flat cakes on hot stones. Anyway, grinding of seeds enriched the menu of our ancestors even before agriculture, and it seems to have been known all over the world.

It is assumed by Washburn and Lancaster that the men who near the end of the last ice age crossed the Bering Straits – which probably were a land bridge at that time – knew this technique of grinding seeds as well. This, they think, might be a plausible explanation for the astonishing fact of a nearly simultaneous and presumably independent discovery of agriculture in the New and Old Worlds. Seeds lost in grinding had been growing and made men realize that plants can be sown.

There is, however, a long way to go from a little horticulture for supplementary food to agriculture as the mainstay of food production. What was it that made men in different parts of the globe go this toilsome way?

Today it is assumed that there were several factors contributing to this development. The end of the ice age brought climatic changes and probably a deterioration of conditions in some regions. Agriculture, in this view, is *an adaptation to changing environmental conditions*, when one cannot continue to live as one did before. The benefit of the new way of life was, at first, not so much an increase in productivity of labour beyond the normal level attainable for gatherers and hunters, but in the possibility of getting a higher yield by *more work* and thus feeding more people than before within a limited area. Before the advent of agriculture 10 000 years ago, there were perhaps 10 million men or even less living on earth. At the time of Jesus Christ the world population is estimated to have been about 200 million. This 'population explosion' had occurred exclusively in those parts of the world where there was agriculture and cattle-breeding. In the other half, where men still lived as gatherers and hunters, population had hardly increased.

Population densities of today's gatherer and hunter peoples are very low – except for a few fishing tribes. Rarely do they exceed 1 person per square mile, often they are 1 to 25 persons per hundred square miles (Lee and DeVore, 1968, p. 11). This is far less than the population density of apes, not to mention baboons which might attain 25 animals per square mile.

'Social groups of nonhuman primates occupy exceedingly small areas, and the vast majority of animals probably spend their entire lives within less than four to five square miles,' write Washburn and Lancaster (1968, pp. 296–7). 'Even though they have excellent vision and can see for many miles, especially from tops of trees, they make no effort to explore more than a tiny fraction of the area they see. Even for gorillas the range is only about fifteen square miles (Schaller, 1963), and it is of the same order for savannah baboons (DeVore and Hall, 1965). When Hall tried to drive a troop of baboons beyond the end of their range, they refused to be driven and doubled back into familiar territory, although they were easy to drive within the range. The known area is a psychological reality, clear in the minds of the animals. . . In marked contrast human hunters are familiar with very large areas. . . The most minor hunting expedition covers an area larger than most nonhuman primates would cover in a lifetime.'

According to Lee (1968) a population of 248 Bushmen which he studied inhabited a territory of 600 square miles with eleven water holes, whereas a rather larger number of baboons in the Amboseli Reserve inhabited a territory of a few square miles with only one water hole. Interest in a large area is typically human, declare Washburn and Lancaster. Man is the only primate that regularly migrates long distances to adapt to seasonally changing conditions.

Today's primeval peoples are claimed to keep their population constant and to live in ecological balance with nature (Lee and DeVore, 1968, p. 11). Generally the carrying capacity of the territory they inhabit does not seem to be fully utilized even in lean years. But did such an ecological balance between man and nature exist *everywhere* before the discovery of agriculture – unless it was disturbed by catastrophic climatic change? Or are those peoples who still live in a primeval state rather a small group who were able to survive as gatherers and hunters *exactly because* they managed to adapt their demography to their way of life, whereas the others, because of their population growth – and not, primarily, because of climatic change – were compelled to resort to agriculture?

Why did men invent ever new and better hunting implements? Why did they start fishing about 40 000 years ago and hunting aquatic mammals soon after? Why did they advance into ever new parts of the globe including the regions of the Far North where life is very harsh indeed even if one can find sufficient food? Why did they build seaworthy ships and search for ever new shores? All this does not look like the behaviour of beings living in good balance with their environment. Rather it seems to be an indication of a species being under continual massive pressure to find ever new hunting grounds and new ecological niches. But what caused this pressure?

To a biologist man is an omnivore, consuming, as a rule, more vegetable than animal food. To a zebra or a giraffe he is, nevertheless, the most dangerous of all predators. For exactly because man can, in case of need, live on vegetables alone, he is much more dangerous to the animal world than all pure carnivores. The lion and the wolf are dependent on the existence of their prey species. Long before they had exterminated them they would have starved themselves. Man can switch over to another diet. Thus he can exterminate his prey species and still survive.

Certainly, animal species became extinct before the advent of man. But can it really be mere chance that a massive disappearance of many animal species within a short time span coincides either with the appearance of new hunting gear in the archaeological record or with the appearance of man in the respective regions? According to the American geo-scientist Paul S. Martin (1966) no less than 26 genera of large mammals, mainly herbivores, became extinct in Africa about 50 000 to 40 000 years ago. In the same period large stone axes, cleavers, bifacial knives and other new stone tools are found in Africa for the first time. In Madagascar where no stone axes have been found the composition of the fauna did not appreciably change in that same period. But 16 genera of vertebrates became extinct there about 1000 years ago, when Melanesians with highly developed hunting techniques invaded the island.

In Australia several genera of large mammals and birds disappeared about 30 000 to 20 000 years ago. The Australian scientists White and O'Connell (1979) assume this to be the consequence of the combined effects of climatic change and human hunting. As mentioned in the last section men came to Australia about 35 000 to 30 000 years ago.

In the New World mammoths and mastodons, giant sloths and giant beavers, camels, horses, antelopes and other large herbivores had existed in an environment without man for millions of years and had not learnt to fear this dangerous predator. When mammoth hunters from Siberia crossed the Bering Straits (or, at that time, the Bering Isthmus) towards the end of the last ice age, they found a true El Dorado. There was no need for battues or for the construction of complicated pitfalls. The large prey animals were not shy and did not flee at the approach of a hunter – and before they had learnt to fear man, they were exterminated. In a time span of not much more than 1000 years, no less than 35 genera of large mammals disappeared in the New World – in North America seemingly a few hundred years earlier than in South America where humans arrived later (Martin, 1973).

Seen in this way the labour productivity of stone age hunters was not too low but rather, as it were, too high. The versatility, adaptibility, and cunning of man enabled him to break the general rule of balace between predator and prey and to overexploit nature. In this perspective the discovery of cattle-breeding seems to have been a way to secure the highly valued animal foodstuffs even after the extermination of many prey species. And the invention of agriculture might have been not a precondition, but rather a *consequence* of a tendency, possibly existent, to multiply excessively and to overexploit the carrying capacity of the environment. The roots of the 'limits to growth' might go back to the beginnings of our species if not even to our pre-human ancestors.

Introduction of agriculture only temporarily solved these problems. Population growth accelerated. Soon the fertile plains had not enough arable land. Hillsides and mountain slopes were taken under the plough with the well-known consequences of soil erosion, lowering of the subsoil water table, etc. The realm of the Sumerians perished owing to such problems 5000 years ago, and many other cultures have followed since.

The lessons have not yet been learned today. World population grows faster than ever before. Crises of supply are precariously 'solved' for a short while by ever more radical environmental manipulation – but causing even graver problems in the long run. One of the things in which we are unique indeed, and seem to distinguish ourselves from all other species, is our ability to destroy our environment much more radically than any other animal would be able to do.

2.14 *Can an animal have a bad conscience?*

A dog that has done something he 'should not have done' behaves as if expecting to be punished. 'He seems to have a bad conscience,' says his master.

But can an animal indeed have a 'conscience'? Or do we, in saying so, rather impute human-like feelings to the dog which he just cannot have? And even if a *dog* might have some feeling of 'guilt' – is it not only because he is a domesticated animal? Could a wolf have a conscience as well?

Certainly a wolf amongst wolves must learn different norms of behaviour than a dog on a farm. But the wolf too must integrate into a society – and a highly evolved one for that matter. He must conform to social norms too. He must not just follow his instincts without any consideration. Life in a group and successful collective hunting would be impossible without such restraint.

What man teaches the dog is the particular content of certain commands and prohibitions. But the *ability* to internalize such rules of conduct is *inborn* to the dog. According to the Swiss psychologist A. Zweig (1959) a dog is able to develop certain traits resembling a 'super-ego'; and this ability is probably inherited from his undomesticated ancestors.

An animal living and hunting solitarily, like a wildcat, need not have a similarly strong control of its social instincts. Hence our cats, descendants of the wildcat, have no 'super-ego' comparable to that of a dog. A cat is by no means dull, but it can be trained only within narrow limits and it cannot be taught to abstain from following its instincts.

128

As long as a dog is well fed it is not too difficult to teach him not to molest piglets, young goats, fowl and other animals on the farmyard. He can even be trained *contrary to his predatory instincts* to become a shepherd's dog, doing useful work without killing his lambs. A cat cannot be trained to supervise a troop of mice, and in its presence one had better not have a tame bird flying around. Even if the cat is not hungry it will try to catch and kill the bird, irrespective of the fact that the two animals might have lived together in the same house for years. The cat will show no signs of 'bad conscience' when doing so; it has a different psychological structure from a dog.

Some species of wild animal too develop norms of social behaviour resembling a 'conscience'. A fully grown hamadryas baboon with his own harem respects the harems of other males, even if one of them might be temporarily absent. In far more than a thousand hours of observation Hans Kummer and his collaborators never saw an adult male copulating with a female belonging to another harem. Yet, as soon as a harem owner is trapped all these inhibitions break down and the females of his harem are incorporated at once into the harems of others (see also Kummer, 1981).

Long before becoming mature, hamadryas females are kidnapped by a young male or recruited with great patience to become members of his future harem. The young male educates his girls, one is nearly tempted to say he 'trains' them as a master trains his dog. By threatening glances and gestures, bites in the neck and a considerable amount of rudeness he creates, as it were, a conditioned response. The females are taught not to flee him when he threatens or attacks them but rather to approach him and always to remain around him.

As a rule this unique educational programme is successful, and the females, when mature, remain with their master as they had been trained to do when still juveniles. 'Adultery' of a young female is a rather infrequent occurrence and nearly always it is committed with a young male of the same clan who does not yet have his own harem. When mating with such a young male the female carefully hides from her master's sight, repeatedly checks on his whereabouts and in between times visits him with very submissive gestures – only to return to her hidden lover whenever possible and to continue mating with him (Kummer, 1978).

129

Is such a behaviour 'sheer hypocrisy' or does the young female really have a 'bad conscience'? Evidently she follows her instincts while knowing at the same time that she is doing something she 'ought not to do'. One cannot find out whether she is merely afraid of being punished by her master or whether she has feelings of 'guilt' when committing 'adultery'. But then, after all, what is bad conscience in man? Is it not closely interwoven with fears of bad consequences just as well? Fears of being punished by parents, teachers, superiors, the state or by evil spirits? Fear of losing eternal salvation or merely of 'losing face' and the esteem of other people? The dividing line between 'merely pretended' and 'real' feelings of guilt is fuzzy – not only in baboons.

The main difference between man and animals in this respect is that our conscience has not only an emotional side but a reflective side as well. Man – and *only man* – can ask himself whether he really *ought* to have a bad conscience for this or that. By intellectual reasoning he might arrive at the conclusion that certain moral norms which he internalized during his education are *no longer valid* owing to changed circumstances. This is a very valuable and indispensable way of adapting to a rapidly changing world.

Anubis baboons, though near relatives of hamadryas baboons, have quite a different family structure with no harems or permanent bonds between individual males and females. An anubis female, when attacked by a male, behaves 'quite naturally': she flees. In spite of the differences in behaviour, hybrids between the two species – some taxonomists consider them as mere sub-species – are possible. In the border region of their respective habitats there is a whole region populated by such hybrids.

In experiments Kummer (1968) trapped hamadryas females and transplanted them into free-living troops of the other species. That hamadryas females quickly adapted to the new conditions and began to flee when attacked by a male in an anubis group might perhaps not be considered as a great surprise. But adaptation was possible the other way round as well. Anubis females transferred into a hamadryas troop were immediately incorporated into the harem of one of the males and *within hours* learned how to behave there – i.e. not to flee when threatened but to stay and approach their master. Thus it seems that a baboon is able to teach a female of another (sub-) species not to behave in the way typical for her species but quite differently. *An animal trains another animal!*

The success of this training is not always permanent. Some of the females eventually reverted to their original anubis behaviour and fled, either temporarily or for good – though the survival chances of a solitary free-ranging baboon female are small indeed.

Yet the existence of a permanent hybrid population seems to prove that members of both (sub-) species are able to adapt their behaviour in such a way that they can permanently live together in more or less stable groups. The social structure of these hybrid groups is a peculiar mixture of elements of hamadryas and of anubis behaviour. Some of the males try to form permanent harem groups but as a rule they are not very successful and their harems remain small and unstable (Kummer, 1971, p. 134; Nagel, 1973).

Chimpanzees have strong emotional ties between members of a troop. Quarrels are rather frequent between these easily enraged animals, but there is also a marked tendency to settle such disputes quickly without asking questions of 'guilt'. According to Jane Goodall (1971, p. 221) a chimp after having been threatened or attacked by an animal of superior rank, 'may follow the aggressor, screaming and crouching to the ground or holding out his hand. He is, in fact, begging a reassuring touch from the other. Sometimes he will not relax until he has been touched or patted, kissed or embraced.' It all looks like a human begging for pardon, but such an impression *is wrong*. When asking for consolation, for the restoration of friendly terms, the chimp *does not* confess any feeling of guilt. 'A female who is attacked for no reason other than that she happens to be standing too close to a charging male is quite as likely to approach the male and beg a reassuring touch as is the female who is bowled over by a male as she attempts to take a fruit from his pile of bananas' (*ibid.*).

No signs of 'bad conscience' were seen in the 'deviant' chimp females mentioned in section 1.6 that hunted for the babies of others. Neither were there any visible attempts to punish them for their 'crimes' or to expel them from the troop. At the moment of their 'crime' their behaviour met with the disapproval of other group members. Males sometimes helped the mothers to protect their babies from the cannibals. But even an animal as intelligent as a chimp does not seem to be able to recognize that another troop member may be a permanent danger. The long established emotional tie presumably obscures the ability to make such an inference (Kummer, 1978).

There seems to be a deep contradiction in the chimps' behaviour towards the cannibals within the group and towards those former members of the group that split off and formed their own band ranging in a border region of the former group territory. Though originally the secessionists had been members of the group and there must have been the usual emotional ties to them as to all group members, and in spite of the fact that there was still personal acquaintance, they were all persecuted and eventually killed.

The rules regulating the coexistence of individuals in animal societies are a result of natural selection. The selection processes are different according to whether behavioural tendencies are inborn or learnt in the course of individual development, but the results in both cases are likely to conform to the rather general rule dealt with extensively in chapter 1 of this book: in the long run only those behaviour patterns can persist that contribute to the genetic success of the individual by increasing its chances to pass on a maximum amount of its own genes, or genes identical to its own, to future generations.

Natural selection is inherently based on competition between conspecifics. To pass on as many genes as possible means passing on *more* genes than others. A feedback between behaviour and selection can only become effective if social behaviour favours *some* conspecifics to the detriment of others: close kin versus distant kin or non-related individuals, members of one's own group versus strangers. The slogan 'all wolves become brethren' cannot work for two reasons. First of all a wolf adhering to that maxim and sharing its prey with any wolf, not only those belonging to its group, would have small chances of survival. Moreover, being kind to every conspecific does not favour those that behave in the same way to the detriment of those that do not. Therefore treating all fellow wolves as 'brethren' does not help natural selection to spread genes for such a behavioural tendency within a population that, on the whole, is less altruistic. Thus general 'indiscriminate' kindness to all conspecifics cannot become the general inborn norm in an animal society by way of natural selection – whereas preferring kin to non-kin can.

On the other hand, to behave in a 'genetically reasonable' way does *not* mean extreme and narrow selfishness. Time and again there are situations of conflict between immediate personal interests

132

and 'genetical obligations' towards descendants, other kin and other members of the group. Inborn and learnt norms of social conduct should help an animal in such a situation to find the 'proper' solution – i.e. to behave in a way that gives the best chances of passing on – directly via descendants or indirectly via other kin – as many genes as possible to future generations. Of course, the animal is not aware of this.

Whereas in social insect societies the individual is 'cheap' and prepared to sacrifice itself and others for the benefit of the colony without hesitation, mammals, on the other hand, have a strong inborn tendency for 'self-realization'. Thus mammalian societies have the problem of finding viable compromise between safeguarding the rights of the individuals and safeguarding general welfare, since otherwise an orderly coexistence in a group would be impossible (see section 1.15).

Australopithecus, the biped with the ape's brain living in African steppes about 3 million years ago, had to solve this problem too. We do not know the details of his solution, but certainly it was not a set of behavioural norms as found in an insect society, but something within the bandwidth typical for social mammals. This is the heritage handed down to us from our animal ancestors. This was the starting point for the evolution of human morals.

2.15 *The evolution of sympathy*

A greylag goose may reach an age of 50 years, yet at 2 years it is mature. African apes live just about as long, but the period of their individual development lasts about five times as long as that of a goose. Female apes reach maturity at an age of about ten or eleven years, males even later. This long time span of development is one of the most important preconditions of the high intelligence of the apes.

Humans may reach nearly twice the age of chimps and their period of individual development lasts about twice as long as well. Moreover, a human infant is born in a particularly 'unfinished' state. The relative importance of learned behaviour as compared to inborn behaviour patterns is much higher in man than in apes. Hence human behaviour is still much more flexible than that of the most intelligent animals; man is able to adapt to an astonishingly large range of external conditions.

133

An animal at the evolutionary level of a goose is by no means totally pre-programmed (see section 1.4, also Midgley, 1978/80, p. xvi). Within a certain bandwith there may be individual variations of behaviour due to personal disposition and experience – and occasionally one goose among millions might invent something new which goes beyond the behavioural patterns hitherto typical for the species.

The bandwith of individual variation is much wider in chimps than in geese and orders of magnitude wider in men than in chimps, but even human behaviour is by no means entirely unpredictable. An individual couple freely decides how many children they want to have – and in the age of the pill they probably will be able to realize their decision – yet demographers can predict with fair confidence how many children are going to be born within the next five years in a particular country. Forecasting the result of an election or the probable trend of rates of criminality is much more than mere guesswork – in spite of occasional failures. A psychologist working intensively with a certain individual will be able to predict fairly accurately how that person will behave in a certain situation.

The influence of instincts on human behaviour is weaker and not as compelling as in animals, but this is a difference in degree rather than a difference in principle. According to Norbert Bischof, a German experimental psychologist working at Zürich University, the spectrum of instincts in man is broadened and more differentiated than in animals. Instincts in man are reduced to the level of emotional tendencies which form the basis for cultural super-structures in specifically human forms.

In Bischof's view (1978, p. 63) the main differences between animals and man are found not primarily in the realm of motivation, but rather in the realm of cognition. An ape is able to imagine changes in his environment, he writes, to assess the advantages and drawbacks of such changes – i.e. to perceive environments that are possible but not existing – and then he tries to realize the most satisfactory alternative. But only man is able to assess not only his present but also his future needs, and to try to realize a state which is most beneficial overall – independent of, or even in contradiction to, his current needs. When planning his actions an ape can think beyond the moment but not beyond the present. Only man is able to project himself into the future with the aid of his imagination. As a consequence he is *compelled* to think about the future and this has drastic emotional consequences.

The future is uncertain, full of dangers and mostly unpredictable. Uncertainty is related to unfamiliarity and causes anxiety which merges with fears characteristic for the particular period – fears of war, plague, nuclear bombs, environmental polution, etc. Only inevitable death is certain. This gives rise to the typically human 'existential anxiety' which is, according to Bischof, the first price we pay for being able to anticipate the future.

As we have seen, animals too can experience conflict situations in view of diverging or even contradictory needs. In man who can – and must – assess future needs as well, the number of possible conflicts increases manifold whilst, on the other hand, the motivating force of present needs is dampened, since otherwise it would not be possible to take proper account of future needs. This, says Bischof, results in a poor stability of motivation, in a typically human 'fickleness' and that's the second price we pay for our awareness of the future.

A third problem arises from the fact that man can imagine himself in future in another place and under different conditions. Not only is he able to recognize his image in a mirror – as chimps are as well – he also can see himself, to a degree, mirrored in *any* fellow man; and he can see in a conspecific an image of what he was in the past, or will become in future. The gap between 'ego' and 'others' is partly bridged by this. As a consequence man is capable of directing social motives like sympathy or aggression towards himself, whilst, conversely, his own selfish feelings may protect others – since he cannot help identifying with them. 'Greedy people cannot bear it when others waste their money,' says Bischof. The capability to identify with others is a source of many new conflicts. Should one care for sick or old members of the group or the family (as one hopes that somebody will care for oneself one day) or should one expel them from the community according to present egoistic interests?

Thus, in Bischof's view, man is influenced by an immense diversity of ambiguous and conflicting motives. They give no clear direction for action, yet take vengeance if neglected; and they are continually overshadowed by the ever-present existential anxiety. These are the special problems to be solved by human morality – and they are

135

moreover included in the more general mammalian problem as formulated by Wilson (see section 1.15) which has to be solved by man as well: to find an optimal compromise between one's own interests and the advantages of belonging to a community.

As a forager, hunter or toolmaker man hardly could have been too clever or inventive, writes Hans Kummer (1978). The more his behaviour was unpredictable to his prey animals the more easily he could outwit them. But since our ancestors probably mostly hunted in groups and certainly lived in communities they must have been able to perform team work and hence their behaviour must have been predictable to the other members of the team.

Certainly there was competition amongst the members of a group of early men or proto-human beings. To be astute and unpredictable would confer advantages to an individual in his competition with fellow group members; yet if such traits were to become too strong, co-operation within the group would become impossible. Hence the more man liberated himself from the rule of instincts and the more he broadened the bandwidth of his behaviour the more urgent became the formation of a strong 'super-ego' to counterbalance his astuteness in the social realm and to enable him to continue to exist as a social being (Kummer, 1978). Once again we find a difference in degree rather than in principle between animals and man. Mechanisms of psychological regulation already present in primitive form in some higher animals evolved to a higher level in our own species.

It can be assumed that the evolution of proto-human and human morals was at first subject to the same general rule of natural selection that is operating in the animal kingdom too: behaviour can only persist if it is 'genetically reasonable'. Altruistic behaviour contributing directly (via descendants) or indirectly (via kin) to passing on a maximum of one's own or identical genes to future generations might have evolved according to the diverse mechanisms described in the first part of this book – by individual selection, kin selection, group selection or mutualism (reciprocal altruism). Moreover, in a being as intelligent as our ancestors can be assumed to have been, one could well imagine a selection of strong aggressive tendencies against individuals not conforming to generally accepted rules of social conduct, or selection of a tendency to look for a mate not too unpredictable in his or her behaviour towards fellow men (Trivers, 1971; D. T. Campbell, 1978).

136

Seen in this way the evolution of 'genetically reasonable' ethics does not pose an insoluble problem for Dawinistic theory. But any such morals clearly discriminate – overtly or covertly – between privileged (kin, members of the own group, the own people etc.) and other men. One can find examples for this from the rituals of tribal people emotionally reinforcing the bonds of clan membership to modern ideologies of racism and chauvinism. The Old Testament too preaches the religion of a 'Chosen People'. Even the famous vision of the prophet Isaiah speaks of conquering the godless and *then only*, after the final victory over the 'heathen', swords will be turned into ploughshares.

Yet there are many examples showing that man is capable of developing moral ideas going far beyond a 'genetically reasonable' altruism that demands favouring certain people to the detriment of others. For Jesus Christ *all* men are children of God, possessing an immortal soul – not only members of the 'Chosen People' but of all peoples, not only males but females as well, not only freeborn but also slaves. Love thy neighbour – any neighbour – as thyself.

Viewed in a Darwinistic perspective it does not seem surprising so much that such ideas are distorted, that they are (ab-)used to justify crusades against the 'infidels' and the burning of 'heretics', but rather that they could arise at all. Yet it is a fact that the ideas of loving one's neighbour, of international solidarity, of 'all men become brethren' ('*Alle Menschen werden Brüder*' as sung in Beethoven's 9th symphony) did arise again and again in manifold forms in the course of human history and that they have a strong emotional appeal and mobilizing power.

According to the principles of genetical cost–benefit calculation and of a morality based on it one cannot explain how there could be people that hid fleeing prisoners of war with whom they could hardly talk and fed them even in times of dire want. How could there be in World War II courageous persons in many countries that risked liberty and life to help persecuted Jews, prisoners of concentration camps or members of oppressed nations? Why are there millions nowadays contributing to help victims of an earthquake or a famine in a far away continent? How is it possible that an organisation like Amnesty International could become an important moral force in world politics; that there are several hundred thousand people working in its ranks to help prisoners of conscience they do not know and whose views they possibly do not even share?

Whether such acts of charity or solidarity are spontaneous or motivated by religious or other convictions, they are only possible because we humans in the course of our evolution attained –together with our intelligence and imagination of the future and, as it were, as a by-product of them – the capability to see an image of ourselves in *every* other man. A wolf is not capable of doing this, and neither is an ape. 'A baboon enters a trap even after having just seen another one being caught in it,' reports Kummer (1978). Even if he might have a certain amount of consciousness of himself it seems that all apes and monkeys lack the insight leading to an inference like: 'I am like him. What now happens to him can happen to me.'

Man has this capability. And he is able to identify not only intellectually but also emotionally with every fellow man.

Chimpanzees do not seem to be able to grasp the condition of a sick or disabled comrade. Survivors of a polio epidemic, moving on their partly paralysed limbs as well as they could, elicited fear when they tried to return to their group owing to their strange appearance. 'When Pepe shuffled up the slope with his useless arm trailing behind him, the group of chimps stared for a moment and then, with wide grins of fear, rushed for assurance to embrace and pat each other, still staring at the unfortunate cripple', reports Jane Goodall (1971, p. 201). 'Pepe, who obviously had no idea that he himself was the object of their fear, showed an even wider grin of fright as he repeatedly turned to look over his shoulder – trying to find out, presumably, what it was that was making his companions so frightened. Eventually, the others calmed down, but, though they continued to stare at him from time to time, none of them went near him.'

Though one would assume that the disabled were still personally known to their group mates, they were treated as outcasts, threatened and attacked when trying to approach the others. Jane Goodall describes the tragedy of an old male paralysed in both legs who repeatedly tried to re-establish contact with his mates: 'When at last he reached the tree he rested for a while and then made the final effort and pulled himself up until he was close to two of the grooming males. With a loud grunt of pleasure he reached a hand towards them in greeting – but even before he made contact they both swung quickly away. . . For a full two minutes he sat motionless, staring after them. As I watched him sitting there alone, my vision blurred, and when I looked up at the groomers I came nearer to hating a chimpanzee than I have ever done before or since' (*ibid.*, p. 202).

When a chimp is frightened and seeks a reassuring touch, the motivation of the one giving the consolation *cannot*, in Jane Goodall's view, be compared with that of a human in a similar situation: 'Humans are capable of acting from purely unselfish motives; we can be genuinely sorry for someone and try to share in his troubles in an endeavour to offer comfort and solace. It is unlikely that a chimpanzee acts from feelings quite like these' (*ibid.*, p. 221).

Even more outspoken is a paragraph in a booklet on *Aggression in monkeys, apes and man* (1980, p. 166) by the Swiss ethologist Walter Angst: 'Last not least aggression research should help to find ways to reduce aggression in its many unwelcome forms. For man does not just accept the biological evolution and function of aggression. He has ethical ideals like equal rights, freedom, human rights etc., that are contrary to the inherited program of aggression. A basis for such an anti-aggression ethics is the human capability to imagine the feelings of a fellow man subjected to aggression. Man, as it were, is able to 'transfer' himself into the other, though indeed he is inferring from himself without really knowing what happens in the other's feelings. This capability for compassion serves as a psychological basis for the ethical demand to control aggressions, since they cause physical and psychological distress to other men.'

In all the voluminous sociobiological literature I have never found a statement similar to that one.

The mere knowledge that we are capable of compassion does not yet explain how such a trait could evolve and persist against inborn egoistic tendencies. Yet it is a fact that man – *and man only* – can identify with every conspecific. We do it far too seldom, but when doing so we put at least the tip of a toe beyond a threshold that is unsurpassable for animals.

2.16 *Once again: What is man?*

As a motto for his booklet criticizing sociobiology Marshall Sahlins (1976) uses a quotation telling how a young scientist at the beginning of this century visited the aged philosopher Benno Erdmann at the University of Jena. They had a warm and friendly conversation on the old philosophers and their systems. But when the visitor tried to talk about contemporary philosophy, Erdmann shook his head, declaring that he could not understand the young men any more. 'In my day,' he explained, 'we used to ask the everlasting question: "What is Man?" And you, nowadays, you answer it, saying, "he *was* an ape".' (Steffens, 1931).

In this second part of my book I have tried to show that the sociobiological approach to this topic can tell us considerably more; and that just its unusual perspective of looking at men as 'through the front end of a telescope', as Wilson puts it (1978*a*, p. 17), can highlight traits and peculiarities of man that are usually not perceived by philosophers or social scientists. Traits and capabilities – for better or worse – in which we are unique and others in which we are different from the animals only by degree or not at all.

Of course, *any* species by definition must have certain traits distinguishing it from all other species. 'Humans, in short, are not unique in being unique,' says Pierre van den Berghe, professor of sociobiology at the University of Washington (1978). But such a statement, though correct, misses the point. *Man is unique in a unique way*, and to gloss over this fact confuses still further an already complicated discussion.

Being human we quite naturally have a tendency to perceive our species as something very special indeed. Sometimes we tacitly tend to assume our uniqueness as 'evident' and people knowing little about animals put forward claims, not always correct ones, that 'only man' is able to do this or that; or actually-existing gradual differences are inflated into non-existing principal ones. The 'unique uniqueness' of man cannot be proved except with facts, and such facts can only be found by thoroughly comparing man with other species.

In the course of human evolution something happened which some scientists call a 'quantum jump'; one might just as well borrow from Hegel and Marx and call it a 'transition from quantity to quality'. Yet both these metaphors do not quite correspond to reality. There was no specific point in our evolution where the animal ended and man began, as there is a point at which a liquid, when further supplied with heat energy, does not get warmer but starts

140

boiling. It was a *gradual* transition, quick according to biological time scales, but nevertheless a process with intermediate forms that were no longer animals and not yet quite human. Evolution of man was no sudden 'revolution' – but it was a unique and very peculiar process with nothing comparable in the history of life on earth.

We are unique in a unique way, but perhaps not as much as some social scientists seem to think. Hence I believe that we might be able to understand ourselves better if we know how we became men; and maybe we might get new insights into man and his evolution if we know more about animals and their evolution.

There are many examples in biological research which show that it can be a very rewarding enterprise to study complicated problems in primitive organisms, since it is easier to observe such processes in them. Of course, knowledge gained in the study of bacteria, yeast cells, nematodes, sea urchin eggs or fruit flies must not be transposed to higher organisms without checking to what extent it is applicable. But in many instances rules applying to all animals have been found by studying simple organisms – rules of metabolism, of embryonic development, of heredity, etc. In other instances the study of simple organisms has at least given valuable cues for research in higher animals or for the solution of complicated medical problems.

I cannot quite see why such a method might not be profitable in the study of behavioural problems as well. Of course, inventions of the oyster catcher or of the macaque, tool-use of Darwin finches or of chimpanzees, the 'conscience' of a dog or of a monkey are more primitive phenomena than even the most primitive human culture. But *just because* all human cultures are complicated, the study of the much more primitive cultural achievements of animals might give us hints for a better understanding of the evolution of human culture. Human peculiarities such as the role of language should not blind us to the fact that once we had ancestors with certain elements of culture like tool-use but presumably without a human-like language. Even less should it blind us to the fact that our pre-human heritage did not simply dissolve into nothing with the evolution of human language and human morals, but that it still exists and influences us.

This book is not intended to be a manual of sociobiology. I did not set myself the task of giving an overview over all aspects where sociobiologists tried – more or less convincingly – to compare animals with men. I rather tried to select a few examples to show that such comparisons can be interesting and that they can help us to grasp similarities as well as differences between ourselves and the (other) animals.

Of course, one should only compare things that really are comparable and should not infer too much from superficial analogies. Yet just this is one of the reproaches uttered by many critics of sociobiology, and it would be very surprising indeed if some of them were not justified. In the euphoric mood accompanying any new scientific achievment its explanatory power inevitably is overtaxed. This happened not only in applying sociobiological ideas to animals (see section 1.9), but even more so in trying to apply them to man.

'The trouble is not – as people often think – that human concepts cannot be extended to other species', writes Mary Midgley (1978/80, pp. 88–89). 'It is that such an extension must be done sensitively. Apparently similar patterns can play very different parts in the lives of different species.' She then reproaches Wilson for his tendency to use too much quantifying comparison across the species barrier, which cannot possibly do justice to these differences. Wilson, she writes, in fact very often sees the differences but fails to see how strongly they demand a non-quantitative approach. Grasping such differences 'is not an obstacle in the way of a unified study, but a condition of it.'

In some twenty or thirty years the wheat will be sorted out from the chaff; by then, most probably, some of the basic notions and approaches of sociobiology will belong to the normal tool kit of scientists studying man and his society. Comparisons between human and animal behaviour will become all the easier the better we understand animals themselves. Even today Washburn who is a harsh critic of sociobiology quite sensibly refers to chimp tool-use to counter prejudices about our early ancestors (see section 2·11); and already in 1966, when the term 'sociobiology' was practically unkown, he made very interesting comparisons on population densities and territoriality in monkeys, apes and man (see section 2.13).

For it is simply not true that 'most human behaviour has no close counterpart in any nonhuman animal' as Washburn stated in the heat of discussion (1978*a*, p. 40; see also section 2.2). What matters is to find a solid basis and a useful methodology for such comparisons that protects against pitfalls.

3

Sex and family in animals and man

3.1 *What is sex for?*

There are things with which we are so familiar that we never get the idea of asking why they are so. Every human being must have a mother and a father, that's obvious, isn't it? But *why* do we humans only reproduce sexually?

The first organisms, from which we are all descended, did not know sex. They multiplied by cell division, and most micro-organisms do not have any other form of propagation even now. Under favourable circumstances they are able to colonize a fitting habitat very quickly in this way. Asexual forms of reproduction can also be found in many multicellular organisms, particularly amongst plants, but also in a large number of lower animals, as for example in the coelenterates mentioned in section 1.12.

By cell division an organism can pass on *all* its genes to its descendants, whereas only half are handed down in sexual propagation. Moreover asexual reproduction is a much more simple process than the complex and easily disturbed mechanisms of sexual propagation which entails every individual starting anew as a 'unicellular organism', as it were, and facing many dangers in embryonal and juvenile development.

In order to beget offspring in the sexual way an organism must produce highly specialized sex cells that only carry half its genes (see section 1.3). Even in the most simple cases, such as oysters which shed these cells into the sea and leave the rest to chance, the sex cells must be able to recognize a fitting partner cell and to distinguish it from other unfit objects like the sex cells of other species. If possible, sex cells ought to be capable of attracting the right partner cells, or to search for them; and in any case they must have a programme enabling them to fuse and form a fertilized egg cell.

On a higher level all this is supplemented by activities of the individuals that produce the sex cells. Many higher plants have brightly coloured and strongly smelling blossoms to allure insects that transport the pollen to other blossoms. Animals attract members of the opposite sex by a multitude of scent, sound and optical signals. They must look for a proper partner and be able to distinguish such a partner from an unfit object of attraction. The cuckoo must 'know' that it is a cuckoo and must not try to copulate with the species of its foster parents. For reproduction the partners need sexual organs and a repertory of well matching behaviour patterns enabling them to copulate.

From all this it is evident that sexual propagation needs a lot of genetical pre-programming: for the production and the 'behaviour' of sex cells; for embryonic and juvenile development; for the development of sexual organs; for the regulation of inborn sexual behaviour patterns typical of the species and/or for the ability to learn such behaviour. Every one of these mechanisms is liable to disturbance, and thus one might well ask why all this great effort is needed, since reproduction is possible in a much simpler way and at much less 'cost' by asexual means (see also Bischof, 1978/79).

Yet it is a fact that sex proved to be a very successful 'invention' which has become the predominant or only form of reproduction in nearly all higher organisms. Obviously the great effort must 'pay' somehow; and biologists can provide a plausible explanation for it.

In asexual reproduction the descendants get exactly the same genes as their ancestors – not counting occasional mutations. They are adapted to their environment just as well as previous generations, but they have no means to 'adapt' quickly to environmental changes. Only in sexual reproduction is there what we have called the 'shuffling of the cards' in section 1.3. Every reproductive act becomes an experiment with an unforseeable result – a kind of genetical throwing of the dice. The descendant gets a combination of genes that most probably never existed before (see section 1.5).

That this explanation is not merely theoretical but is close to reality can be seen in animals that have sexual as well as asexual reproduction, for example aphids. As long as the environment is

145

stable they reproduce asexually. In case of environmental changes a generation of sexual animals arises that produces progeny with new combinations of genes, i.e. with a certain bandwidth of different traits. Of this new generation, only those that are best 'adapted' to the new circumstances survive.

To achieve a 'shuffling of the cards', however, one would not need two *different* sexes or different kinds of sex cells. Yet, if an individual 'wants' to have a large number of progeny – or, to be more exact, since natural selection puts a premium on mechanisms or behaviour patterns having such an effect –there are different and *contradictory* methods to get to this end. One way is to produce as many sex cells as possible, which, of necessity, must be small in size, and in this way to increase the chances that at least some of them will reach the right partner cell. Possibly such cells should have a small motor mechanism, a bit of 'propellant' and a homing device for finding partner cells. The other method is to increase not the number but the survival chances of the sex cells by giving them a rather large amount of 'foodstuff' on the way and perhaps a protective cover. Thus one gets rather large cells, the number of which, of necessity, is small.

If every sex cell had to exist on its own, evolution most probably would have created a large range of compromise solutions in different species to comply with both demands to some extent –as there are a large number of forms of fertilized plant seed that are subject to the same sorts of contradictory selection pressures. Fertilization being an act of fusion of *two* cells, however, it was easily possible for evolution to go in both directions simultaneously, producing two types of sex cell with different sets of optimal traits that supplement each other in a most convenient way: a large number of small, highly mobile male sperm cells which search (and compete) for a much smaller number of fairly large female egg cells which have stored rather large provisions (see also Parker *et al.*, 1972). Very simply, one could say *that the male principle puts its stake in the success of quantity, the female one in that of quality.*

To produce different types of sex cell one does not necessarily need individuals of different sex. Actually the large majority of higher plant are monoecious, i.e. they are hermaphrodites. Within one and the same bloom they have anthers producing pollen as well as a pistil leading to the seed-vessel, containing what would be called in animals the female egg cells. Some lower animals too, for example earthworms, are hermaphrodites, fertilizing each other in both ways. In higher animals, however, two opposite sexes are the rule, with each of the sexes having typical, sex-specific behaviour patterns. Yet these different behaviour patterns do rest on a general basic attitude common to both sexes: an inborn urge to have the highest possible reproductive success. The animal, of course, does not know this; it does not 'want' to pass on a maximally possible amount of his genes to future generations. Neither can it be assumed that the animal knows about the connection between copulation and reproduction.

Biologists and ethologists speaking about 'sex strategies' are using, as it were, a sort of mental shorthand, since it would be too tedious to repeat again and again that natural selection puts a premium on those behaviour patterns that lead to maximal reproductive success. Yet the fact remains that in the process of selection only those survive who not only possess sexual organs but who know how to use them optimally. The evolution of a sexual reproduction going beyond the mere shedding of sex cells into the sea, the evolution of sexual organs that can bring sperm cells close to the egg cells, demands a concomitant evolution of a sexual drive: a strong urge to use one's sexual organs appropriately.

The sexual drive is an *emotional superstructure* which –particularly in man – can achieve a certain amount of independence, but which nevertheless serves (or has, at least, evolved to serve) biological ends which the actor does not need to know. Since natural selection puts a premium on reproductive success, men and sexually propagating animals have a strong sexual motivation. In order to get a sex partner they take considerable risks. Even animals that usually are very shy forget, in the 'turmoil of their senses', the most elementary precautions that are usually an integral part of their behaviour.

In humans of our cultural sphere, most sexual activity nowadays does not serve the original biological end. Reproductive success is not desired; in many instances it is even considered as a snag. We have sex for its own sake because we like it. But *why* do we like an activity which is biologically useless – though we know very well that the feelings of pleasure we get in this way are but an emotional superstructure for a biological end that we usually do not want to achieve? Why is it that men and women use in their love affairs well-known ancient sex-specific strategies of behaviour which, with

147

appropriate modifications, are used by animals as well? Strategies that serve, even if the individual does not realize it, to achieve the maximal possible *success of reproduction* – even though we humans usually do not wish such reproductive success?

The sexual drive is inborn, in us as well as in other species reproducing sexually. To satisfy this drive the two sex partners need a rather large repertory of well matching and precise behaviour patterns. Even in higher animals these behaviour patterns are not pre-programmed to the very last detail – and still less so in humans. Learning and education certainly play a considerable part in their development. On the other hand, however, there can be no doubt that nature confers on a sexually reproducing organism not only a drive, but also a set of 'recipes' by which he or she can satisfy this drive – a set of inborn basic patterns of behaviour that can be refined and supplemented by learning processes and experience.

3.2 *Are females handicapped by nature?*

A male and a female producing progeny together are, biologically speaking, both 'interested' that their children should grow up to be fit and to produce, on their part, a maximal possible number of descendants. Thus the parents, though as a rule not kin, have common 'genetic interests' in the thriving of their children. Yet this does not exclude that they might have different and even contradictory interests as well.

Amongst sociobiologists, especially Robert Trivers dealt with this problem in a seminal paper published in 1972. Basing himself on deliberations of early population geneticists (see for example Richards, 1927; Fisher, 1930; Bateman, 1948) Trivers spotlighted the different kinds and amounts of effort that each parent spends for his or her progeny. In principle, Trivers claims, every animal has an inborn tendency to induce its mate to invest as much as possible into their common progeny whilst trying to keep its own investment as small as is compatible with reasonable survival chances for the young. There are all sorts of solutions for this conflict of interests, different from species to species and often even from individual to individual. As a rule, however, males have an advantage in this conflict owing to their biologically more favourable starting conditions.

Even if a female does no more for her progeny than to shed egg cells into the sea, maternal investment, according to sociobiological reasoning, is much larger than the paternal one, since an egg cell is bigger than a sperm cell. The difference in size of the sex cells is particularly conspicuous in reptiles and birds, but even in man the microscopically small egg cell is still 85 000 times larger than a sperm cell (Wilson, 1978a, p. 124). Parker et al. (1972) even suggest that the sperm, as it were, 'parasitizes' (their inverted commas) on the large provisioning of the egg cell, but such an argument does not really seem fair to me and it can easily be turned round: most of the egg cells, on the other hand, would never be fertilized at all, if there was not a large number of highly motile small sperm cells around to do so. In other words the male *must* produce a very large number of sperm cells if there is to be a reasonable chance that at least some of them might reach an egg cell. This is not only true of oysters that shed their sex cells into the sea, but even for mammals where fertilization occurs inside the female body. For, to the tiny sperm cell which is ejaculated into the lower regions of the female genital organ, an egg cell travelling in the oviduct is still a very distant goal that is not easily reached.

In humans a healthy male produces about 80 to 150 million sperms in one ejaculation. If it is 85 millions, his initial investment is about a thousand times *larger* than that of the woman whose egg cell is about 85 000 times as big as a single sperm cell. This large initial male effort is by no means extravagant. Males producing only a few thousand sperm cells per ejaculation are practically infertile. Their chances to produce offspring in the natural way are exceedingly small. If they want to have children one must collect many of their ejaculates, concentrate the sperm and use it for artificial insemination (McLaren, 1970).

The decisive contribution of the female in humans and other mammals is not the size of the egg cell but the fact that the mother provides, as it were, a protective nest for her progeny in the interior of her body; that she feeds the embryos, while they grow in her womb, via her blood circulation; and that she provides them with milk after birth. This causes a difference in investment which cannot be fully compensated even by a large male contribution to brood care.

Of course, many forms of what Trivers calls 'parental investment' (PI) are much more easily defined than measured or evaluated

149

against each other. Even respective energy investment of mother and father cannot serve as a general yardstick. In many socially living species males do not contribute anything to routine brood care, but they defend the young in case of danger. In total this probably requires much less energy than the daily devoted efforts of the morther, but the males risk their health and even their lives in fighting predators, and what they contribute might be no less important for the survival of the offspring than maternal brood care.

A 'division of labour' between the parents, with the mother caring for the young and the father defending them, may conform to traditional human conceptions, but it is only one of many possible behaviour patterns. In quite a number of species, from song birds to gibbons, there is a state approaching true 'partnership' with mother *and* father contributing to the care of the brood as well as to their defence. At the other end of the spectrum there are animals, some of them very high on the evolutionary ladder, with a paternal 'investment' strictly confined to fertilization and nothing else. The mothers of such species have to carry the full burden of caring and defending their young and they do so either as solitary individuals, as in orang-utans, or in groups of closely related females, as in elephants.

The amount of biological inequality is most clearly visible when comparing the maximal number of offspring that can be produced by a male versus a female of particular species. Cases like the honey bee, with a queen that must copulate with up to a dozen males to get enough sperm for fertilizing all the eggs she presumably will lay during her life (see section 1·13), are rare exceptions. In the large majority of higher animals, and particularly in mammals and birds, a male theoretically can produce many times more young than a female.

In humans a woman under optimal reproductive conditions might give birth in the course of her life to more than 20 children – assuming that she has no miscarriages and gives birth to twins several times. This is not a mere theoretical calculation. Very large numbers of children were not uncommon in Europe in the nineteenth century. The Austrian president of 1919 and 1945, Dr Karl Renner, was born in 1870 along with a twin as the seventeenth and eighteenth children of a peasant family in southern Moravia, then part of the Austrian empire. The famous singer Enrico Caruso was born as the nineteenth of 21 children, about 1875 in the vicinity of Naples. A male, on the other hand, might beget several hundred children within a year if he can find enough female partners, and theoretically could father several thousands in the course of his life. The American Mormon chief Brigham Young was said to have fathered nearly 500 children.

It might be asked why there are, as a rule, about equal numbers of both sexes, if a much smaller number of males would be sufficient to fertilize a much larger number of females. Yet the main biological 'end' of sexual reproduction is not to get a maximal number of offspring which would be easier accomplished by asexual propagation, but rather a 'shuffling of the cards', as mentioned in the last chapter, to achieve genetical diversity amongst the progeny. And a maximal bandwidth of variation requires about equal frequency of both sexes. Moreover, competition amongst males is in itself part of the selection process.

Arguing in this way, however, assumes evolution for the 'benefit of the species' and therefore is not convincing to strict Darwinists. But individual selection works in the same direction, as was shown by the great population geneticist R. A. Fisher in 1930. If there were many more females than males, parents of sons would have a genetic advantage; they would pass on many more genes to future generations than parents of daughters. Thus, since the frequency relation of the sexes is itself subject to genetical regulation, genes for having more sons would spread in the population until a state of about equal numbers of sexes is reached. There might be exceptional situations to which this reasoning cannot be applied (see for example, Hamilton, 1967), but as a rule, at least in higher vertebrates, there are indeed about equal numbers of males and females.

3.3 Female and male sex strategies

Having different biological starting conditions each of the two sexes needs a different kind of sexual strategy to be successful in the genetical sense. A male will have maximal reproductive success by copulating with as many females as possible – unless there are other limiting factors. Females, on the other hand, can also mate with many males – and in some species like chimps they indeed do so – but they can hardly increase significantly the number of their offspring in this way.

151

As a rule all females are fertilized and hence (if there is enough food to go round) the number of surviving offspring of one individual female is independent of the reproductive success of the others. A male, on the other hand, cannot increase the number of his progeny except by curtailing the reproductive chances of other males. Thus it is usually the males that are fighting for access to the females and not the other way round, and those that are victorious father *significantly* more children than the losers of such contests, whereas the difference in the number of offspring of individual females is much smaller.

In a group of elephant seals 4% of the males were observed to account for 88% of all copulations (LeBoeuf, 1974); in sage grouse 85% of the copulations were performed by only 7% of the males (Wiley, 1973). These, of course, are extreme examples, but there are many species, among them some primates, in which a few high-ranking males monopolize most of the matings – especially when the females are at the peak of their oestrous period and most likely to be fertilized – whereas other males only have rare chances of copulation or none at all (see for example, Hausfather, 1975; Packer, 1979).

In other species, as, for example, in lions or hamadryas baboons, all males, or at least most of them, have a fair chance to conquer a harem when they are in their prime, but they are unable to hold such a position for an extended period. After only two years or three they lose their females to younger competitors and after such a defeat the older males, though still fertile and sexually interested, hardly ever have a chance of access to a female again.

Since males must compete for females they are jealous of each other. For a female, on the other hand, jealousy, biologically speaking, does not 'pay', unless she gets from the male more 'parental investment' than mere fertilization.

Since the 'demand' for females is usually much greater than the 'supply' – even if females mature earlier or mortality among males is higher – it is the males who, as a rule, court the females and not vice versa. 'We cannot fight for love, as men may do; we should be woo'd and were not made to woo', says Helena in Shakespeare's *A Midsummer Night's Dream*.

Normally, there is no danger of a female being 'left over' and finding no mate – unless there are other limiting factors like, for example,

152

lack of enough appropriate breeding territories. Thus the female can afford to be choosy and to select a highly valuable male – whatever that may mean in a particular species; or she might demand some initial investment of the male such as building of a nest or possession of a good territory before being prepared to copulate with him. Again we see that females, to achieve reproductive success, must look for quality, whereas males striving for quantity, i.e. for as many copulations as possible, do not care so much about the 'worthiness' of every one of their mating partners.

'The male has little to lose by courting numerous females and by attempting to fertilize as many of them as possible,' writes the well-known American zoologist Ernst Mayr (1972, p. 91). 'Anything that enhances his success in courtship will be favoured by selection. The situation is quite different in the case of the female. Any failure of mating with the right kind of male may mean total reproductive failure and a total loss of her genes from the genotype of the next generation.'

In species with a paternal contribution to brood care monogamy – or, to be more exact, a male as little polygamous as possible – seems to be the best solution from the female's point of view. Under such conditions true 'partnership' with maximal 'equality of sexes' might evolve. Song birds, greylag geese, jackals or gibbons are classic examples.

There are, however, some good biological arguments for non-monogamous *female* behaviour as well. By copulating with several males, a female minimizes the risk of losing an entire breeding season because her mate was infertile. For females giving birth to a larger number of young in one litter or clutch, copulation with several males might have genetic advantages too: having different fathers for her young might expand the bandwidth of variations amongst them and thus their respective capability of being 'adapted' to *different* environmental conditions. Irrespective of whether these attempts at an explanation are right or wrong it is a fact that in many species not only males but *females too* strive for copulation with a rather large number of partners. This applies to animals practising 'free love' (promiscuity) like chimps just as well as to species forming harems in which female 'adultery' seems to be a fairly common occurrence (see section 1.4).

On the other hand, polygamous (or, as scientists like to say, 'polygynous') behaviour is not always the best strategy for males – especially if the living circumstances of a particular species demand a certain paternal contribution to care and defence of the brood. Under such conditions being a 'Don Juan' probably will not 'pay'. For even if such a male can find sufficient mating partners whom he leaves after copulation he must leave with them their young – his own progeny – as well. Having no father caring for them their chances of survival will be low; hence the 'Don Juan', though fathering many children, might have very few grandchildren.

How sexual behaviour, even in animals, is influenced not only by 'emotions' but also by 'cold materialistic calculations' can be seen in wrens. As a rule these birds live monogamously, but if a male has a good territory with several good nesting caves a second female might prefer to settle in this realm instead of mating a poor male with an inferior territory. The male with the rich territory thus might become a bigamist. If all goes well he can in this way increase his reproductive success, but he probably must increase his own working burden as well, since he has now to contribute to the feeding of two clutches. Bigamy is a luxury that only a 'well-to-do' wren male can afford.

Basically the same problem on the human plane is shown in the humoristic Italian film *L'immorale* with Ugo Tognazzi playing a successful conductor and violinist who besides his own wife has two other women and children with all three of them. He tries to be a good husband to all three of them and a good father to all his children. In the end he dies from a heart attack.

'Institutionalized' polygamy as found in many birds and mammals from domestic poultry to hamadryas baboons is an attempt to combine the advantages of having several wives with a certain amount of paternal investment in the care and particularly in the defence of *all* the young of a father. The essence of such a 'harem' is that the females do not have 'separate households' as in the case of the bigamist wren, but that every one of the mothers with her children constitutes a sub-group of a larger family with only one male head who, as a rule, is the father of all the children.

For the male this kind of solution diminishes the dangers of cardiac disease. For the female, on the other hand, it might be genetically advantageous to be one of several wives of a strong and successful male, for inasmuch as the success of this male is due to

154

inherited traits there is a fair chance that his sons too will inherit these genes and be successful again. Hence a female mating with a successful male will probably have many grandchildren and thus be able to pass on many of her genes to future generations. Moreover belonging to a harem is bound up with many advantages of living in a large group. Of course, there is another side of the coin as well. Jealousy and rank order fights amongst female members of a harem as well as attempts to get advantage for one's own children to the detriment of others are common in harems of animals and of humans.

Institutionalized polyandry can be found in some bird species. It has two very distinct forms. One might better be called 'wife sharing' between two brothers as in the Tasmanian rail (see section 1.8). The other one is a true swapping of sex roles with a female acquiring a sort of 'reversed harem' of several males who, apart from laying eggs, do all the brood care.

The evolutionary root of this second form probably is so-called 'second clutch strategy' as found in some shorebirds and wildfowl, like the red-legged partridge (Emlen and Oring, 1977). The female first lays one clutch that is incubated solely by the male and then a second clutch that she herself incubates. In some species both clutches usually have the same father, in others the female might look for a new male. Going still further, the female might produce more than two clutches within one season that are incubated by different males.

An extreme form of polyandry and role swapping is found in the Middle American Jacanas. They are water fowl building their nests on floating vegetation. In the breeding season the males hold territories and defend them against other males. The much bigger and stronger hens try to conquer several of these territories with their males and defend them against other females. The female copulates with a male, lays her eggs and then goes on to the next male to repeat the procedure. Only the males incubate the eggs and look after the chicks. The female remains in the territory but only to chase away predators or other females (Jenni, 1979).

There are limits to the number of males that can be in one harem. Even the strongest Jacana hens cannot produce more than three or four clutches in one season and hence cannot 'utilize' more than three or four males. Thus the difference in the biological starting

155

conditions restrains the possible size of 'inverted harems'. Similarly these unequal starting conditions mean that polygyny is much more common in the animal kingdom than polyandry.

In birds it is at least technically possible for the males to incubate the eggs all by themselves and rear the young after hatching. In mammals a male cannot possibly take on the burden of bearing and nursing the young, and this, presumably, is the reason why there is no mammalian species with a family structure even remotely resembling the 'feministic' social order of the Jacanas.

3.4 ... sees Helena in every woman

The bandwidth of male sexual behaviour is rather wide. It ranges from the greylag gander who is a loving and, as a rule, faithful husband and a devoted father, to the organ-utan male who not only does not contribute anything to the care and protection of his children but even, on occasions, rapes a female not complying with his wishes (Angst, 1980, p.16). Nevertheless there are some 'generally male' traits of behaviour that can be observed in the vast majority of species. Males are more easily aroused and more active in courtship, they take more risks to get a mate and they are not usually very selective in the choice of their mating partners. The 'typical male'– inasmuch as such a type exists at all – 'sees Helena in every woman' as Goethe put it, who had ample pertinent experience. Not quite as poetic but no less to the point is the joky saying about a man: 'He has good luck with women – he likes any one of them'

'Males are very easily stimulated to engage in courtship, while females are often inactive and respond to the overtures of the males not at all or only after long-continued male displays', writes Ernst Mayr (1972, p. 91). A male rat might even cross an electrically charged grid to get to a female, reports Norbert Bischof (1978/79, p. 48), whereas a female is not prepared to do so.

According to Mayr (1972, p. 98) 'it is well known that the mating drive of males of many species is so strong that they display not only to females of their own species, but also to females of related species. If the females were equally lacking in discrimination, an enormous amount of hybridization among closely related species would take place.' For the male, programmed by his 'nature' to strive for copulation with as many females as possible it is not a great risk to mate for once with a partner belonging to another species and to beget a hybrid of low fitness or even unable to reproduce like a mule. For a female who can produce only a limited number of offspring giving birth to such a bastard might significantly reduce the number of genes she passes on to future generations.

In the absence of females a male might even court another male of his own species or of a related species – particularly if the differences in outward appearance between the two sexes are small as, for example, in greylag geese (see section 1.4). And if he has no display partner at all a male might even court less appropriate objects.

In many so-called monogamous species males seem to be much more interested in sexual escapades than females (see section 1.4). A 'married' sparrow male can easily be induced to copulate with a widow in the vicinity. He thus becomes a bigamist and eventually may have to contribute to the care of two clutches. He will also mate with the 'wife' of another male if he has the chance (Welsh, 1975; Smith, 1978).

Female 'adultery' has been observed or experimentally proved in a number of species forming harems (see section 1.4). Similar experiments with females of 'monogamous' species seem to be lacking. In many of these species females tend to be more closely attached to the real estate than to the male. If the 'husband' is absent and does not defend his territory and the 'possession' of his wife, she might readily accept another male. On the other hand Lorenz (1963/66) reports that female greylag geese as a rule mourn much longer for a deceased partner than males. This might be taken as an indication that 'matrimonial fidelity' probably is stronger in female geese than in males as long as the partner is alive as well.

As mentioned in the last chapter there are a number of good biological reasons not only for males but also for females to commit 'adultery'. Nevertheless in monogamous species with a sizeable male contribution to brood care the risks associated with such female behaviour seem to outweigh the possible benefits. For males that invest heavily in their offspring are programmed by natural selection to be careful that they really raise *their own young* and avoid cuckoldry. They harshly attack putative adulterous wives and might even repudiate them if they easily can find another female. The American zoologist David Barash (1977, p. 63) created faked *'in flagranti'* situations in experiments with the monogamous mountain bluebird by putting a stuffed male near the nest when the resident male was absent. On return the latter would vigorously attack the strange male *and his 'wife'* and in one case the female subsequently left her mate or, perhaps, was driven away by him. Repeating the experiment later in the season when the breeding period was over, the eggs were laid, and hence cuckoldry no longer possible, Barash observed less aggressivity of the 'husband' towards the strange male and no attacks at all on his 'wife'.

Monogamous species with a significant male 'parental investment' usually have long and complicated courtship rituals. Often they have a considerable period spent as 'fiancés' but not yet copulating. Such a behaviour pattern has advantages for both partners. The female can test the male in this period and find out whether he really has 'serious intentions'. By refusing an early copulation she counteracts the general male tendency of being easily aroused by any female and soon cooling down after. The future mates forage together and in some species feed each other, they build a nest together, but the female refuses to copulate with the already highly aroused male during this period of 'engagement'. In this way the bonds of emotional attachment between the 'fiancés' are strengthened. Simultaneously, the fact that the male has invested time and energy into building a nest, etc. is some sort of guarantee that he will not be going to leave his 'bride' after copulation, for he would have to write off all these investments, and even if he finds another female he probably would have to repeat the same procedures again before being able to copulate.

For the male, on the other hand, such a long period of 'engagement' increases the probability that the young he will care for are indeed *his own* progeny. Trivers (1972, p. 145) even suggests that in species with large paternal investment a male should be likely to follow a mixed strategy: 'to help a single female raise young, while not passing up opportunities to mate with other females whom he will not aid'. Under such circumstances, he speculates 'a male would be selected to differentiate between a female he will only impregnate and a female with whom he will also raise young. Toward the former he should be more eager for sex and less discriminating in choice of sex partner than the female toward him, but toward the latter he should be about as discriminating as she toward him.' He does not provide any evidence that animals do indeed behave in such a 'human, all-too-human' way, but the possibility that some species might do so cannot be ruled out.

When fertilization occurs outside the body as in most aquatic animals paternity is often clear and cuckoldry excluded. These are good preconditions for a rather large paternal investment. Actually there are some species of fish in which the female even deserts the male after laying the eggs, leaving to him all the worries about the brood; and the stickleback combines polygyny with exclusively paternal brood care. He builds a tunnel of love and allures females who deposit their eggs in there and leave. The male fertilizes the eggs and looks after the brood (Barash, 1977, p. 190).

Not only in man but also in animals the emotional superstructure of sexuality might attain a certain amount of independence from its biological ends. An interesting example is found among tropical hummingbirds. They forage on flowers and compete for feeding territories. Since the males are more aggressive they usually end up with most of the available flowers, forcing the females to make do on other foods. Only in the breeding season are females tolerated in the territory of a male to feed there. But in at least one species of hummingbird females can be seen in territories of males even outside the breeding time. On close observation it turned out that the females have to 'pay' for this favour by allowing the male to copulate with them. They 'sell' their sex for food as in human prostitution (Wolf, 1975, quoted after Barash, 1977, p. 159).

Seem from a purely genetic angle the male hummingbirds seem to behave unreasonably. Copulation outside the breeding period is expenditure of time and energy without producing offspring. Maybe the males establish emotional bonds in this way to a future mate, but this is mere speculation. Yet, even if it should turn out to be true, such a copulation seems to be 'alienated' from its original biological purpose.

3.5 Male competition, female choice

Two big stags are fighting. In the roaring contest they were about equal. In the actual fight they seem to be well-matched too. It takes a long time before one of them proves to be the stronger. Meanwhile the hinds are not supervised. What do they do?

'It is a common observation in cervids that females placidly await the outcome of male strife and go with the victor,' writes Trivers (1972, p. 170). According to the theorists such behaviour makes sense, biologically speaking. A female waiting to be inseminated by the winner of a contest has a good chance to beget sons that will win contests again and hence will inseminate many females. Mating with the winner thus gives rise to the prospect of having many grandchildren. The hinds actually behave as they 'should' do according to theoretical deliberations.

Do they indeed? In this book we have seen time and again that, as a rule, statements about how 'the' members of a certain species behave are of only limited validity. Animals do not all behave alike. There is a certain *bandwidth* of more or less typical behaviour, and this applies to hinds too. On close examination it turns out that there are always some young stags around such tournament places – sexually mature males that, however, are not yet strong enough to fight a fully grown adversary. They wait for chances for a quick, sneaking copulation while the strong males are fighting and cannot supervise their hinds, and more often than not they are successful. They find one or other 'frivolous' hind ready to accept such a young lover.

Why some hinds behave like that whereas others do not is a matter of speculation. But it is a sort of behaviour observed time and again – and not only in deer. Maynard Smith and his colleagues used to speak about this phenomenon at first in rather crude terms, but eventually they felt that they should coin a proper expression for it; thus they called it 'kleptogyny' – theft of wives.

As explained above, mating with the contest winners seems to be the best strategy for hinds according to theory. Why do some of them not 'know' that? Is this again a case of an emotional superstructure becoming independent of its original biological purpose? Or do 'frivolous' hinds actually gain some advantage for the proliferation of their genes?

So far one can only speculate about this question. Presumably, to be a successful young lover a stag needs genes other than those needed to become a winner of contests. His sons probably will inherit these genes and be successful lovers as well. They will already have progeny at an age when the sons of tournament winners have not yet started their careers. Thus a hind mating with a young lover, though having less grandchildren than those waiting for the contest

160

winners, will have these grandchildren earlier. When the other hinds get their grandchildren she might already have great-grandchildren. This might be a sort of smuggler's path to proliferate one's genes.

One can always find seemingly plausible explanations for what is observed in nature. Whether the explanation is true in this case would have to be checked. But anyway, it is a fact that kleptogyny and female adultery are relatively common occurrences. Such behaviour patterns seem to 'pay' somehow although only a minority of female does engage in them.

The question of who mates with whom is thus decided by the concurring effects of male competition and female choice; and male competition is by no means confined to tournaments or the use of brute force to prevent a rival from mating. Already in 1871 Darwin wrote that 'the power to charm the females has sometimes been more important than the power to conquer other males in battle'. But how do you charm a female?

There is no general rule to answer this question and, in most cases, not even one general answer applicable to *all* females of a certain species. There are, however, certain trends related to the respective ways of life of different species.

For a female eagle that is to be fed by the male during a long incubation period, and even afterwards as long as the fledgling is small (see section 1.6), it is essential to find a mate that is a good hunter. Thus it seems reasonable that these birds have complicated courtship rituals with pieces of food exchanged in the air. To do this, almost acrobatic abilities are required as well as good co-ordination of muscles and vision. A bird successful in such courtship rituals most probably will be a good hunter (Barash, 1977, p. 149).

If possession of a territory is a precondition for raising a family it is, as a rule, the males that conquer such territory and defend it against competitors. The females seem to consider first of all the quality of the territory (food supply, nesting sites, etc.) which in itself is to a certain extent a proof of the male's abilities, while giving only minor attention to the male's personal traits. A male of such a species does not need an imposing appearance.

A lack of conspicuous marks distinguishing the sexes indicates a monogamous species with paternal participation in brood care, whereas polygamous species show marked sex differences. At

161

first glance even an expert might not be sure whether he sees a goose or a gander, but every layman knows the difference between a cock and a hen. Such so-called 'secondary' sex differences need not neccessarily be *visible*. Many nocturnal animals or species living underground can recognize the sex of a conspecific by its smell and even a human with his rather poor olfactory sense can recognize the characteristic odour of a male goat.

In species practising 'free love' or polygyny, males nearly always are considerably bigger and stronger than females, even if they do not contribute to the defence of the young. Elephant seal bulls, having no natural enemies in their habitat, spend a lot of time fighting for females that are only a third or a quarter of their size. They need strength to fight their rivals, but also, it seems, to charm the females. A male hamadryas baboon weighs about twice as much as a female. His strength is as important for defending his harem against young rivals as for protecting females and young against predators. In non-monogamous birds males often have beautiful bright colours charming the females – but attracting predators as well. The females often have camouflage colours, particularly in species nesting on the ground – the pheasant being a well-known example.

In wildfowl and some other bird species, cocks assemble on 'leks' at mating time, fighting for territories of only symbolic value. Females visiting the lek wander singly or in small groups past the males and indicate their choice by crouching. The strongest cocks occupying the central positions of the lek usually have most of the copulations. There are, however, some hens who, for unknown reasons, prefer other cocks. Even those males that could not get any lek territory on their own and must settle as sort of 'sub-tenants' on the territories of the strongest cocks may achieve reproductive success. Though they must behave very inconspicuously in order not to be chased away some of the hens approach them in a clearly visible choice and crouch before them (Selander, 1972, pp. 216–18).

For reproductive success a male needs those traits which charm the females – even if they are features of no survival value. The extremely long tail of the male peacock certainly is a hindrance when the male is trying to escape a predator. Yet the peacock-hen must be stimulated by the display of the tail to be ready for copulation. A peacock with a short tail would certainly have better chances of survival, but he would have practically no chance of reproductive success. The same applies to the wings of male Argus pheasants decorated with beautiful eye patches. The wings are so big that the cocks can hardly fly, yet they are indispensable to get a mate.

In species with 'free love' a female might copulate with one male after the other in quick succession. A female chimp in heat goes to a male, presents herself, and after copulation goes directly to the next one. Jane Goodall (1971, pp. 82, 173) reports observing such scenes without any indication of jealousy between the males. On the other hand she reports some females which, for reasons not obvious to the human observer, did not respond to the courting of one particular male though they copulated with others.

In such forms of promiscuity, the biological competition between the males does not end with the mating. With several males copulating with one female within a quarter of an hour the sperm of any one of them might eventually fertilize the egg cell. Presumably the chance for reproductive success will be directly proportional to the number of sperms released by the male in ejaculation as well as to the motility of the sperms. Thus it does not seem to be surprising that the testes of chimpanzees are of enormous size. Natural selection evidently favoured the production of a large number of sperms (Harcourt and Stewart, 1977).

In many species dominant males try to prevent low-ranking ones from mating. In some primate species there is a certain liberality at the beginning and the end of the oestrous period, yet at the peak of the oestrus, when the probability of fertilization is highest, dominant males try to monopolize the females. According to Harcourt and Stewart this applies to chimpanzees as well. To avoid competitors a male, particularly a lower ranking one, sometimes withdraws from the group together with a consort for a few hours or even a few days. Such a behaviour has been observed in chimps (Goodall, 1971, p. 177) and in several other species. It is, of course, only possible if it corresponds to a common intention of both partners; it presupposes a kind of *mutual affection.*

Even in a society seemingly as male-dominated as that of hamadryas baboons, female choice turns out to be much more important than commonly assumed. Field observations of Kummer and his collaborators and experiments of Bachmann and Kummer (1980) have shown that males seem to be able to assess female choice and to act accordingly. Lower ranking males in particular are motivated not so much by their own preferences as by their assessment of the female's choice. 'Under a given dominance relationship between the two males, a female with strong preference for her present owner is too costly a prize for the rival in terms of herding effort and the risk of losing her again,' write Bachmann and Kummer. 'However, if a rival is informed that the female will not choose her present owner, his attack may temporarily free her from the owner's herding and permit her to exert her choice in favour of the rival.'

This corresponds with observations in the field that fighting amongst males can induce massive transfer of females between the males. On the other hand, mothers and daughters separated in such large-scale fights had worked their way back into the same unit several months later (Abeggien, 1976).

Even when young males conquer the harems of older ones females do not seem to be mere passive objects. As a rule the older males lose *all* their females in these fairly rare and heavy encounters. In one instance, however, J. J. Abegglen, a pupil of Kummer's, who died prematurely, observed that one of the females remained with her previous 'owner'.

3.6 *Animals' family structures and their causes*

Why do lions form 'prides' while tigers live solitarily? Why is the society of the gorilla a stable group with only one fully adult male whereas chimps have loose groups of rapidly changing composition with no permanent bonds between individual males and females?

One can give rather simple answers to such questions. The lions in the savannah do not seem to be very proficient hunters when solitary. Co-operation in a pride makes it easier for them to get their prey. The tiger in the jungle can stalk its prey in the dense cover most efficiently if it hunts alone. Gorillas feed on leaves, blossoms, shoots of bamboo, fruits, and other vegetable food all of which are widely distributed. Chimps are omnivores, primarily depending on fruits which are distributed patchily and irregularly in time and space. Their flexible social structure with changing sub-group size allows quick adaptation to the size and location of particular food sources.

Certainly such answers are incomplete. They do not take account of all the factors influencing family and group structure, and do not explain all the pertinent phenomena. Why, for example, do lions not have a 'normal' harem with only one male, but instead the unusual family structure of a 'group marriage' with two or three kin males living with a larger number of equally kin females and their young (see section 1.8)?

It would be tempting to devise a simple scheme which, to a first approximation at least, could show how family structures adapt to ecological conditions. Basing himself on papers of H. S. Horn (1968) on birds, of W. W. Denham (1971) on primates and many other pertinent sources, Wilson (1975, pp. 52, 524) tries to sketch some elements of such a scheme. The basic idea is a correlation of resource availability and family structure. As long as food is distributed evenly in space and time, the best solution seems to be to parcel out the territories so that an animal or a family gets (or, rather, must conquer and defend) its lot. Many birds mark the possession of their territories by their songs; many mammals lay down scent marks (urine or faeces). A territory is defended against conspecifics as long as the energy expenditure for the defence is smaller than the energy gain accruing by monopolizing the possession of the food within this territory. The larger the territory the greater the energy costs of defending it. In many species individuals only defend the core of their region intensely, whereas the outer borders on neighbouring territories remain fuzzy.

When food is distributed sparsely but evenly, animals might live solitarily, defending their territory even against members of the opposite sex – at least outside the breeding season. 'Among vertebrates, male territory owners are often highly aggressive and frequently inclined to respond aggressively to any intruder upon their domain, whether male or female,' writes Barash (1977, p. 148). 'In situations of this sort, courtship often involves the display of certain physical characteristics that distinguish males from females.'

With food more abundant and evenly distributed, joint defence of a territory by a monogamous couple might become the optimal strategy. Usually the males have to conquer the territories first, then attract the females. Where there are significant differences in the quality of the territories possessed by the individual males, the best ones might be suitable for supporting more than one female with her young. Thus the 'polygyny-threshold' might be passed (Verner, 1965; Orians 1969).

When food distribution is irregular in space and time, formation of larger groups generally seems to be more advantageous than dividing up a territory into individual lots (see section 1.1).

Such a very simplified scheme shows why there might be different forms of family structure within one and the same species in varying environmental conditions. As mentioned before many males of 'as-a-rule monogamous' birds may be able to attract additional females if the external conditions and the carrying capacity of the territory makes it advantageous for females to accept polygynous matings (Orians, 1969; see also Emlen and Oring, 1977).

There is however more to the 'quality' of a territory than mere food supply. For birds like the wren (see section 3.2) appropriate nesting caves might be even more important. Gulls never try to parcel out their hunting grounds in the sea, but they vigorously defend the nesting places in their colonies since these are a limiting factor.

Thus any attempt to explain family structures only (or even mainly) by food distribution is simplifying too much and bound to fail, since there are also other ecological factors influencing the way of life of a species. Lions or wolves form groups mainly for better hunting success, whereas sheep form herds to improve their survival chances and to be better able to protect their young (see section 1.1).

Ecological conditions often pose divergent or even contradictory demands, and the actual social structure realized by a species is a compromise for performing all these tasks as well as possible. Hamadryas baboons sleep in herds of up to several hundred animals if there are only a few good sleeping rocks in their territory. Food distribution, on the other hand, demands that the herd be divided up into small sub-units. The one-male groups (harems) are most appropriate 'single-tree-foraging-units', because the females and young enjoy the protection of at least one strong male and they still have plenty of acacia blossoms and seeds left over for them on the thinner branches after the heavier male has collected all he can reach (Kummer, 1971, pp. 44, 60). When approaching the water-hole at noon usually all the one-male groups of a band meet (see section 2.5), and this is very adaptive too, since predators like to hide near

166

water-holes and can most easily be fended-off if there is a group with many strong males.

Ecological conditions are, however, but one factor of several that influence family structures, since different species owing to their different genetic endowment tend to react to similar environmental pressures in different ways. 'When a new or changing environment requires of a species an adaptation of one of its features, several solutions may be feasible,' writes Kummer (1971, p. 91). 'But the immigrant or surviving population is probably not capable of realizing every one of these solutions within a tolerable time span. A solution arises partly from long-standing predispositions and partly from adaptations to former habitat.'

A social structure that would seem to be very functional in certain ecological conditions may not be within the bandwidth of the behaviour patterns that a certain species is able to realize. The flexible system of the chimpanzees, with groups of quickly changing size and composition, would probably be very adaptive for many primates living in tropical forests, but surprisingly it has not been found in any one monkey species (Kummer, *ibid.*). Presumably this way of organizing is not within their repertory of inborn or easily learned behaviour patterns.

Simple rules that relate the group sizes of different primate species to features of their preferred habitat often turn out on close observation to be incapable of explaining the real complexities of the situation. Generally, ground-dwelling species of monkeys form larger groups than species living mainly in the trees; but there are exceptions, such as the extremely terrestrial patas monkeys with their small groups that disperse and flee when danger threatens (Kummer, *ibid.*, p. 55).

According to Stephen Emlen (1976) it should be possible 'to interpret and partially to predict the social structure of a species on the basis of a limited set of environmental or ecological variables. . . Ecological parameters impose limits on the range of types of social organization that will be adaptive. With differences in the dispersion of a critical resource, the availability of mates, and other factors, optimal social strategies shift, resulting in a fine tuning of social organization to ecological constraints.'

In their paper of 1977, Emlen and Oring point out – like Kummer – that there are *not only* ecological but also genetical constraints to the

167

range of behaviour patterns a species is able to realize. 'The environmental potential for polygamy depends on the degree to which multiple mates, or resources critical to gaining multiple mates, are economically defendable,' they write. But the ability of an animal to utilize such a potential is subject to phylogenetic constraints as well.

In birds more than 90% of all species studied are monogamous (Lack, 1968) – or, at least, as a rule monogamous. 'The prevalence of monogamy among birds,' write Emlen and Oring, 'is due primarily to the inability of most species to take advantage of any environmental "polygamy potential". Considerable parental care by both parents is often required for successful rearing of the young. Thus, losses to an individual parent accrued by withholding care from one set of offspring while courting and mating with additional mates may be greater than the gains resulting from such behaviour.'

For the large eagle species whose males have to cater for the females during their long incubation period and are not able to bring enough food for more than one fledgling (see section 1.6) the 'bigamy threshold' presumably cannot ever be reached, whereas a male wren or sparrow, as mentioned before, might become a bigamist under favourable circumstances. Polygamy as the dominant form of family structure is found mostly in bird species with 'precocious' young, i.e. those able to walk and to feed themselves immediately after hatching; yet even among these species some are monogamous like, for example, the greylag goose.

In mammals only a few species, like the jackal or the gibbon, are monogamous. Many live solitarily, such as the badger. The young are always dependent on their mother for food (milk). The paternal contribution to brood care, if any, is protection from predators and, possibly, feeding the lactating mother, as in jackals. The young may be 'precocious' inasmuch as they might be able to run very soon after birth to escape predators (hares, many ungulates); or they may be very helpless after birth and remain hidden in a nest cave, like rabbits or wolves; or such young might be carried about by the mother – in a pouch like the kangaroo, or clinging to the mother's fur coat, like young apes and monkeys.

Many ungulates live in small groups for part of the year, while forming enormous herds with hardly any internal social structure in times of plenty. Permanent mammalian social groups are, as a rule, either harems with only one adult male or mixed groups without any permanent bonds between sex mates. Elephants have a society of females and their young only, with the males leaving the group at maturity (see section 1.8). In many mammalian species sub-adult males form bachelor groups living at the margin of an established group or as an independent band. The ecological and genetic factors producing such a large variety of mammalian society structures are as yet by no means fully explored.

Man intruded into a multitude of ecological niches and adapted to them with his family and society structures. Research, comparable to that in animal species, on the ecological influence on these structures is only just beginning. Of course, our species too is subject not only to ecological but also to genetic constraints and cannot realize every social structure that might be conceivable in a certain environment. Nevertheless one can expect many new insights from applying an ecological approach to human societies.

3.7 *Primate family life*

This section repeats in part things stated elsewhere in this book. But before starting to speculate about what the family structure and society of our pre-human ancestors might have been like it might be useful to have a comprehensive overview on pertinent features in our closest relatives in the animal kingdom.

Apes and monkeys are very 'altricial', i.e. helpless after birth, and spend a rather long period of development with their mothers. As a rule they are born singly; hence they have no litter mates as does a young wolf or young lion. But they are still far from being mature when the next child arrives. A mother with several children of different ages is the smallest social unit in most primate societies. If the eldest child were a male near maturity a casual observer might think he sees a family with father, mother and children.

In chimps the time space between the births of two children of the same mother is normally 5 to 6 years. As a rule weaning is not completed before the fifth year or on the arrival of a younger sibling. Older siblings, sisters in particular, start playing with the infant very early on. At an age of about 5 months the child makes its first steps and starts climbing a bit, at 7 or 8 months it begins to play with other children but always remains near the mother. Not before a chimp is about 6 years old does he or she start moving around without the mother for short periods and temporarily join other groups. Puberty starts at 8 or 9 years; girls have their first sexual swellings at that time. Males copulate with them, but the young females are not yet fertile. Their first infant is born when they are 12 or 14 years old. Males attain their full social maturity at bout 15 years. Chimps may reach an age of about 40 years. In the course of its life a female might give birth to six or seven children (all data after Jane Goodall).

A long attachment of children to their mother, a rather long period of socialization as compared with total life span, strong bonds between siblings of different age and a great importance of play in the development phase are typical of all apes and monkeys. Apart from that there is large variation in the patterns of family and social structure, even when comparing closely related species (Data after Wilson, 1975, and others).

The gibbon is, as it were, the 'song bird' amongst the apes, living in monogamous families without any superior social structure. The parents co-operate in rearing their young until they leave the parental territory at maturity.

The orang-utan lives solitarily. Groups, as a rule, comprise a mother with her children. The adult males move about alone and approach females only for copulation. On reaching puberty, the children leave their mother, the young females remaining in the vicinity, the males wandering far afield and making a new home somewhere quite distant from their place of birth.

The gorilla's society is, according to Harcourt and Stewart (1977), 'something approaching a harem'. A typical group consists of one fully mature male with silver-grey back, up to half a dozen females with their young of various ages and sometimes one or two young males, probably sons of the dominant male, tolerated by him at the margin of the group. The very strong males, weighing up to 180 kilogrammes, reach a height of up to 2 metres. Within the group behaviour is very gentle. Quarrels seem to be very uncommon in a gorilla family.

Schaller (1963) reports that he only saw two copulations of gorillas, both by non-dominant males in the presence of the group leader who tolerated it – but, maybe, these were exceptional situations. Harcourt and Stewart assume that, as a rule, the dominant male is the only one to mate with the females of his group. Young females sometimes leave the group on reaching maturity and join another one. Most young males also leave their native group and wander about alone or in small bachelor groups. These wandering males try to recruit young females or females from other groups, which may lead to encounters with the dominant male of the group, either in form or display contests or in real fights with the antagonists bearing wounds for days or even weeks afterwards.

Chimps live in loose groups of about thirty to eighty animals dividing into sub-groups of varying and rapidly changing composition. Females in oestrus seek the company of males and mate with several of them within a very short time. One act of copulation does not last more than a few seconds. Loose pair-bonds lasting even beyond an oestrous period were sometimes observed by Jane Goodall (1971, p. 177/178), but they seem to be an exception rather than the rule. Paternity is never quite certain in chimps, though there are instances where the father can be guessed with considerable confidence (Goodall, 1979). The males are friendly towards infants, but the burden of caring for them and protecting them rests on the mother and on older siblings. Young females often leave the group and join another one. Young males remain in the group and hence are all kin. This might be the reason why there is not much jealousy amongst them. Brothers (i.e. sons of the same mother) still know each other in case of strife within the group.

Amongst the apes, chimps are the only species that forms groups with a larger number of fully adult males and females. For social monkeys this is nothing exceptional, and there are all sorts of society structures.

In rhesus monkeys a group of kin females, as a rule a mother with her daughters and grand-daughters form the core of the group. When a group divides, one of the daughters with her daughters forms a new independent group (Chepko-Sade, 1979). Males – or, at least, some of them – leave the maternal group on reaching maturity. Often they form bachelor groups before joining another group. The males defend the group but do not contribute otherwise to brood care. As a rule paternity is unknown.

Anubis baboons live in mixed groups without permanent pair bonds. There is fierce – and cunning – competition for access to females in oestrus (see section 1.11). Sometimes a male succeeds in withdrawing with a consort from the group for a few hours or days, but this seems to be an exception rather than the rule. Usually

171

a female copulates with several males and paternity is not certain. All males, including sub-adults that probably do not have any children as yet, contribute actively to the defence of the group against predators (see section 1.1).

The two species of monkey living in open land, hamadryas baboons and geladas, are the only ones to form large groups with a social structure on several levels (see Kummer, 1968 and 1971; see also sections 2.5, 3.5). A hamadryas baboon herd, counting up to several hundred animals is subdivided into bands and into clans. Owing to the similarity of their outer appearance and to other indications it is assumed that all males of a clan are kin. According to Kummer's observations in the sixties, sub-adult males get the basic stock of their future harem by kidnapping female children that are as yet far from maturity and herding them – a behaviour that is tolerated, astonishingly enough, by the girls' parents. Ableggen (1976) and Stolba (1979), on the other hand, have observed in another herd that the young males try to recruit girls with much patience and gentleness. The girls are always from their own clans. An exchange of animals between different herds seems to be a rare exception. The whole system results in frequent matings between rather close kin.

The young males are also interested in mature young females belonging to other males of their clan and sometimes have secret affairs with them. When reaching full maturity, a young male conquers a harem of an elder male of his clan – i.e. of a male to whom he probably is a close kin. Such fights, leading to the transfer of whole harems, are infrequent but fierce, sometimes causing serious wounds. For the older males the loss of a harem seems to be an irreversible occurrence (Ableggen, 1976). After they have lost their females they soon show signs of getting old. They remain within the clan as 'seniors' and in difficult situations their vote still carries considerable weight (see section 2.5).

One of the main differences between hamadryas baboons and geladas is in the role of the females, which is much more active and independent in the latter species (Kummer, 1971, p. 109 *et seq.*). Sub-groups of a gelada herd are either harems or bachelor groups. Within the harem there is a strong dominance hierarchy amongst the females. In captivity it has been observed that the highest-ranking female helps her male to herd the other females. Gelada females can move about in their herd rather freely, without male interference. The bond between a male and a female is formed and maintained by the activities of both partners. 'To win a female over from another group, a gelada male has to do more than just defeat her owner,' writes Kummer (1971, p. 110). Thus the coherence of the gelada family rests, as it were, on *mutual* emotional bonding, whereas in hamadryas baboons it is mainly the male who supervises and herds his females, like a shepherd (or, rather, a shepherd's dog) does with sheep.

3.8 *The society of our pre-human ancestors*

The two species most closely related to us, chimpanzee and gorilla, have very different structures of family and society. Hence the 'steppe apes' that most probably were our ancestors (see section 2.6) might, on their part, have had again a totally different social structure. All that we can deduce from our phylogeny with confidence is that our ancestors, like ourselves, were similar to apes inasmuch as their infants most probably were born very 'altricial', with a long development period after birth and long-lasting ties to the mother (or, maybe, to both parents). Apart from that everything is open to speculation.

Some possibilities can be excluded, however, on ecological grounds. Like hamadryas baboons and geladas our ancestors were living not in dense forests but on open land – yet they were not pure vegetarians, as are those two species. On the other hand they were not pure carnivores either, like lions or wolves. They were predators, hunting most probably much more than chimps, but they were also prey. This is a unique position with no parallel amongst big mammals.

As hunters no less than as prey, our ancestors needed cooperation in groups. Thus most probably the species preceding us in our phylogeny were not living solitarily like the orang-utan nor in isolated monogamous pairs like the gibbon. Even the group of the gorilla with only one fully mature male would presumably have been too small for the conditions in the steppe.

A flexible society with sub-groups of rapidly changing composition, such as in chimps might, ecologically speaking, have been useful for our ancestors. Indeed even present-day gatherer and hunter peoples often have similar flexibility, with groups of seasonally changing size and composition. On the other hand the rather low degree of jealousy amongst chimp males and the lack of permanent pair bonds do not seem to be a human-like pattern.

173

It could be imagined – though not proved – that the 'steppe apes' might have had a society structure with several hierarchical units similar to that of geladas or hamadryas baboons, which also inhabitate open land. The fact that we are not as closely related to these species as to the apes does not exclude this possibility. Gibbons and song birds are much farther apart phylogenetically and yet have the same sort of family type.

A social structure organized on several levels still leaves open many details. The gelada example shows that *mutual* bonding of sex partners can be very important in firmly cementing smaller familial sub-units within a larger group. There are good reasons for assuming that such strong partner bonds might have been important in the evolution of man, too. For our species differs from other primates not only in its higher intelligence. It has also another unique distinguishing feature that apparently is in no way connected either to the size of our brain or to our upright posture: the human female has no noticeable oestrous period.

Ape females, as a rule, are only sexually active and attractive to the males when they are 'in heat'. At the time around their fecund days females of many primate species have brightly coloured swellings of their genital region visible over large distances and moreover a special scent. These signals arouse and attract males. The females themselves are very active, when in heat, and behave quite differently than at other times.

In humans there is nothing comparable. Women do not feel when they have their fecund days and men do not notice it. One cannot do anything other than look at the calendar – and most people who still remember the time before the advent of the pill know all too well that this is not a very reliable method. On the other hand, it is just this 'handicap' from the point of view of family planning that confers on women a sort of 'equality of rights' not enjoyed by any other primate female: the possibility of *continual* sexual activity which in all other primate species is the sole prerogative of the males.

To realize the enormous significance of such a state of affairs one must think what life is like for a primate female with a normal oestrous period. For a chimp female the full cycle lasts 35 days, ten to twelve of which she might be in heat. In young females sexual swellings might appear even in the first months of pregnancy, and about a year after giving birth to an infant first indications of swellings might reappear though the females are not yet receptive at that time

174

(Goodall, 1971, p. 179). Space between two births is about 3 to 4 years in young females and 5 to 6 years in older ones, and with increasing age it takes longer and longer for oestrus to reappear after a female has given birth to a child – in older females up to 5 years. Thus one can calculate that a chimp female in the 30 years or so of her adult life has something like 1 000 days –approximately one-tenth of the total time – when she is sexually active and attractive to males.

Compared to the gorilla this is still quite a lot, for the females of this other species closely related to us are in heat only one or two days in a period (Harcourt and Stewart, 1977). If one assumes that animals like to have sex, just as we do –and there cannot be any doubt about that – the females of the great apes are definitely handicapped in comparison to human females as well as compared to the males of their own species.

But do they themselves really feel it that way? One might assume that their sexual interest would disappear with the end of the oestrus and the accompanying hormonal changes. Yet Jane Goodall reports otherwise. One chimp girl, after the end of her first oestrus, continued to offer herself to the males and was visibly disappointed when they no longer took much notice of her (1971, p. 167/168). Old and experienced females were markedly jealous whenever a new young female in heat appeared in the troop.– and if no males were present to protect the newcomer they even beat her up and chased her away. Once, one day after the appearance of such a young female that attracted the attention of all the males, one of the old females of the troop even developed what might be called 'hysterical swellings' though having given birth to an infant only 14 months before. They lasted for 1 day only, but were sufficient to arouse the attention of the males. The next regular swellings on this female did not appear until 4 years later! (*ibid.*, p. 120/121.)

As compared to humans, ape and monkey males, though capable of sexual activity throughout the year are 'handicapped by nature' as well. For they are living in a society in which the large majority of females is sexually 'unavailable' – as they are either pregnant, or lactating, or just not in heat. Though by sheer numbers there are about as many females as males there is a skew in what Emlen and Oring (1977) call the 'operational sex ratio', leading to intensified competition for access to the few remaining 'available' females.

Polygamy does not solve this problem –not even for the fortunate

175

strongest males who are the harem owners. 'Repeatedly we have seen a hamadryas baboon pasha with a large harem, but all his females were either pregnant or lactating and not available for sex,' Hans Kummer told me. 'And next to him another group with two females in oestrus might pass by.'

'And what does the male of the first group do?' I wanted to know.

'He turns his head to the other side. But certainly he is experiencing considerable emotional stress.'

The fact that human females are nearly continually sexually 'available' and attractive – even when lactating and far into pregnancy – certainly diminishes this sort of stress amongst human males. Competition amongst males is reduced in this way, co-operation between them made easier (see also Crook, 1972, p. 249; Wilson, 1978a, p. 141).

It seems to me that *this* aspect of our sex life might have been no less important in human evolution than the other one usually much more emphasized: the possibility of cementing a partner bond by continual sexual activity. Human children are even more 'altricial' than ape children; and human females have no fur for a baby to cling to. Thus, early in human evolution women continually had to carry their small infants and were hampered in their mobility for months or even years. To have a male partner in such a situation who helps the mother and protects her is evidently advantageous.

The unique features of human sex – continual availability of both sexes with neither oestrous periods nor seasonally fixed breeding periods – seem to provide good preconditions for a long and stable bonding between two mates. Thus one might conclude that the ancestral form of the human or pre-human society might have been a group organized on several levels with the monogamous couple as smallest unit, and not a harem group as in geladas or hamadryas baboons. Ecologically such a societal structure might have been well-fitting to the habitat of our ancestors. There are, however, important *biological* arguments that cast doubt on to a purely monogamous past for man and his ancestors.

3.9 *Are humans polygamous 'by nature'?*

Men have beards and women have breasts. Men have more body hair than women, but are apt to get bald-headed. Male voices change in puberty whereas women's voices retain their higher pitch. Men, on the average, are taller, heavier, and stronger than women. A man can be dressed up as a woman which could not be done with a hamadryas baboon male, even after having shaved off his mane; and one might not be able at the first glance to tell the sex of a young human being with long hair and blue jeans – yet, on the whole, secondary sex characteristics are definitely more pronounced in humans than in greylag geese or gibbons, though not as strong as in peacocks or gorillas.

In animals it is, as a rule, very difficult to distinguish between the sexes in monogamous species, whereas strong differences in outward appearance are a token of polygamous species. Hence one may conclude – now, what do you think? No, it is not as simple as all that; one might conclude something else as well. Speaking at an international interdisciplinary conference on 'Female Phenomena' held in Paris in 1976, Norbert Bischof referred to the striking discrepancy between a conspicuous human sexual dimorphism and 'human monogamy'. He therefore concluded 'that monogamy may be a rather recent acquisition of *Homo sapiens*'. This, moreover would be in agreement with the rather frequent occurrence of polygyny in primary human societies (in Sullerot, 1978).

Actually, however, institutionalized polygyny today is by no means confined to primary (= 'primitive') societies, but can also be found in highly cultured Islamic countries with hundreds of millions of inhabitants – not to mention marginal phenomena like the Mormons in the USA. Thus I cannot quite see how the well-known Italian demographer M. Livi-Bacci could speak at the same conference of 'the monogamy of the human species' (*ibid.*). Are Muslims or tribal people not to be considered as true representatives of *Homo sapiens?*

Even Richard Dawkins who in his book *The Selfish Gene* (1976) does not seem to worry much about making shocking and simplifying statements is very restrained on this topic. 'Most human societies are indeed monogamous,' he claims (p. 177). 'On the other hand, some human societies are promiscuous, and some are harem-based.'

Only Wilson seems to face the issue squarely: human males are larger than females, he writes (1978*a*, p. 20), and in apes, monkeys, and other mammals this has a specific meaning – there is a direct correspondence between such size differences and the degree of polygyny. When values for humans are plotted on a curve based on other species of mammals it turns out that a successful human male should, on the average, have more than one female but less than three. This theoretical prediction, Wilson claims, is close to reality. 'We know we are a mildly polygynous species.' In about three-fourths of all human societies, he continues (*ibid.*, p. 125) the taking of multiple wives is permitted by law and/or custom, and the ostensibly monogamous societies 'usually fit that category in a legal sense only, with concubinage and other extra-marital strategems being added to allow de-facto polygyny.'

In a review of Wilson's book the British biologist Steven Rose (1978) comments sneeringly: 'Don't blame your mates for sleeping around, ladies, it's not their fault, they are genetically programmed.' But cynicism, after all, is not a convincing argument and does not prove that Wilson's claim is incorrect.

But is Wilson right? Is there indeed a tendency to polygyny *inherent in human nature*?

One must ask precise questions if one wants to get reasonable answers. Concerning this issue it seems to me that there are several questions that ought not to be mixed up. The first is what human behaviour is like in reality and whether it might be justified in some sense to speak of 'the monogamy of the human species' as Livi-Bacci and Bischof do. The second question is whether the actual reality is an expression of a biological 'human nature', i.e. of inborn behavioural tendencies, or rather a consequence of existing social relations. The third whether 'human nature', if there exists such a thing, shows polygamic tendencies only (or mainly) in males whereas women's 'nature' is monogamous. The fourth question to ask is whether existing natural (inborn) human tendencies might or even ought to serve as a basis for ethical or legal norms.

As to the first question there is a large body of solid evidence showing that polygyny is by no means confined to 'some' human societies as Dawkins claims; even Wilson's three-fourths seems to be an understatement. According to the well-known ethnographer George Peter Murdock who compiled data on 849 human societies, a male may have more than one wife in 708 of them, whereas there

178

are only four societies with institutionalized polyandry (quoted after Daly and Margo Wilson, 1979).

The asymmetry shows even more strikingly if one adds that polygyny, where it is legally sanctioned, is a luxury for the well-to-do, whereas polyandry, on close inspection, turns out to be wife sharing for the poor. In the Himalaya region and in Tibet polyandry is practised in the poorest peasant regions when individual farm lots are so small that they cannot be further divided without sinking below subsistence level. In such situations two brothers sometimes take a wife together to live with them on their jointly owned farm (Crook, 1980).

An investigation of customs in small 'primary' societies is, of course, very important to find out something about 'human nature', i.e. about the heritage we got handed down from our semi-human ancestors. But quantities ought not to be overlooked either. Many of Murdock's 708 societies practising polygyny are rather small groups; moreover, in most of these societies only a minority of married men indeed has more than one wife. On the other hand a majority of humans live in societies considering monogamy as the only possible institutionalized form of matrimony. Even if there are many actual transgressions against matrimonial fidelity in these societies, there is still a difference between such a loosely practised monogamy and a harem. Seen in this way it is not so far off the mark if some scientists speak of 'human monogamy' as a predominant feature – though I believe that they are generalizing rather too much in doing so.

To my knowledge there is no human society practising total promiscuity as chimps do; neither is there a human society that can do without the idea of matrimony. There is some evidence on what might be called 'temporarily institutionalized promiscuity' in tribal societies and also in reports on the customs of ancient peoples. As a rule this is embodied in some religious rites of festivals when existing norms are temporarily cancelled.

Non-institutionalized 'promiscuity', i.e. a certain amount of extra-marital relations, probably existed at all times and in all societies. Total marital fidelity of both partners seems to be very rare in humans even in so-called monogamous societies, much rarer than in greylag geese who, as we have seen in section 1.4 also have many 'exceptions to the rule'.

179

In humans as in most animal species women are the sex for which there is more 'demand' and hence they can sell themselves or be sold or bartered by others. In two-thirds of all human societies the bride's family must be compensated with money, gifts, or labour (Daly and Wilson, 1979). Thus in the Dogrib Indians in Northern Canada the young husband must work for the family of his father-in-law until the birth of the first child (Helm, in Lee and DeVore, 1968, p. 121). In the Scriptures Jacob must work twice seven years for Laban to get Laban's daughters Lea and Rachel. How bride barter is working in Israel today where members of very different cultures meet is told in the nice film *Sallah* after a text of Kishon.

Since women are the coveted sex they have better chances than men to marry upwards – i.e. a man of higher social rank than that of their own father (Berghe and Barash, 1977). Extra-marital relations often are part of the same female strategy. Female sex has been sold for millennia and the market for it never seems to have been saturated. 'Reverse prostitution' is a fairly rare occurrence.

Where there is slavery, male slave owners, as a rule, have sexual rights over their female slaves. In feudal societies the noble lord had a *'ius primae noctis'* – the right to spend the first night with the bride when one of his serfs was married. (In Mozart's *La nozze di Figaro* – and still more in the play of Beaumarchais which served as source for the libretto – this is a central theme.) In our own modern society it is common practice that a male superior behaves as if he had 'rights' on women subordinate to him. Compulsion of women and even outright rape are much more frequent than shown by criminal statistics.

All these phenomena have something in common: Women are 'used' as mere objects of sex; the man does not bother to know whether there is any indication of *mutual* love. Apparently a large majority of human males do not consider such a situation as being repulsive; they even seem to be able to find a certain amount of satisfaction in it.

In my view it would be wrong to call such a male behaviour 'brutish' (in the sense of being animal-like). Rape is a rather rare occurrence in the animal kingdom. As a rule the male has to woo the female and must charm her (see section 3.5), before being able to copulate. Nevertheless all these male behaviour patterns are 'inhuman' in a very deep sense. For man *and only man* can identify with a conspecific, and it is just in the 'act of love' that he can realize an amount of identification with a partner and a state of emotional harmony that cannot be reached by an animal.

'I cannot conceive chimpanzees developing emotions, one for the other, comparable in any way to the tenderness, the protectiveness, the tolerance and the spiritual exhilaration which are the hallmarks of human love in its truest and deepest sense,' writes Jane Goodall (1971, p. 178) who certainly does not tend to underestimate the animals to whose observation she has dedicated the work of her life. 'For chimpanzees usually show a lack of consideration for each other's feelings which, in some ways, may represent the deepest part of the gulf between them and us.' In sex without mutual love this gulf disappears. Man moves down to the emotional level of a chimpanzee.

Institutionalized and de-facto polygyny are very widespread amongst our species and so are asymmetries in the behaviour patterns of the sexes. But does this prove that such phenomena are due to 'human nature'? Might they not just as well reflect existing social power relations? Left-wing critics have repeatedly claimed that sociobiology justifies unsatisfactory social conditions by declaring them to be 'natural' and in this way hampers efforts to change them. Such a reproach ought not to be dismissed lightly.

No sane biologist would deny that human behaviour is the joint product of inborn tendencies, education, and other environmental influences. There is no 'either–or' between nature and nurture. The ideas on which role males and females ought to play in a certain society are, as it were, inoculated into boys and girls from their earliest childhood and shape their future behaviour. But these role expectations themselves do not come out of nothing. Man as an organism is subject to the laws of nature. Hence, as Norbert Bischof puts it very cautiously, the possibility should at least be considered that human behavioural norms 'are not blindly superimposed onto human nature but, rather, can be understood to paraphrase, interpret and eludicate this nature' (in Sullerot, 1978).

After all Wilson has a rather strong argument for his thesis: actual human behaviour conforms to predictions that can be deduced from general biological rules. Observations in the animal kingdom, made without a sideglance at man, have led to the formulation of the rule that species with clearly visible secondary sex characteristics – as can be found in humans too – are polygamous. Man would be an exception if he was monogamous – and in fact he is not.

Stating this does not 'justify' anything. What is 'natural' need not be right; and what has been biologically reasonable in the past need not be so in future under changing circumstances. Yet, exactly if one wants to change unsatisfactory social conditions one ought to ask on what basis socio-cultural superstructures rest. It is reasonable to assume that a sexually propagating species like ours has a sexual drive that is inborn and not a product of a social superstructure; it is equally reasonable to assume that such a species might have something like *inborn* tendencies of sexual behaviour as well. But – what, indeed, is inborn in women? 'Human nature', after all, is not only the 'nature' of males.

3.10 A 'natural' sex code – for women as well?

Man is not a greylag goose, but even less is he a jacana. Swapping of sex roles as done in that species is no useful model for us. The many asymmetries mentioned in the previous chapter are *not only* consequences of existing social conditions, they also have biological causes. One cannot simply reverse such things and ask what would be if... Even a strong woman cannot rape a weaker man. She can only seduce him – and in a society with maximal equality of sexes this would be no different.

In feudal times there occasionally were noble ladies or queens with real social power. It is known that such women often used their social independence to enjoy more sexual liberty than had been generally customary for their sex. But could one imagine such a lady introducing *de jure* or *de facto*, a reversed *'ius primae noctis'*? The idea seems absurd – and not for social but for *biological* reasons. The noble lord might not have bothered if some amongst his serfs were his own children or children of his father. But for the noble lady it could not have been a very tempting prospect to give birth to a child of which perhaps she might not even know who of her many serfs was its father. The basic biological fact that a man can produce many children, but a women only a few, and that therefore she has to look for 'quality' cannot be removed by any change of social power relations.

As a general tendency females in species with a paternal contribution to brood care strive to achieve male monogamy, for this is the best way to maximize paternal investment. But this is only a tendency and not a strict rule. As we have seen a female wren might prefer to be the second wife of a male with a rich territory rather than the only wife of a male in a poor region (see section 3.3).

In wrens such a behaviour pattern probably is inborn and not the result of conscious calculation. A human female, on the other hand, is able to ponder about such a problem. And she might decide that she is better off as a second wife of a good hunter than as the only wife of a bad one; or that she might do better as the mistress of a rich man than as the respectable spouse of a poor one. Monogamy of the husband is no absolute goal in itself for a women.

Different mating systems in animals are, as we have seen, adaptations to different external conditions. Even within a species there might be alternative behaviour patterns for different environmental conditions. The wren is by no means the only example.

A most prominent feature of 'human nature' is that man is able to adapt to a large set of different environmental conditions and to intrude into the most diverse ecological niches. Thus it can be assumed that for this reason alone the bandwidth of human mating behaviour should be very wide and that different marriage and family systems in different human societies are – at least to some degree – adaptations to different ecological niches in which humans live – or their ancestors did live. 'Human nature' is a wide range of varying behaviour patterns – in sex as well as in other realms. And in every environment men and women will try to look after their own interests as well as they can.

A large bandwidth of behaviour patterns does not mean, however, that there is no basic tendency that can serve as a yardstick if one wants to discern more or less general features. The data show that more than 700 of 850 human societies know institutionalized polygyny, and that so-called monogamous societies do fit this category in a legal sense only. Whatever the differences in detail, which are due to adaptations to varying environmental conditions and/or, maybe, to autonomously working factors of the socio-cultural superstructure as well, polygyny seems to have been the originally predominating tendency, and this, as we have seen, conforms well with the biological expectations.

Hence, if we ask after the 'nature' of women we must start from this fact and ask how females behave in polygynous species. With all reservations required in such comparisons we will in this way probably get nearer to truth than if we compare human males with gorillas or hamadryas baboons, but human females with greylag geese or song birds.

Not much is known about female matrimonial fidelity of ostensibly monogamous song birds. Presumably 'adultery' is more frequent in males than in females, but there is no support for the claim that female infidelity would be 'unnatural'. As for species with polygyny it has been *proved* that female adultery is within the normal range of behaviour patterns, though the frequency of such occurrences seems to be different in different species. The sterilization experiments on the redwinged blackbird mentioned in section 1.4 have shown that in this species nearly half of the females have occasional extra-marital relations. In hamadryas baboons, on the other hand, female adultery is, according to Hans Kummer, a rather infrequent occurrence. But he and his collaborators did not systematically study this phenomenon, and a behaviour pattern which the animals themselves try to conceal might not have been noticed by a human observer who did not concentrate on it. Anyway, there is no doubt that matings of young females with young males are within the bandwidth of normal behaviour patterns in hamadryas baboons too; and the harem owners violently attack their females if they suspect adultery.

For a human male who, as a rule, contributes much more to the care of his children than a hamadryas baboon does, male jealousy is all the more biologically justified. He certainly acts in conformity with his 'nature' when he himself tries to be polygynous but at the same time demands marital fidelity of his wives, since he wants to care for his own children only and not for those of others. According to Wilson (1978, p. 83) jealousy and suspicion of adultery are amongst the most common motives for murder in tribal peoples.

Social norms or laws allowing polygyny and sanctioning only very mildly male adultery whilst being harsh against female extra-marital relations, as found, in particular, in Islamic cultures, are certainly in accordance with the nature of men (males), but not with 'human nature', since they impose an *unnatural* straightjacket onto the behaviour of women. Only from the male point of view are they a cultural superstructure paraphrasing nature. At the same time they are concomitant to the fact that men hold the power in their hands most conspicuously in Islamic countries and write down social norms according to their 'nature'. This goes hand in hand with a sometimes truly barbaric supression of women as symbolized by female 'circumcision' (clitoris removal) practised widely in Islamic countries.

In many 'monogamous' societies too, especially in Southern Europe, laws and traditional role expectations are very far off from equal rights. Adultery is treated much more leniently in males than in females, premarital sexual intercourse is a matter of course for men whilst being condemned in women. This goes so far that a bride in Spain might accompany her bridegroom right to the doorstep of a brothel, or that a young man in Greece might refuse to take as a wife a girl with whom he had intercourse, since he could not be expected to marry a woman who is not a virgin.

Even in Western and Central Europe skewed ideas about monogamy are by no means a thing of the past though they are being gradually removed by the course of general social development. A growing number of women who are earning their own money and are no longer dependent on a man refuse to be pressed into norms that only conform to male 'nature'. The pill makes it easier for them to indulge in those tendencies of their 'nature' that are not neccesarily monogamous and at the same time facilitates a separation of sex and propagation.

This is not to say that women, if they have the chance, are 'just as keen' on polygamy as men. Different biological preconditions entail different 'natural' emotional tendencies, and within the range of a very large bandwidth of behaviour patterns for both sexes it probably is 'normal', even in modern industrialized society, that, on the average, women have less 'affairs' than men. But this does not mean that female extra-marital relations ought to be considered, overtly or covertly, as 'deviant' or even as an offence against a law of nature.

Comparisons with the animal kingdom cannot give more than clues for analogies. We need not look to the redwinged blackbird or to the hamadryas baboon if we want to know how a human being 'ought' to behave. But if we want to find out what is 'natural' we must look for species whose behavioural tendencies are in some ways comparable to ours – not only in the case of men but also in the case of women.

It is certainly true that one can find occasionally 'masculinistic' accents in sociobiological or ethological literature – as one can in the works of many psychoanalysts, sociologists or philosophers. Yet the claim that sociobiology is masculinistic ('sexist') by its very nature and that it *inherently* must justify existing social conditions is not well founded. One of its major concepts is that there are *naturally existing conflicts of interest* between the sexes as a consequence of different biological starting positions, as has been shown convincingly by Trivers. This applies to humans too, and hence there cannot be a 'natural' code of sexual behaviour fully conforming to the biological interests of both, men *and* women.

Like all other sexually propagating species we too have to find viable compromises between the diverging interests of males and females; and even more than other species we have to adapt to varying external conditions with varying mating systems and family structures. Thus there is no point in looking for a generally applicable 'natural code of sexual behaviour', since norms that are, or were, sensible under certain conditions might easily become outdated, injurious, or unrealistic in other circumstances.

Having read the first draft of this chapter Mary Midgley pointed out to me that there is another side of the coin as well: 'It is that the conflict of interests between males and females is not just a crude economic battle, but also a conflict *between rival traits within the nature of each,*' she writes. 'A brutal patriarch, when he treats the women of his family as chattels, is destroying his own sensibilities and losing the chance of normal human happiness – and the same is true of a brutal matriarch. In general, our nature constantly sets us these dilemmas, and compromise is called for *within* each individual as well as between competitors.'

There are many good arguments for monogamous relations as a rather good adaptation to conditions existing in our modern industrialized society. They can serve as a solid basis for a viable compromise between the divergent interests of man and woman. In such a relation both partners have the chance of a rather high degree of self-realization; they can find equality and mutual esteem while preserving their own human dignity. Moreoever, monogamy creates a good environment for the bringing up of children. If the norms of such monogamy are not applied too restrictively, they are probably compatible with 'human nature' – of men as well as of women.

Presumably, the historical trend goes towards a gradual spreading of conditions of such a 'loose monogamy'. But this is a long way off from the claim that man is a 'naturally monogamous' species. Even less does it justify an attitude that treats polygynous tribal people as 'savages' not yet to be considered as true representatives of our species.

3.11 *Women – objects or subjects?*

'In our previous publications, [hamadryas baboon] females appeared as mere possessions which the males conquered, herded, and lost without regard to the females' own preferences,' write Bachmann and Kummer in their 1980 paper mentioned in section 3.5. 'Various observations and arguments suggest that this view was too simple.'

'Do you think that a woman scientist in your place would have made the same error?' I asked Kummer, when I visited him in his institute in Zürich.

That was a rather difficult question to answer, he replied. He did not think that he was wearing specially masculine spectacles in his work. But when studying a species for the first time in the field, one looks at what is most prominent. In baboons the adult males simply catch the eye. They are more than twice as tall as the females, they chase and threaten each other conspicuously, and, actually, they do play a dominant role within the family group. The first thing to be seen in a hamadryas baboon herd is a movement of harem groups. 'Only after having observed a herd for some time does one get the eye for smaller details and less conspicuous changes, and then one can see that females too play an active role, though they nearly always do it in a much more subtle way than the males.'

Critics from the human and social sciences and from the left and feministic camp might easily be tempted to use the above quoted paragraph as a confirmation of their preconceived view that sociobiologists and ethologists generally tend to see their objects from a one-sided masculine point of view –and that for this reason (amongst others) comparisons with humans ought to be taken with a large grain of salt. For, actually, it is not only in hamadryas baboons that males attract the main attention of an observer by their larger size, their brighter colours or their more conspicuous behaviour. And not

187

all scientists do finally realize, as Bachmann and Kummer did, that this might induce them to view what they see in an unbalanced masculine perspective. But can such a tendency only be found in biological sciences?

When I read the paper of Bachmann and Kummer it suddenly occurred to me that I had sometimes been struck by the very same impression when studying anthropological sources for this book: there was an obvious tendency to depict women as mere objects – as in Kummer's earlier works on baboons. Many examples for this can be found in the papers read at the symposium on *Man the Hunter* (Lee and DeVore, 1968) mentioned in chapter 2 of this book. Claude Levi-Strauss, one of the grand old men of anthropology, writes that 'in human society a man must obtain a woman from another man who gives him a daughter or sister' (p. 211; see also Lévi-Strauss, 1966). Exchange of women in his view is a sort of 'communication' between different tribes or clans. The Australian anthropologist L. R. Hiatt challenged this view and maintained that it was not daughters or sisters but, as a rule, nieces that used to be exchanged by the aborigines of his continent (Lee and DeVore, 1968, p. 165 *et seq.*, 211 *et seq.*). But in both presentations women are seen as *objects of barter without own intentions and purposes*; objects for which there was great demand since Australian aborigines practised polygyny.

The society of these peoples is sometimes called a 'gerontocracy' (old men's rule), though, on close inspection, it turns out that these 'old men' are about 35 to 55 years and at the peak of their social influence (Rose, in Lee and DeVore, p. 205; Woodburn, *ibid.*, p. 209). These men used to have several wives that were twenty and more years younger than they themselves, whereas a young man, according to a report of the German anthropologist E. Eylmann from 1902, either had no wife at all, 'or if he does, she is old enough to be his grandmother'.

Thus, it turns out that male dominance and bartering of women – contrary to widely held beliefs – did exist already in primeval communities that had not yet experienced the 'fall of man' that led to the formation of societies based on class divisions. Male dominance and bartering of women continues to exist in many cultures up to this day. Man is able to treat a fellow human as an object of barter or to sell or buy him or her like a commodity. Not only bride barter, but also slave trade and prostitution prove this. Though we have the ability to identify with every conspecific – an ability distinguishing us from all other animals – we far too seldom use it.

But do Lévi-Strauss or Hiatt really tell the whole story? Is it indeed credible that women of some tribal peoples have less possibilities to influence their own fate than even the females of the hamadryas baboon, a species with very marked male dominance? And is it indeed always 'the' men who treat 'the' women as objects?

Reading anthropological papers carefully one can find an occasional hint that older influential women (mothers, grandmothers, aunts, depending on the family structure) often play an active role in bride barter too and might, in doing so, follow their own interests not always coinciding with those of the men (see Hiatt, in Lee and DeVore, 1968, p. 174). On the other hand there are quite a number of cultures where not only young women but also young men might become objects of barter. Even in our Western societies cases like this are – or, at least, were – by no means unknown, with emotional resistance being ruthlessly overridden when 'higher' dynastic or material interests of the family were at stake.

On the other hand, a woman, if she has the chance to choose her partner herself, often does *not* follow 'the voice of her heart' but rather is led by sober calculations whether the mate she is going to choose will be able to provide for her and her children properly. This is by no means 'unnatural'. As we have seen, a female wren might do just the same.

If we assume as a working hypothesis that women in Australia perhaps, after all, were *not only* objects of barter but active subjects themselves, we might ask whether the peculiar marriage system found in that continent might have been of some benefit for them as well – since, if it was not, it probably would not have lasted for centuries or even millennia. The East-German anthropologist Frederick G. Rose (not to be confused with the British biologist Steven Rose mentioned in a previous section) holds the view 'that it was the women and not the men who took an active role to establish polygynous units and that this type of family provided the optimum conditions for the rearing of the younger generation'. The women, according to him, 'tended to aggregate themselves in collectives of co-wives around the men at the peak of their productive capacity and this tendency reached its maximum when women had their greatest child-bearing and child-rearing burdens' (in Lee and DeVore, 1968, p. 206). The most successful or socially most influential men could most easily provide meat for their families. Moreover, it was the women who gathered vegetable food and for a pregnant or nursing woman it evidently was advantageous to belong in such times of reduced mobility to a family in which other women continued to provide such food.

Actually an Australian often took his second wife at a time when the first one was in an advanced stage of pregnancy or nursing – and the motivation might have been less the sexual gratification of the male than the carrying of the co-wife's burden, i.e. to get additional labour for vegetable food gathering. For the second 'wife' often was a girl of about 9 or 10 years that had been promised to the man even before she was born, but that just now was coming into his house, when her labour was needed, though sexual relations were delayed until she reached puberty (Rose, *ibid.*, p. 205, and discussion by Pilling-Rose, *ibid.*, p. 210).

Extra-marital relations of young women and young men presumably were more frequent than one would guess by the sparse hints to be found in anthropological papers. But being married to a much older man need not, of necessity, be unsatisfactory to a young woman. There are many species of mammals in which females reach maturity much earlier than males, but none where it is the other way round. This is one of the biological mechanisms for coping with the higher 'demand' for females. Equally, there are many human societies in which women, on the average, marry several years earlier than men. Even in our modern industrialized society in which women, as a rule, enjoy a fairly free choice of mates there are many couples of lovers or spouses consisting of a younger woman and a much older man, whereas stable bonds between younger men and considerably older women are rather infrequent. Finding a man who can provide material safety might in such cases be motivating young women, but this is by no means always the predominant factor.

It is a fact that many human societies tend to treat women as objects of barter or as commodities. Yet an anthropological or sociological perspective seeing *only* this trend is just as skewed as the description of a baboon herd that assumes the males to be the only active force in all social occurrences. Females – in baboons as in men – often have more subtle ways than males to reach their goals, but they certainly are able to influence, as subjects, what is happening in their society.

3.12 *Are women different by nature?*

When comparing male and female chimp children, writes Jane Goodall (1971), only a few differences can be observed. Chimp boys prefer a more rough-and-tumble way of playing and in their play they more often practise patterns of aggressive behaviour and of imposing gestures. Moreover, they start to threaten and attack others earlier than females.

Only a few differences, but they are significant ones nevertheless. Hans Kummer (1968, p. 91) reports on similar observations in hamadryas baboons; and others have found the same pattern in other primate species: young males go farther away from their mother when playing and are more rough and aggressive.

In human children it is just the same. Speaking at the conference on Female Phenomena the French child psychologist René Zazzo (in Sullerot, 1978) reported more motile activity and roughness in boys, whereas girls of the same age have more contacts, co-operate more, and have more verbal activity. According to the American psychologist Eleanor E. Maccoby (*ibid.*) boys and girls after the age of two show some fairly clear differences in social behaviour. Where they have the choice they prefer to play with children of their own sex. Girls tend to play in smaller groups than boys, and they are more sedate in the sense that one seldom sees the bursts of wild running around, rough-and-tumble play and mock wrestling, which are typical for boys. 'Girls fight very little, and although their verbal ability is at least as great as that of boys, they do not use verbal taunting and teasing with their age-mates as frequently as boys.'

The facts are well known and presumably need no further elaboration. The real question is whether these differences of behaviour are *inborn* or whether they are mainly a product of education and of role expectations held in society.

The fact that sex-specific behavioural differences in human children are very similar to those found in other young primates supports the idea that they have, at least, a strong inborn component. Or are such phenomena in monkeys and apes also a product of sex-specific differences in 'education'?

191

'We never did specifically investigate this question,' Hans Kummer told me when I asked him about that. 'But I know of experiments with pregnant monkey females to whom the male sex hormone testosterone was administered. When they gave birth to daughters these showed a strongly masculinized behaviour. Thus sex specific behavioural differences seem to be influenced by testosterone before birth.' (See also Goy, 1966.)

Meanwhile I have seen a report according to which rhesus monkey mothers treat their small daughters in a distinctly different way to their small sons (Flad-Schnorrenberg, 1978). It is, however, not easy to interpret these differences.

This example shows very strikingly, that seeing all things as a dichotomy of nature and society might not always be fruitful. Rhesus monkey children apparently are educated differently according to their sex, yet it seems that this sort of educational behaviour is inborn in their mothers.

As concerns hormonal influence on the behaviour of human children an inadvertent experiment was made in the United States in the fifties. A drug given to pregnant women to prevent miscarriages later turned out to cause hormonal disturbances in some cases. Thus a few female embryos were exposed to male sex hormones in the womb of their mother. Some of them were born as hermaphrodites; their internal sexual organs were fully female, but their external genitalia had to be surgically altered after birth and they were then reared as girls. Others appeared to be true females at birth. Yet, most of these girls, those born as hermaphrodites as well as those born as anatomical females, tended to show boyish behaviour later on. They had greater interest in athletic skills, were readier to play with boys, preferred slacks to dresses and toy guns to dolls (Wilson, 1978a, p. 131–2, citing Money and Erhardt, 1972; Reinisch and Karow, 1977).

Of course, there is a broad spectrum of partially overlapping behavioural tendencies in both sexes. When a girl likes to play football with her brothers or school mates, or when a boy likes cooking or doing some needlework, one need not necessarily assume that such children are unrecognized hermaphrodites. According to Wilson (1978a, p. 129) inborn behavioural sex differences are rather modest; the divergence is almost always widened in later psychological development by cultural sanction and training. Behavioural sex differences might be reduced or perhaps even cancelled by a different sort of education, he thinks. Yet, actually, the realization of such a programme has so far never succeeded. In the early times of the Israeli kibbutzim, a generation of women and men with strong ideological motivation tried to abolish traditional role clichés and to establish full sexual equality. At first they almost succeeded. Yet the children and grandchildren of this pioneer generation, though they had been educated in a *milieu* of maximal equality of sexes, strongly tended to regress to the 'natural' distribution of roles (Tiger and Shepher, 1975, cited by Wilson, 1978).

'The differences between the two sexes is one of the important conditions upon which we have built the many varieties of human culture that give human beings dignity and stature,' writes Margaret Mead (1949, p. 7). 'In every known society, mankind has elaborated the biological division of labour into forms often very remotely related to the original biological differences that provided the original clues. . . Sometimes one quality has been assigned to one sex, sometimes to the other. . . Some people think of women as too weak to work out of doors, others regard women as the appropriate bearers of heavy burdens. . . Whether we deal with small matters or with large, with the frivolities of ornament and cosmetics or the sanctities of man's place in the universe, we find this great variety of ways, often flatly contradictory one to the other, in which the roles of the two sexes have been patterned. But we always find the patterning. We know of no culture that has said, articulately, that there is no difference between men and women except in the way they contribute to the creation of the next generation; that otherwise in all respects they are simply human beings with varying gifts, no one of which can be exclusively assigned to either sex. . . However differently the traits have been assigned, some to one sex, some to the other and some to both, however arbitrary the assignment must be seen to be . . . although the division has been arbitrary, it has always been there in every society of which we have any knowledge.'

According to this view it is only the *existence* of different sex roles that is a common feature of all human cultures, but not their actual content; and indeed one can always find exceptions to the rule, or to quote Martin Daly and Margo Wilson (1979): 'the universality of sex-role stereotypes can be refuted if one marshals examples of unfamiliar roles in unfamiliar cultures'; nevertheless, a general trend is clearly emerging from ethnographic statistics.

In the vast majority of hunter and gatherer peoples only men hunt (see Lee and DeVore, 1968, *passim*). Women might help as beaters in hunting big game, or catch small animals such as rabbits, but as a rule they do not have hunting weapons of their own and autonomous female hunting of big game is a rather rare exception (Watanabe, *ibid.*, p. 74; Yengoyan, *ibid.*, p. 187; see also, Agnes Estioko-Griffin and P. B. Griffin, 1981). Similarly, technically more complex forms of fishery are solely a male task, whereas women gather shellfish or do simple basket fishing (Murdock, 1968, p. 335).

This, says Wilson (1975, p. 567), does not warrant the conclusion that it must have been just the same in our ancestors. In chimps most of the hunting is done by males, yet sometimes hunting females were observed as well (*ibid.*, p. 542, quoting Teleki, 1973). *When* in human evolution hunting became a predominantly male prerogative is a matter of speculation. Anyway, it is a fact giving food for thought that the ancient Greeks and Romans did not have a male god of hunting but a goddess: Artemis and Diana, respectively.

Tabulation of a large number of anthropologists' reports by George P. Murdock (cited by Daly and Wilson, 1979) shows that production of weapons nearly always is an exclusively male occupation. Carrying of water, on the other hand, in some regions a very toilsome business requiring *hours* of work, is an exclusively female task in more than three-fourths of all human societies or a task of older children; even today children in some Bolivian villages have no school in the dry season in order that they have enough time for carrying water (Agarwal, 1980).

That cooking is a strictly female activity in more than three-fourths of all societies and an exclusively male task in only 5 out of 200 does not come as a surprise. Moreover, what is the meaning when the ethnographic statistic says that both sexes may cook? In our society many hotels or restaurants have a male *chef de cuisine*, but at home the kitchen is usually the domain of the woman – even if both spouses are working.

Men that must go to the restaurant if they do not want to starve when their wife is absent or in hospital are becoming rarer in our society. Similarly, in the younger generation there are many who do not fear to lose their male identity by pushing a pram or sewing on a button. Moreover, the basic idea of partnership in matrimony is *not* that both spouses necessarily must be able to do every kind of

194

housework just as well as the other. Rather the *total* burden ought to be shared equitably. Nor does adherence to the idea of equal rights for both sexes imply that any thought of naturally existing differences between men and women *a priori* has to be rejected as reactionary.

This is a point of leverage for the French sociologist Evelyne Sullerot who, as a leading member of the French women's movement, gradually and with growing intensity became aware that, as she puts it, 'some feministic arguments lack scientific rigour'. Facts not fitting into preconceived notions are rejected, or mentioning them is considered to be atrocious in feministic circles. This, Sullerot thinks, leads to the danger of weakening all feministic arguments – even those that are justified and well founded.

She talked about these problems to the Nobel laureate Jacques Monod, and both of them eventually agreed 'that hitherto existing taboos ought to be disregarded and differences between the sexes should be openly discussed ... be it to cut them down to their proper size, to correct them or to recognize consequences following from such differences' (Sullerot, 1978). During these conversations the idea emerged of holding the previously mentioned workshop on *Female Phenomena.* Monod himself, though actively participating in its preparation, could not attend this conference. He had died shortly before it was held.

At this meeting Evelyn Sullerot spoke very openly about the problems she had encountered in her sociological research: 'I am studying choices of occupation of adult women in France and I just completed an investigation on occupational choices of girls and women in seven European countries, East and West,' she reported. 'When starting on this work about ten years ago I was convinced – as my writings prove – that it is exclusively social conditions and education that are responsible for all the differences in choice of occupation and achievement of success which exist between men and women. I still believe that this is true for a great many of those differences in interests and fancy that lead to the choosing of a certain occupation. But my sociological belief has been shaken by hard facts. Thus I went the opposite way of many others who lately tend to overemphasize social factors. I could not explain solely by social analysis all the causes for the distribution of sexes within certain occupations; neither could I explain certain

195

failures of educational and vocational training experiments that intended to change stereotypes and thus I began to take account of differences in spatial representation in boys and girls.'

This refers to the fact that boys from about ten years of age onwards are, on the average, considerably better than girls in reading maps, blueprints or other two-dimensional representations of three-dimensional things, and that they are much better at turning objects round in their mind's eye (see also Sandra Witelson, in Sullerot, 1978). This, Evelyne Sullerot thinks, is probably why women nearly always perform unqualified labour in mechanical industries, whereas in the chemical industry in France they earn, on average, even more than men – which shows that they occupy a greater number of qualified jobs.

'I have investigated special sectors of the mechanical industry,' she continued, 'for example watch-making which does not demand strength, is not a dirty occupation, nor one performed in a *milieu* polluted by the stench of oil. But I had to take notice of the facts: women, everywhere, assemble watches and clocks very quickly and very well. But with very few exceptions they neither invent nor design clockworks, nor do they repair them. In the Soviet Union boys and girls originally were sent to the same vocational training centres for watch making. Today these schools have two divisions – one for assembly and one for repair. In the first one there are only girls, in the other one only boys. This sort of division of labour was not intended, there were even efforts to prevent it; yet, in the long run, it just asserted itself.'

On the average rather weak spatial representation is, of course, not the reason why women have worse career expectations in many jobs that have nothing at all to do with this special ability. Rather this is due to the prejudices of those who have to decide on promotions, and to some extent it is also due to the fact that many men consider it as a kind of 'discrimination' if they have to work under a woman superior. Thus even a manager who himself has no 'sexist' prejudices will hesitate to appoint a woman as a leader of a department where men are working, since he knows that this most probably will cause trouble.

As a rule a woman must be much more able than her male competitors to get a responsible job. Thus it is no surprise that feminists are rather allergic to any hint that there might be natural differences

196

in the abilities of men and women. They fear – and with good reason – that every such hint might be used to the detriment of women.

Yet facts remain facts. And discrimination against women in vocational life – certainly a fact too! – cannot be abolished by countering male prejudices with feministic counter-prejudices. Natural differences between men and women often are exaggerated and interpreted in a biased way to the advantage of men. They must be, as Monod said, reduced to their actual size. On the other hand one would, in the long run, render a bad service to the cause of women by denying their existence.

3.13 *Of world records and IQ tests*

Men, on the average, are not only taller and stronger than women, their organism is also better able to mobilize energy reserves quickly. They have a higher metabolic rate, a higher 'vital capacity' (breathing performance), more red blood corpuscles per cubic centimetre of blood, and a higher heart beat capacity (Crook, 1972, p. 247; Zazzo, in Sullerot, 1978).

When you are going to have some of these body functions tested in a medical laboratory you might get the result on a form stating different, though overlapping, 'norm values' for men and women. Other laboratories consider these differences as unimportant and use the same norm values for both sexes.

As far as there are differences it is not always certain whether they are strictly speaking 'inborn', i.e. *directly* caused by genetic factors. Lower average values of red blood corpuscles in women for example might be 'indirectly inborn' – a consequence of regular monthly blood loss in menstruation.

There are many diseases occurring at different frequencies in men and women. Some of them like colour-blindness or lack of blood coagulation are caused by a faulty gene on the X-chromosome of which men have only one, whereas women will suffer from such diseases only if *both* of their X-chromosomes contain the same faulty gene. For many other diseases the reason for different frequencies between the sexes is not yet clear. Empirically it is claimed that men more frequently have gastric ulcers, whereas women more frequently have gall-stones, that some kinds of mental disorders are more frequent in women and others in men (Eisenberg, in Sullerot, 1978), but to what extent these and other differences are due to genetic causes and how much they are influenced by differences in occupation, life style, smoking and drinking habits, etc. is an open question. Statistical correlations not taking account of *all* possible causal links do not tell us much.

There is no doubt that women, on the average, live longer than men. Statistics from all parts of the globe prove this. In developing countries the average difference in life expectancy is about two to three years, in highly industrialized countries four to seven years. In the past, life expectancy in industrialized countries was lower and the difference between the sexes smaller. With rising affluence and improvement in hygiene and medical services the differences are widening to the advantage of women.

This too might be a composite effect of several factors. With a continuing trend of women proving their 'equal rights' – for instance by smoking and drinking just as much as men – lung cancer, cirrhosis of the liver and other diseases will probably become more common amongst women and, maybe, sex differences in life expectancy might decrease in coming decades. Yet, even disregarding differences in life style and in the frequency of vocational diseases, the female organism seems to have more general resistance against many disorders.

Lower 'risk acceptance' of women presumably is a further reason for their higher life expectancy. Contrary to widely held prejudices women, according to accident statistics, are, on the average, the better, or, at least, the more responsible car drivers. Counted per kilometre travelled, they have less accidents than men, in particular less grave accidents. On the other hand, men between 18 and 25 – but not women of the same age class – are particularly accident prone. How far this is due to an *inborn* tendency to take risks and to 'show off' and to what extent such tendencies are further reinforced by conventional social clichés is not quite certain.

Taking account of the bodily differences it does not come as a surprise that men are superior in most sports. World and national records in running, jumping, swimming and speed-skating show differences of about 5 to 20%. Throwing contests cannot be compared since women use lighter javelins, discus, etc.; nevertheless men throw farther. Even when testing men and women of equal size

198

or weight men, as a rule, are superior in these sports (Wilson, 1978a, p. 127).

This is not to say that *all* differences in performance are exclusively due to biological factors. Though a woman having reached the rank of a top athlete most probably will be cared for just as well as her male colleagues, there certainly are differences in the population at large. Sporting exercise is still encouraged more widely amongst boys than amongst girls. Hence the base from which top athletes are drawn is smaller for women than for men.

Actually the differences between male and female world records declined within the last twenty years. In running contests they were 12 – 20% (average 15%) in 1956; the differences were reduced to 9 – 12% (average 10.5%) by 1976. The same trend can be observed in swimming where differences in the same time span came down from 10.5% to 8.5% The trends were computed by Ken Dyer (1977), a lecturer in social biology at the university of Adelaide, Australia, and referring to them she boldly claimed that 'women may one day run and swim as fast as men'. Ultimate sportive equality between the sexes could be reached, according to her, 'perhaps within 3 to 4 decades'. Anyway, she thinks, it has now become 'absolutely clear' that the reasons for past differences in performance were 'more social than biological'.

Ludwig Prokop, an Austrian authority on sports medicine, considers such claims as completely unfounded. 'A female organism works in a different way than a male one,' he told me. 'There are inborn differences in the design of the body, in muscular strength, etc., and this cannot be eliminated by any amount of training.'

Moreover, it is a fact that male sex hormones are used for doping female athletes. Being 'masculinized' in this way women achieve a higher performance (Baulieu and Haour, in Sullerot, 1978). Thus, an extremely feministic position ascribing all differences to social discrimination of women does not conform to the facts – but neither does an extremely 'masculinistic' position claiming male superiority for *all* sport's disciplines.

'In one event equality has already been essentially attained', writes Ken Dyer. 'Women hold the speed record for swimming the English Channel in both directions, in each case the difference amounting to about 40 minutes in the time of about 9 hours required to cover the distance.'

This, by the way, is not what I would call 'equality', but rather female superiority. However, quite apart from this aspect of the story it is just such facts that refute Dyer's own arguments. For it is by no means obvious why factors of social discrimination should be less effective for Channel swimmers than for those competing in short track swimming or running. Might one not at least consider the possibility that there are biological factors at work as well? Women have more fat underneath their skin, their blood vessels are situated deeper in the body; they have, as it were, a better 'heat insulation'; hence they do not cool down as rapidly as men when in the water and they need less energy to maintain their body temperature – meaning that they can expend more energy in swimming.

As concerns *endurance*, Prokop says, women are not inferior to men, the difference is in muscular strength. Therefore certain sports disciplines are a sole prerogative of men – but hardly anybody will consider it as a 'discrimination against women' if there are no female weight-lifters or boxing champions.

In disciplines requiring a fine tuning of muscles, as in gymnastics or horse riding, women are equal or even superior to men, according to Prokop. In horse riding and sailing women and men compete together in one class and, as a rule, women do no worse than men. In clay pigeon shooting – according to traditional view a typically 'male' exercise – women seem to be even slightly superior to men.

In chess, on the other hand, which certainly does not require either strength or fine-tuning of muscles, men are so strongly superior that joint competitions for both sexes are ruled out. Promotion of chess playing for boys *and girls* in the Soviet Union has resulted in practically all female chess champions being Soviet – yet they do not attain the level of their male colleagues.

Thus one might ask whether there are sex specific differences not only in muscular strength and metabolic rate but also in the working of the brain. The Canadian neurologist Sandra F. Witelson answers this question with a clear 'yes'. Essentially, the differences she found concern 'lateralization', i.e. the assigning of specific tasks to one side of the brain or the other. Originally the localization of brain functions had been studied mainly in men whose brains had been damaged in war. A picture emerged according to which verbal, logical, and analytical skills are concentrated on the left hemisphere, whereas the right hemisphere seems to be specialized for spatial and synthetic processing. Lesions of the left side of the brain (the linguistic centre) often lead – in men! – to disturbances of speech or reading ability. In women, however, the frequency of similar disturbances after the same sort of lesions is much lower and/or the disturbances slighter. This was one of the starting points which led Sandra Witelson to assume that lateralization and specialization of the brain hemispheres is more pronounced in men than in women. After many investigations and experiments, the description of which which would be beyond the scope of this book, she concluded that the brains of men and women are organized in a different way and work differently in some tasks (in Sullerot, 1978; see also Witelson 1976; 1977).

Most pertinent investigations are of rather recent date and many of the details have still to be cleared up, yet there seems to be hardly any doubt about the basic facts. 'In ten years time it will be generally recognized that there are sex-specific differences in the organization of the brain,' I was told by Jerre Levy who is studying brain lateralization too, when I met her at the Dahlem Conference on *Animal and Human Mind.*

Such differences in cerebral organization might be one of the reasons for the fact that women and men, on the average, perform differently in certain kinds of tests. Thus males, as mentioned before, generally are superior in spatial tasks, whereas women generally show a slight verbal superiority.

Sex averages, of course, do not tell anything about the special capabilities of a single person. Mrs X applying for a job that requires geometircal skills might be superior to all her male competitors; presumably she would not have applied if she was bad at geometry. There is much common sense in the feministic demand that job advertisements ought to be 'sex neutral' and that experts, when asked to evaluate the results of written tests, ought not to know the sex of the testee. Yet taking the *average* of a large number of test subjects – say of all the pupils of a certain age class – it will turn out that there are always the same sex-specific differences in the frequency distribution of certain kinds of capability.

When the first experiments were made with the historic Stanford-Binet IQ test boys seemed to perform better than girls. The testers felt that this was unfair and *adjusted* the differential scoring items until both sexes had equal chances to attain the same *total* score

(S. Rose, 1979a). There are, however, still characteristic differences in the results for the single scoring items: female superiority in verbal tasks, male in spatial tasks.

'Intelligence' is an ill-defined composite notion, summing up a whole range of different talents. These single capabilities can be weighted differently when calculating the IQ score. Yet the fact that scoring items *can be adjusted* in a way that makes the test 'sex neutral', whereas other combinations of scoring items are not, does prove that there are sex differences in the performance on single components contributing to the general IQ result. On the other hand, IQ tests *cannot* give evidence as to whether such sex differences are inborn or the result of different education.

Whereas it is widely known that there are sex-specific differences in the frequency distribution of certain intellectual skills, few people seem to realize that there is another sex-specific difference as well: the bandwidth of results is considerably larger in boys than in girls (Sullerot, 1978). In other words, there are many more boys than girls deviating far from the average in a single capability or in the total score – and this higher incidence of male deviation goes *both ways*: to the upper *and* lower regions of the frequency bandwidth. There are, it seems more male geniuses but also more male imbeciles.

According to the child psychologist René Zazzo (in Sullerot, 1978) the percentage of pupils that have to repeat a year in French schools is 'significantly higher' amongst boys than amongst girls. For children coming from the most underprivileged circles (children of non-qualified manual workers) the proportion of pupils passing school in normal time without repeating a class is 29% in girls and only 6% in boys. Amongst the children of the most privileged (those of higher civil servants, office workers in responsible jobs) the respective figures are 80% for girls and 67% for boys.

Failure at school need not necessarily be due to lack of intelligence; it might just as well be caused by lack of motivation. Yet, be that as it may, these figures do not fit well to stereotype clichés – neither of 'male intellectual superiority' nor, on the other hand, of 'general discrimination against women'.

'The higher frequency of light and grave debility amongst boys is irritating and one tries not to mention it,' says Evelyne Sullerot (1978). 'On the other hand most societies have long-established institutions for the higher education of their brightest boys – hot-

202

houses, as it were, for the promotion of their intellectual and social success... In recent times some countries are opening the doors of these breeding places of 'egg-heads' for girls too... yet the handicap for a female minority amongst this highly talented minority is enormous.'

Before these developments of the last decades, some very brilliant women had been able to overcome even greater handicaps and to surmount barriers of prejudice in order to follow a scientific career. A Madame Curie or a Lise Meitner asserted themselves in most 'unfemale' disciplines, but in doing so they had to put up with many assaults on their human dignity. It may seem to be a triviality, but it is typical of the atmosphere of that time that at the Kaiser-Wilhelms-Institut in Berlin, where Lise Meitner was working, there were, of course, no wash-rooms for women scientists... Today nobody doubts any more that a woman can be an outstanding scientist, though they are still a rather small minority.

Literary history at the first glance seems to be a predominantly masculine affair too – in spite of the higher verbal ability of women. Yet everybody with some knowledge of literature will be able to enumerate at least some outstanding female poets and writers from Sappho to Selma Lagerlöf – and in our times female writers no longer are a rare exception.

In music the picture is different. Women certainly are not less musical than men and there are many female interpreters (singers, pianists, etc.) of the highest rank. Female occupation with music has a long-standing tradition in Europe and there certainly were no opera houses in the last century without garderobes for female artists. That there are hardly any female conductors might have to do with the prejudices of male orchestra players who do not like to work under the baton of a woman. But why, in half a millennium of European musical history, is there *not one* female composer of the same rank as Selma Lagerlöf attained in literature or Madame Curie in science? That male prejudices should have been so much greater amongst publishers of music than amongst publishers of literature seems hardly credible (see also, Sullerot, 1978).

For me there is no doubt that women indeed are discriminated against in our society and that they have to overcome many additional handicaps in their vocational life. But the significantly different degree of female success in the various disciplines of science, arts, and sports cannot be explained *solely* by social factors. If equal rights do mean, first of all, the chance of self-realization for all people without regard to their sex – a chance that is severely restricted for males as well in our society – one should expect that the frequency distribution of inclinations and talents might be naturally different amongst the sexes not only in sports and arts. Rejecting the common practices of today's discrimination a priori against women, which tries to force them into specific 'female' roles irrespective of their individual talents and aspirations, should not lead to the converse error of expecting that women, when enjoying 'equal rights', ought to be represented in *all* social and vocational roles in the same numbers as men – for such an attitude probably would again override their specific individual talents and aspirations.

3.14 *Is there kin selection in humans?*

When we tend to favour near relatives as compared to other people this seems to us a matter of course. Even the law recognizes that. A witness before court has to tell the truth and nothing but the truth. However, in many countries the law takes account of the fact that a witness would be in a conflict of conscience if he had to give testimony against his parents, his children, his spouse or other near relatives. In such a situation he can be relieved of his duty of testimony. On the other hand, where the defendant is a good friend of mine I nevertheless have to give testimony; and if I try to help him, by not telling the truth or by concealing something I know, I might be punished.

Inheritance laws too recognize the kin principle. When somebody dies without leaving a will the closest kin are the heirs. Thus one can inherit a fortune from an uncle in America though one may never have met him, whereas those who were nearest to him during his life might get nothing. In many countries – though to my knowledge not in Britain – the spouse and the children have a legal claim to part of the estate of a testator irrespective of what has been said in the will; only of the rest (usually half of the estate) can the testator dispose freely. Illegitimate children, on the other hand, have either very limited or no hereditary claims at all in most countries – even if parternity is clear and has been recognized.

For tribal peoples kinship is even more important than for us.

Often their languages have a great number of words to denominate all sorts of complicated kin relationships which in modern European languages require indirect definition. Thus in our languages 'uncle' might mean the brother of either parent, whereas the languages of tribal peoples, as a rule, have different words for each and a different emotional evaluation as well. According to Tacitus (Germania, chapter 20), a German of his times would look on the son of his sister as his own son. When taking hostages the sister's son was considered to be a stronger guarantee than the own son of the one to be bound.

Kinship relations in tribal peoples entail all sorts of mutual rights and duties such as hunting in the territory of certain classes of kin's people, visiting their camps and being received as a welcome guest, or even settling there; moreover kinship might be the basis for claims to certain women related to a man in a certain exactly defined way – for example, the *right* of a man to get the daughter's daughter of the brother of his maternal grandmother as his wife (see for example Hiatt, in Lee and DeVore, 1968, p. 165 *et seq.*).

According to Richard Lee (*ibid.*, p. 152) gatherer and hunter peoples show much flexibility in applying all these rules. Discussions among anthropologists of whether members of a certain tribe are 'matrilocal' or 'patrilocal' – meaning whether they live with the family of their mother or that of the father – are, in his view, removed from reality. Actually, he says, most of them behave in a way that could best be described as 'pragmatilocal', i.e. they make their residence arrangements from purely practical considerations. As a rule a group is composed of a core of people bound by some kin ties and their spouses, and a young couple will join a group in which one of them has kin.

Edward Wilson in his book *On Human Nature* (1978a, p. 136, quoting Gutman) reports that amongst negro slaves in the USA families were frequently broken up and their members dispersed and yet knowledge of kin relations was faithfully preserved for many generations (more about that in section 4.3). This, in his view, proves that principles of kin selection are important for humans too.

The well-known anthropologist Marshall Sahlins denies this. Tribal people, he says, often use kinship terms that do not correspond to biological reality. Cousins, for example, are often called brothers. Though this phenomenon is widespread, there also is evidence that peoples using such terms know the real (biological) relations quite well. Cousins are called 'siblings' amongst Indians in Northern Canada, yet, according to June Helm who studied these peoples, they can distinguish quite well their cousins from their siblings (Helm, in Lee and DeVore, 1968, p. 151).

The main part of Sahlins' booklet on the *Use and Abuse of Biology* deals with this question. He enumerates many examples as evidence for his thesis. Disregarding many variations in detail one basic principle clearly stands out: peoples still living in more or less primeval conditions are organized into clans or similar groups that are regarded as groups of kin though the actual biological degree of kinship is often only very slight. Thus, cousins of the third degree have, owing to their common ancestors, only a hundred-and-twenty-eighth of their genes in common, less than 1% yet, if they belong to the same clan they treat each other as if they were close kin.

As a rule marriage between members of the same clan is forbidden. Biologists consider this to be an unconscious mechanism of incest avoidance though many anthropologists doubt this (more about that in the next section). The details of the marriage rules vary in different peoples, but one of the spouses must in any case leave his or her community and join the community of the other partner. This entails that in future he or she will no longer co-operate in everyday life with his or her own kin but with the kin of the partner or with their spouses. Thus a man living in the family of his wife might hunt or work together with the husband of this wife's sister.

The children can belong only to one clan – as a rule to that in which they grow up. For them members of this clan are close kin, whereas relatives that are just as close biologically, not belonging to the same clan, are considered as remote kin. Sahlins (1976, p. 52 *et seq.*) quotes examples of Polynesians who know exactly the actual biological relationships but nevertheless consider a cousin of second degree belonging to the same clan as close kin, and a cousin of first degree not belonging to the same clan as remote kin.

Thus kinship ideas in the thinking of tribal peoples are a product of culture and in Sahlins' view cannot be reconciled with a biological theory of kin selection. However, in claiming this he does not take account of the fact that the basis of sociobiological kin selection theory is a genetical *cost/benefit calculation* and not merely a statement of degrees of relatedness. Nor does he take account of the fact

206

that actual realities in the animal kingdom are very similar to those in humans.

In men as in animals living in structured groups, the core of the group is made up of individuals related by real, though not necesarily strong, ties of kinship. Members of a group behave to each other *as if* they were kin though they are not always really so (see section 1.10). What the anthropologist Sahlins considers to be a typically human cultural superstructure can be found with appropriate modification in the instinctive behaviour of animals as well.

In the first part of this book we have noted several times that in animals group-interests have a higher rank than kinship ties – *even if the latter are known to the animals*. The splitting of a chimp troop mentioned in section 1.6 eventually led to the killing of all males of the secessionist group by members of the main group – though the victims evidently were close kin and known as such to the murderers. In humans it is very similar. The interests of my own group containing my closest kin, i.e. my children, are of higher rank than kinship ties to members of other groups. This is in no way in contradiction to the theory of kin selection, since, according to this theory, I ought to support kin *only if that is advantageous* to the maximal spreading of my genes (or genes identical with mine) in future generations.

In humans as in animals members of one sex as a rule leave their own group to join the group of their mate (or, respectively, join another group to find a mate there). Though such 'immigrants' are *not* kin to the members of their new group they are accepted and treated, more or less, as if they were kin.

Moreover, if there are quarrels within a group of monkeys, apes, or humans, close kin help each other against other members of the group. Parents try to promote the interests of their children, siblings help each other, 'nepotism' is well known in humans as well as in animals. This is one of the strongest arguments supporting the theory of kin selection, but on this phenomenon Sahlins has nothing to say at all.

Kin selection is not the sole and only true theory that can explain all phenomena of social behaviour in animals – still less can it explain everything in the social behaviour of men, and even its most ardent proponents have never claimed that. However, certain behavioural tendencies in humans might perhaps be seen in a new and better perspective when applying the ideas of this theory.

The Yanamamö Indians in the Amazonian basin, like many tribal peoples, use terms of kin relationship that do not correspond to biological reality. Yet, if a village divides and a new one is founded, division is effected according to the *real* (biological) and not according to the nominal (cultural) kinship ties; thus the average degree of biological relatedness is higher in the newly formed units than it was in the original unit (Chagnon, 1979). This is exactly the same phenomenon as has been observed in rhesus monkeys when a group splits (Chepko-Sade, 1979).

Evidently the actual 'ties of blood' uniting a clan are, as a rule, rather weak; they are reinforced and, as it were, given extra value by myths and cultural superstructures. Yet it is remarkable that practically all primeval people do this by defining an actually existing community of interests in a group as a kinship community resting on the basis of the mythical descent from a common ancestor. Most probably they would not do so if it was not part of human nature to consider kinship ties as very strong ties.

3.15 *Is the notion of incest an 'invention'?*

At the Max Planck Institute for the Physiology of Behaviour in Seewiessen, Norbert Bischof once reared two young wild geese. The animals were imprinted onto him, he told me, and they followed him as others follow their mother. As they grew up they often flew onto the lake, but when he called them they came back to him. They always stayed together like a pair of spouses, though at that time they were far from sexual maturity.

This lasted for nearly a year until the next spring. Then one day they did not come when Bischof called them. As he went along the lake shore to look for them he soon found the female. Yet, when he greeted her she did not approach him as she always used to, but ruffled her plumage – an indication of a conflict situation – and withdrew. After a while he found the male too. When Bischof tried to approach the bird attacked him. The two geese were still far from maturity, which they reach in the second spring, but the period of puberty had started and old family ties had been disrupted. From now on they were looking for new mates.

In ostriches, which live in harem groups, the pattern of puberty conflicts is somewhat different. According to the German scientists

Franz and Eleonore Sauer (1967), who studied these birds in their native habitat of South Africa, the highest ranking hen drives away the youngsters when they are about one year old and show their first sexual urges. As a rule she is supported by the male who threatens the young birds with raised wings and tail, and hits out at them with beak and legs. For days on end the yearlings try to remain with their parent group, sometimes even slightly counter-threatening when attacked, but at long last they give up and start to form independent bachelor herds.

Other species have still other behaviour patterns in puberty. In song birds the young females, as a rule, migrate much farther from the parental territory than the young males; in many mammals it is the other way round (Harvey et al., 1980; Feldman et al., 1980). Monkeys and apes still know their mother when adult and treat her as an animal of higher rank with whom her sons cannot copulate. In rhesus monkeys or anubis baboons the young males usually leave their group when reaching puberty, in chimps and gorillas it is the young females. When a female chimp remains in the group of her mother she is, according to Jane Goodall (1971, p. 168) 'extremely reluctant to be mated by her brothers', screaming a lot when she is approached by one of them.

These variations in actual behaviour patterns all have the same effect: incest, i.e. mating between siblings or between parents and children, becomes rather unlikely.

There are sound biological reasons for incest avoidance. First, every organism inherits from its parents some faulty genes. Such a gene does not manifest itself as long as the homologous normal gene was inherited from the other parent. If, however, the same gene inherited from both parents is faulty, the organism will be unable to live or will be severely handicapped in its normal functions. Close kin have more genes in common than unrelated individuals, hence in incestous matings there is an increased danger that the progeny inherit *the same* faulty gene from both parents.

Some of this progeny will not live at all or die before reaching the reproductive age. If the others that evidently carry faulty genes are excluded from reproduction one can, in the course of several generations, eliminate most of these bad genes from a population. By further inbreeding one can produce 'pure lines' of animals or plants that all have more or less the same genes –

209

almost like identical twins. Under stable laboratory conditions such animals, for example strains of inbred mice or rats, might be able to live more or less like normal beings, but they have lost the major advantage of sexual reproduction – the 'shuffling of the cards', i.e. the formation of ever-new gene combinations in each new generation, which gives the chance that a population can adapt quickly to environmental changes. This is the second disadvantage of incest, and for these two reasons natural selection seems to favour behaviour patterns that render it, at least, very improbably (see also Bischof, 1975).

Animals, of course, do not realize this. As a rule they avoid mating with partners with whom they were reared together – be they real siblings or merely foster siblings – but they prefer mates that are only slightly different from their parents or siblings and not too unfamiliar in their visual, auditory and olfactory characteristics. Experimenting with brown Japanese quails that had been reared in random groups, Patrick Bateson (1978) found that the cocks clearly preferred an unknown brown hen to a foster sister. If however they had to choose between a white hen and a foster sister they preferred the latter. In free choice experiments both cocks and hens preferred first cousins significantly more often than any other category of partner (*New Scientist*, 1982).

The biological disadvantages of incest manifest themselves in humans as well as in other sexually reproducing species. Even frequent marriages between near relatives as practised in some Middle Eastern societies result in a significantly increased rate of genetic diseases (Feldman *et al.*, 1980). In Czechoslovakia an investigation of 161 cases of children begotten by incestuous matings showed that 15 of them were still-born or died within the first year; of the rest more than 40% suffered from various physical and mental defects. In contrast, of 95 children born to the same mothers through non-incestuous relations 5 died in their first year of life, none had serious mental deficiencies, and only 5% had physical abnormalities (Seemanova, 1972, quoted in *Time* magazine).

Friedrich Engels (1884) basing himself on the ideas of scientists of his time, in particular on the work of the American anthropologist Lewis H. Morgan, calls the idea of incest 'an invention – and a most valuable one at that'. According to this view sexual intercourse among parents and children could have been, before this 'invention', no more repulsive than other matings between persons of different generations. As for siblings, Morgan and Engels believed that intercourse between them had originally been a matter of course. According to what we know today about incest avoidance in animals, this seems highly unlikely. If even a young chimp female in heat, which is sexually very active and interested, tries to rebuke the advances of her brothers, it seems very likely that it would have been the same in our ancestors. The 'kinship family' postulated by Morgan as the original human state probably never existed. Seen in the light of today's ethological knowledge it must be assumed that the notion of incest was not 'invented' at all, but rather that men inherited from their ancestors unconcious behaviour patterns of inborn incest avoidance that later were woven into their culture. Actually there is today hardly a human society without incest taboos or laws against incest. In sociobiological perspective this is indeed a paradigmatic case how inborn behavioural tendencies are interpreted by a later cultural superstructure.

Yet, just this is doubted by many human and social scientists. For them the sociobiological explanation is too simplifying. Incest taboos, in their view, are 'a conglomerate of a great many different practices, with different roles to play in different societies' (Solomon et al., 1978). They should not be all lumped together as serving the same ends, but rather must be understood in their socio-cultural context. Moreover, it is pointed out that sibling marriages were allowed and even the rule in ancient Egypt, in Bali and in Hawaii.

In my view this last argument misses the point. Biological 'laws' cannot be applied like physical laws. Rather they are rules that are not invalidated by a few exceptions. 'While many exceptions to this rule are known,' writes the British anthropologist Robin Fox, '[the incest taboo] is nevertheless one of the more universal of all rules and its significance has to interpreted.' (1972, p. 281).

For the human scientists the main function of this taboo is to preserve the integrity of the family and to prevent role conflicts. Fox also refers to the idea of Lévi-Strauss (1949) that the essence of the incest taboo is to define 'own' women as 'objects of exchange' rather than as 'objects of use' – with barter of women being a main base for the formation of alliances and power structures.

211

According to Washburn and Lancaster (1968, p. 301), the incest taboo was intended moreover to prevent a young man from begetting children before he is able to provide for them sufficiently. This, they think, in no way contradicts the other arguments. 'A set of behaviors is more likely to persist and be widespread, if it serves many uses,' they claim.

One might as well go one step further and say that all these explanations do not exclude the sociobiological assumption that men as well as animals have inborn behaviour patterns leading to incest avoidance. That incest would be a disruptive element in normal family relations seems obvious to us – but why are we constructed in a way that we feel incest to be irritating, whereas most primeval peoples accept polygamy as a matter of course?

According to Norbert Bischof humans, like animals, have an inborn tendency to avoid sex with persons with whom they are familiar from their earliest childhood. This seems to be corroborated by experiences in Israeli kibbutzim where all the children of kibbutz members are brought up together as if they were siblings. It turns out that two people who have grown up together in the same peer group hardly ever marry (Shepher, 1971). There is no rational reason to avoid such marriages, nor would they be disapproved of by society, but there seems to be an emotional barrier between such persons.

Similar experiences come from Taiwan where parents in the traditional Chinese way still look for spouses for their children when they are still quite small. Sometimes young girls of a few years of age are brought to the family of their future bridegroom and grow up there, whereas in other cases the bride does not enter the family of her husband before the wedding. In the first case marital difficulties later become much more frequent. When asked for the reasons, people tend to smile embarassedly and eventually may confess that sex does not work well among partners that grew up together as children.

There are, however, examples to the contrary as well. Speaking at the Dahlem workshop on Morality as a Biological Phenomenon the American cultural anthropologist Clifford Geertz referred to customs on Bali. There marriage between cousins is quite common and often they grow up together when they are children; according to his observations these marriages seem to work well. On the other hand A. Jenner pointed out in the same discussion that father-daughter sex is a not uncommon problem to be dealt with in British. psychiatric practice (Solomon *et al.*, 1978).

Incest regularly turns up in criminal statistics and there is good reason to assume that only a small fraction of these cases comes to the knowledge of legal authorities. A court reporter of an Austrian paper told me that he could write about such a case every week; but since the public practically always is excluded from the proceedings newspapers do not find it interesting to report on such cases.

Most incest cases coming to court happened in underprivileged strata of society and in very crowded living conditions. Often the incest is effected by compulsion, if not rape, or the seduction of girls of minor age. Whether incest is indeed less frequent in higher social strata or whether more privileged people are merely better able to 'hush up' such incidences is an open question. Anyway, incest motives can be found not only in old myths but also in modern literature as, for example, in Thomas Mann's *Wälsungenblut* or Jean-Paul Sartre's *The Enclosed of Altona*.

The spectrum of human behaviour is very broad and apparently there is a small band in it where incest seems possible. It would be too simple to reduce the reason for this to a mere faulty gene, as in colour-blindness; and even a comparison with kleptomania is not quite fitting. Incest, unless combined with compulsion, requires *a common deviant behaviour of two persons.* Assuming a general male tendency to see 'Helena' in every woman the main responsibility for avoiding incest probably lies on the female side.

For incest to take place a usually existing barrier must break down simultaneously in two close kin, and this might require inborn genetic defects as well as special environmental conditions. Yet the fact that this occasionally happens in humans in no way proves that such inborn inhibitions do not exist *as a rule*. In animals too these inhibitions are not always a hundred-percent effective, but they obviously do exist. It would be very strange indeed if the incest taboos existing in nearly all human societies were pure cultural products without any base in our inborn natural tendencies to behave in a biologically reasonable way.

3.16 *Pecking order, aggression, and sex*

The groups of most socially living animals have a hierarchic structure. Sometimes such a structure is called a 'pecking order' since this phenomenon was first observed in the henhouse (Schjelderup-Ebbe, 1922). Such an order of rank is vital for the undisturbed co-existence of individuals within a group. It prevents members of the group from starting to quarrel about every piece of food, every sleeping place, or every route to be taken. The pecking order fixes priorities which are only seldom challenged.

An individual of higher rank need not necessarily always insist on his priorities; neither need there be the same rank order for all sorts of questions. An old hamadryas baboon might no longer be able to defend a harem – having lost his rank as concerns access to females – but his vote might still have considerable weight when there is disagreement about the route to be taken (see section 2.5). In certain circumstances even animals of lower rank have certain 'rights'. When a low-ranking chimp has had hunting success, a more dominant member of the group will *beg* him for a piece of the prey, but, as a rule, will not rob him. Usually, every animal has its fixed position within the group and knows what it may do and what not.

For maintaining a hierarchic order recognized techniques of submission are essential. They are part of the 'lubricant' that keeps the system running smoothly. When two gelada males unknown to each other are brought into an enclosure they start fighting, and a winner soon emerges. The loser then avoids his opponent whereupon *the behaviour of the stronger male changes.* He starts to approach the loser with friendly gestures. After a few hours the loser nervously presents his hindquarters in a gesture of submission, i.e. he behaves like a female. The winner then cautiously mounts him and makes a few symbolic movements as in a copulation. By this ceremony peace is ratified and a clear order of dominance established. The two males start to groom each other and on the next day they will forage side by side and behave in a relaxed way (Kummer, 1971, p. 112).

When two gelada females are put into the same situation, fighting will be shorter and less fierce, but a dominance order will nevertheless be established, and it will be sanctioned by the same ceremony of ritualized presenting and mounting. This has nothing to do with homosexuality. It is a sequence of submissive and reassuring gestures. It should be noted that submissive gestures, as a rule, are elements of female or infant behaviour, whereas superiority is shown by ritualized male behaviour patterns.

Patas monkeys do not have comparable gestures of submission. They live in loose groups of one male and several females. The male is programmed to attack violently and chase any other male – even his own sons as soon as they reach puberty. When two patas males are brought into an enclosure they also start fighting, but the loser cannot flee, and no matter how much he tries to withdraw from the winner the latter will seek him out and chase him every few minutes. 'After an hour or so the fleeing male would begin to scream, a rather unusual behaviour for an adult primate male', reports Hans Kummer on such an experiment (1971, p. 111–12). 'Eventually, after a day or two, the loser lay passively in a corner and refused to eat... Had he not been removed, he probably would have died from stress, although he was not wounded.'

High rank (dominance) is not always achieved by mere bodily strength only. Experience, intelligence, descent from a high-ranking mother or a clever 'policy of alliances' might place an individual in a much higher rank than might be expected from his bodily condition. Jane Goodall (1971, p. 109 *et seq.*) reports how a fairly young chimp male rose to the top of the hierarchy by using empty paraffin cans in his charging displays. With them he made such a hell of a noise that he intimidated even the most high-ranking males.

To achieve a high rank an animal must be bold, active, and aggressive. Aggressivity, as a rule, goes with a high level of the male sex hormone testosterone. By administering this hormone to an animal its aggressivity might be increased and it might move up a few steps on the dominance ladder in consequence (Wilson, 1975, p. 251; see also Allee *et al.*, 1939).

In experiments with mice, Dan Ely of the University of Akron, Ohio, found (1981) that dominant males had significantly higher testosterone levels than others and a much higher blood pressure. When a dominant male was removed from his group and kept alone his blood pressure returned to normal within a week, whereas the next one on the dominance ladder in the group who now occupied the top position developed hypertension within a short time. Castrated males had low testosterone levels and failed to establish a dominance order.

In socially living mammals or birds, males, as a rule, have a higher rank than females. One of the few exceptions is the hyena. 'Equal rights' in the sense of an individual dominance order irrespective of sex does not seem to exist in any species of higher vertebrates.

215

As mentioned before, high-ranking males have a monopoly, or at least a privileged position, as concerns access to females. High-ranking females, on the other hand, seem to copulate *less frequently* than females of lower rank in quite a number of species. In domestic fowl a high-ranking female seems to have difficulty in finding a mate, since only males of still higher rank are able to copulate with her (Wilson, 1975, p. 283, referring to Schjelderup-Ebbe, 1922, and Guhl, 1950). Similar problems seem to exist for high-ranking females in some monkey species as, for example, in rhesus monkeys (Wickler, 1969).

The reason for this seems to be that mating itself requires a strongly dominant behaviour of the male in many species. A successful male, writes K. Selander (1972, p. 215) about wild fowl like grouse 'must threaten and appease in a proper balance, so that the female will not flee but will, nonetheless, be completely subordinate and remain in a fixed position for copulation.'

In solitary species like martens a courting male approaching a female might first be considered as an intruder and be attacked. Such female aggressivity might have a selective advantage, since only strong males that are not intimidated by the female attack will eventually copulate.

In males of species with a seasonally fixed rutting period the level of sex hormones and aggressivity rise steeply at that time, and they start attacking not only actual rivals but everybody and anything. 'Hikers are well-advised to give adult male bison a wide berth in late September and October, although bison are relatively placid the rest of the year,' writes David Barash (1977, pp. 215–16). 'The frequency of collisions between Alaskan bull moose and automobiles rises dramatically in the autumn, and even freight trains are not immune!'

In females aggressivity rises conspicuously when they have small young. Hikers in Europe do not have a chance to meet a free-living bison as David Barash did in the USA, but when wandering in regions where there still are wild boars they had better avoid an encounter with a mother sow in spring time.

Dominance first of all means privileged access to food, and males, when they are the sex of higher rank, do use this prerogative without any hesitation. Even in lions where it is the females who, as a rule, do the hunting, the males take priority of access to the slain prey (see section 2.12). In quite a number of species from eagles to wolves the male very affectionately cares for a brooding or lactating female. On the other hand, there seems to be no species where stronger males let weaker females have a general priority. Such 'galantry' is a specifically human behaviour pattern.

3.17 *The myth of the matriarchy*

Amongst nearly 150 species of monkeys there are only a very few, like vervets and Sykes' monkeys, in which females are dominant (Wilson 1975, p. 291, quoting Rowell, 1971). In all ape species males have the superior rank. Thus there is every reason to assume male dominance amongst our animal and semi-human ancestors as well. Moreover, differences in body size, weight and strength also point to male superiority in humans.

In today's tribal peoples chiefs are practically always males. Amongst the North American Indians of the 19th century, studied in particular by Lewis H. Morgan, it was the same. According to his reports men *and women* voted when electing a chief, but there is no indication that a woman might have been elected to this office.

That human society in its primeval state had a matriarchal structure was first claimed by the Swiss scholar Johannes Jakob Bachofen. He was one of the first who, in a voluminous work published in 1861, had investigated the history of the human family. Bachofen was not an anthropologist but a scholar of old languages, and in his work he deals very thoroughly with ancient classical sources. The pivot of his ideas was the assumption, generally held in the nineteenth century, that unlimited promiscuity was the general rule in the animal kingdom, and that the primeval state of humans had been very similar to this. Since in such conditions paternity could not have been certain, descent could only be considered in the maternal line. The mother, according to Bachofen, was the highly respected head of the family. Therefore, he concluded, unrestricted power of women must have been the general rule in olden days.

Speaking at the Paris conference on *Female Phenomena* (see Sullerot, 1978) the French anthropologist Françoise Héritier declared that in her discipline these ideas are considered as mere myths. 'Matriarchal societies never existed,' she added. Actually, there still are some so-called primitive societies in which descent

217

is considered with respect to the maternal line. In such 'matri-linear' societies, membership of the group is bound to women and the name is taken over from the mother (and not from the father). But this, Héritier pointed out, does not mean that power is in the hands of women. The possession of ground, inheritance and political power – in the village or in larger units – is in the hands of men. Whereas in patrilinear societies fathers pass on possessions and power to their sons, in matrilinear societies they are passed on from the mother's brother to the nephew (See also Dahlberg, 1981, p. 19).

At the same conference Evelyne Sullerot said that believing in the idea of the matriarchy is something like an act of faith for the feministic movement. Many important groups of women, well educated and active in public life, tenaciously stick to this convic-tion. Any doubts on the existence of a matriarchal past or even a mere hint that it might only be a myth are considered as treason to the female cause.

Yet myths do not come about by mere chance, and Bachofen had studied the ancient literature very thoroughly. It is a fact that the myths of many peoples report a great upheaval when old matrilinear clans of deities were overthrown and power was taken over by new patrilinear clans of gods. Certainly such myths must have some sym-bolic meaning. How can they be explained if there never has been a human society organized on matriarchal lines?

What I am going to offer here is my own tentative explanation. Today we know that the pivot of Bachofen's ideas – considered obvious in the nineteenth century – is very weak indeed. Promiscuity is by no means the 'natural' state in all animal societies. It is rather unlikely that 'free love', as in chimps, was the general rule for evolv-ing humans. If the family of our ancestors had a polygamous struc-ture as do hamadryas baboons, geladas and (probably) gorillas there might never have been a state of affairs in which paternity was uncertain in the sense that Bachofen assumed.

Thinking in the last century, however, was tied so much to the idea of a primeval state of promiscuity and subsequent changes in family *structure* that it did not even consider the other side of the coin: that a patrilinear structure of society presupposes *the know-ledge* (the realization of the fact) *that every human being has a father.* Animals certainly do not know this, even if they live in a family struc-ture which, for a human observer, makes paternity as evident as in

218

a monogamous couple. And reportedly there were Australian tribes even in our century who did not yet know the causal link between sexual intercourse and procreation (F. G. Rose, 1968, p. 200).

Actually, this link is by no means as obvious as it seems to us today. First of all, there is a long time lapse between cause and effect. Secondly many acts of sexual intercourse remain without consequences. Girls in tribal societies may be sexually active for several years before becoming pregnant for the first time. Nursing mothers, as a rule, do not conceive – at least in living conditions of a primeval peoples. There are infertile women and others who, by mere chance, do not become pregnant for a while though having a normal sex life. Thus, recognizing the causal link required much observation and hard thinking.

Moreover, the idea of paternity includes that a human can have *only one father* even if his or her mother had intercourse with several men; and that children of the same father are siblings and kin no less than children of the same mother. If the original human way of life was a polygynous family the realization of this fact must have been of enormous practical and emotional importance.

An ape or a monkey still knows its mother when it is adult, and respects her. The emotional notion of a father as experienced by children in a modern human monogamous family is known only to the few monogamous species like gibbon or siamang. In the emotional world of a chimpanzee or an orang-utan there seems to be no father at all. For a young gorilla or gelada the presumed father, i.e. the dominant male, is an important but rather remote authority – certainly emotionally much farther away than the mother or the (maternal) siblings. How such a situation influences the emotional life of a human child will probably be better understood when the psychology of people who grew up in a harem has been as thoroughly investigated as that of people of the Western world.

In most monkeys and apes there are strong emotional ties between children of the same mother, ties that persist in adult life. The emotional and still less the 'intellectual' notion of a paternal (half) sibling does not seem to exist at all for a chimp or an orang-utan, and for a gorilla or a gelada these paternal half-sibs are other members of his group, but farther removed than the other children of his own mother who, presumably are mostly his full siblings.

Irrespective of whether the original human group was promiscuous as in chimps or polygamous as in gorillas or geladas, it can be assumed that in the psychological make-up that we inherited from our ancestors the mother and maternal siblings are figures nearer to us than the father. This was the very ancient basis of 'mother right' stemming from pre-human days and deeply rooted in the emotional constitution of early man. Thus the transition to the ideas of paternity and paternal rights must indeed have been a veritable psychological revolution, and it is not surprising that this is a repeatedly recurring theme of horrible old myths of many peoples.

The high respect of monkeys and apes for their mothers does not alter the fact that males are the dominant sex in nearly all monkey and ape species. Neither can a matrilinear organization, as presumably was customary in early human societies, be considered as a proof against male supremacy. Friedrick Engles' view, presented in his famous book *The Origin of the Family* . . . that *de facto* subordination of women did not start before the end of primeval societies, i.e. with the transition to private property and the division of society into classes, most probably is wrong. In nomadic peoples living as gatherers and hunters young women are bartered by elder men (see section 3.10). This, of course, does not exclude that with the transition to new social conditions *new forms* of supression of women emerged that were not known before.

Most tribal peoples have a strict role division between men and women – exactly the contrary of what the women's movement demands today. And women, it seems, were at a disadvantage in this role division since the most ancient times. The males as a rule, did the 'noble hunting', which was considered as something of a sport, whereas the women collected the vegetables which served as staple foods. Even if gathering of nuts, seeds, berries or roots did not require more than a few hours a day it still was rather monotonous work – much more of a toilsome labour than the thrilling hunting.

When I had written the above paragraph for the German version of this book several women readers pointed out to me that I might have looked at this problem through masculine spectacles. They *like* gathering jobs such as picking berries, they told me, and did not consider them to be toilsome or boring. 'I have never wanted to hunt in my life, but I love nutting, berry-picking and foraging generally,' Mary Midgley wrote to me. 'I don't think it is convincing to suggest

220

that a distribution of labour which rested solely or mainly on the grabbing of the best jobs by the top boys would be possible in a hunter/gatherer group. Social good feeling matters to everybody; you can't make people work at things they don't like when you haven't got either a developed wage-system or a police force.'

If one looks at modern society there is, of course, no absolute dichotomy but rather a strongly different frequency distribution of inclinations in men and women. In a large sample one probably will find a few women who like hunting and a few men who don't; on the other hand there will be many women but probably much fewer men who like berry-picking. The very rigid sex-linked division of labour as practised in most of today's hunter/gatherer tribes might have a 'natural' base but it probably forces a minority of women as well as of men to do jobs they don't like.

In chimps both sexes gather, whereas hunting is a predominantly but not exclusively male occupation. We do not know when and how sex-linked division of labour evolved in our ancestors. Possibly there really was a *previously* existing difference in inclinations (as it were, a 'pre-adaptation') in pre-humans or early humans. On the other hand today's differences of inclinations might be a *consequence* of an adaptation to external circumstances that favoured a sex-linked division of labour in our early ancestors.

Anyway, the main demands of the women's movement of our days – equal chances in vocational life and partnership in matrimony, with equal sharing of the joys and the burdens – are intrinsically modern demands. In may view they are justified and in no way 'contrary to human nature'. *For it is natural* for any social creature to adapt to new environmental conditions with new social structures. Hence I believe that these demands have a good chance of being gradually fulfilled. But their implementation *would not be a return* to a natural state when all men and women were living in freedom and equality. There never was such a primeval golden age.

221

4

Is sociobiology a reactionary science?

4.1 *Pseudo-science or real science?*

With the advent of modern science in the seventeenth century several branches of former scholarly tradition were relegated to the realm of pseudo-sciences. Amongst them were astrology and alchemy, and also phytognomy, a branch of knowledge that ascribed medical powers to plants according to their suggestive shapes – for instance, assuming that a plant with heart-shaped leaves would be apt for treating heart trouble.

Phytognomy could draw from millennia of folk tradition. There was a wealth of accumulated empirical knowledge on the medical powers of plants. Asking *why* certain plants have certain medical effects was by no means unreasonable. But the way in which phytognomy tried to answer this question and to bring existing experiences into a system was inherently wrong.

Today we know that plants have medical powers because they contain certain active substances. One can extract these substances or produce them synthetically and one can define their pharmacological effects. But *why* they have such effects is not yet clear in many cases. Even today medicine is often a merely empirical science. But we know at least for sure that the medical powers of a plant cannot be predicted or deduced from its shape. Phytognomy was rightly considered as a pseudo-science giving worthless answers to non-existent problems.

There are scientists nowadays who would like to relegate sociobiology also to the realm of pseudo-sciences. According to the American philosopher Richard M. Burian, the establishment of sociobiology as an autonomous discipline only would lead to the production of pseudo-solutions to pseudo-problems (in Caplan, 1978, p. 393). Of course, nobody denies that the question of how social behaviour did evolve is a real problem demanding an answer consistent with Darwinian principles. But sociobiology, in the view of its critics, tries to find the answer with a wrong approach: by simplifying the influences of genes on behaviour.

Burian, along with the well-known population geneticist Richard Lewontin (1977), and others too, reproach sociobiology for 'explaining too much' (see also Allen *et al.*, 1976). By referring to *all* mechanisms dealt with in chapter 1 of this book, i.e. to individual selection, group selection, kin selection, recriprocal altruism, etc. 'it becomes a highly amusing parlour game to see who can devise the best evolutionary account showing how an arbitrarily chosen behaviour could have become fixed in a given population,' they say (Burian, 1978, p. 382); but in their view it is impossible to test the correctness of such a set of assumptions as is required in any serious science.

I, for my part, do not think that such a critique is convincing. Animal behaviour, after all, is complex, and subject to many factors influencing it. To try to explain all its phenomena with one single theory would seem much more unscientific to me. For instance, as I see it, Wilson ought to be criticized for relying *too much* on kin selection and sometimes giving not enough consideration to other possible explanations (see section 1.15).

Meanwhile the claim that sociobiology inherently can only produce untestable ideas has been refuted. The assumption of Trivers and Hare (see section 1.14) that in social insects parental investment into the two sexes should be within the limits of 1 : 1 to 1 : 3 in favour of female reproductives is testable – and turns out to be wrong. In many instances the above limits are widely exceeded on either side. This does not mean that all the pertinent deliberations of the two authors need necessarily be wrong, but evidently there are other factors too influencing the numerical relations of reproductives in insect colonies.

Hamilton's idea that evolution of social insects can be explained by the fact that sisters in hymenoptera have more genes in common than mother and daughter can be tested – and turns out to be insufficient. As I have tried to show in sections 1.13 and 1.14 of this book, there are a number of facts that cannot be explained by this hypothesis – but manipulation by the queen alone cannot explain

223

all the facts either. Neither idea is mutually exclusive, and if one relies on both of them and on some others as well one can get a fairly plausible story consistent with known facts of how social insects *might* have evolved. Of course, this is only a preliminary hypothesis that needs further testing. Presumably one will find new facts in future work and will have to develop new hypotheses to replace the old ones that no longer fit the facts–but that is a perfectly normal process in the progress of science and not a peculiarity of sociobiology.

'Different social groups arise and persist for different reasons, and no general theory is possible that will ever satisfactorily explain every case,' states one of the group reports of the Dahlem Conference on the Evolution of Social Behaviour (Oster *et al.*, 1980); and the authors, amongst them several with a rather critical attitude towards sociobiology, continue: 'Indeed it is doubtful whether unequivocal explanations are in principle obtainable, and we will always have to be satisfied with a set of "most plausible" stories.' Theory, they add, cannot but provide a list of possible mechanisms which give some qualitative insights into one of the major mysteries of social behaviour: the origin and maintenance of altruism. These theoretical models, they conclude, 'must be applied to a great number of specific systems before general principles are likely to emerge'.

For many scientists studying the behaviour of individual species in the field, sociobiology has brought a wealth of new ideas, turning their attention to questions hitherto not investigated, and this has led to the discovery of quite a number of new and interesting facts (see sections 1.8 and 1.9). To me it seems that this is the most important test for the usefulness of a new theory. Field-workers spurred by Hamilton's ideas to elucidate kin relations in animal societies can hardly be said to deal with mere pseudo-problems of no more importance for animal behaviour than the shapes of plants are for their medical powers.

Certainly sociobiology is as yet a very young and immature branch of science and like every new discipline it has to start with certain assumptions, working hypotheses, and thinking models that must as yet be tested for their validity and their possible range of application. This, in my view, is sometimes not sufficiently emphasized by either its adherents or its critics; in particular, such a

224

cautionary note seems to be badly lacking in some of the more popular accounts (see for instance, Dawkins, 1976; Barash, 1977; Wickler and Seibt 1977).

In science there often is a long way from the first idea to its verification or – partial or total – rejection. It takes time to sort out the wheat from the chaff, to uncover inconsistencies, to formulate newly arising problems of second order and to refine originally crude general insights. Sociobiology has as yet only started to go the first steps on this way. It certainly will be considerably modified and transformed in the times to come, because the mere fact that somebody recognizes a problem and asks sensible questions does not necessarily mean that he will find the correct answers. Today it is certainly far too early to pass a final judgement on the value or otherwise of the sociobiological enterprise, but I cannot see a reason why a new discipline that has given such a valuable impetus to so many scientists should be relegated to the realm of pseudo-sciences right from the start. 'Regardless of the whether socio-biology has or has not any substantial achievements to its credit, it would be downright cranky for any biologist to deny that the professed general scientific goal of sociobiology is intrinsically worthwhile,' writes Gunther Stent (1981), a German biologist, now professor at the University of California in Berkeley, though he holds a rather critical view of this new discipline.

4.2 *Colloquial language as technical terms*

'To be fit' has a definite meaning in ordinary every-day language. Yet when Darwin used the phrase of the 'survival of the fittest' he certainly was thinking of *more* than a mere good bodily condition. But what, indeed, did he really mean?

'"Fitness" has the special technical meaning of reproductive success,' writes Richard Dawkins (1976, p. 146). Hence 'the fittest,' is the one with the highest reproductive success, and if one is not careful 'survival of the fittest' can become a circular definition, saying that 'the fittest' (the one with the highest reproductive success) survives because ... he has the highest reproductive success and therefore passes on most genes to future generations. Quite rightly, Dawkins remarks (*ibid.*, p. 147) that by using the term 'fitness' one easily treads on slippery ground. Moreover, by

225

using the term in a technical way but without quotation marks one can arrive at very odd sentences indeed. What would you think when you read that 'a male harem master is more fit than a female harem member' (Barash, 1977, p. 178)? That he does more sporting exercises than his wives? (What is really meant, of course, is that he has more children than any of his wives – but why not say so?)

Not only 'fitness' but 'survival' as well has another meaning in Darwin's phrase than in ordinary language. The male mantis being killed during copulation by the female – she might start eating his head whilst his sperms still flows into her genital tract –'survives' in a Darwinistic sense, since he has begotten progeny. A male wanting to survive in the ordinary sense of the word and therefore avoiding such a dangerous mate does not achieve any Darwinian 'fitness' at all, since he will pass on no genes to future generations.

Neo-Darwinists, in my view, would have been well advised to coin a very highbrow Greek or Latin term for Darwinian 'fitness'. Laymen would at least notice at once that they do not know the meaning of it, whereas experts, one hopes, would really know what they are talking about. For, after all, the idea of the 'survival of the fittest' is by no means a vacuous or merely circular definition, but a very deep insight. 'Fitness' can be *measured* in reproductive success, but it is not simply identical to it, as Dawkins writes. Rather it means a certain genetic constitution *enabling* an individual to achieve high (or low) reproductive success; or, to be more exact, conferring on an individual the statistical probability of having a certain reproductive success in the average of many future generations.

For this to become true, many factors must contribute: a good bodily constitution is just as necessary as learning ability, the capacity for finding a good mate (even if it might cost life as for honey-bee drones or for the mantis male), and perhaps the ability to rear young properly. To be fit, one must be well adapted to existing environmental conditions, yet nevertheless be able to produce progeny with a certain bandwith of traits enabling some of them to intrude into neighbouring slightly different environments or, if necessary, to 'adapt' to environmental change. Thus 'fitness' means in many cases first of all *the ability to find a viable compromise* in order to be able to fullfil diverse and even contradictory demands that nature poses to a certain individual or species (see section 1.5). It is not so easy to be 'fit' in a Darwinian sense.

Ethologists and sociobiologists unfortunately followed this Darwinistic tradition of using words of the every-day language as technical terms with a special connotation. In this way not only laymen sometimes get confused. Biologists speak of 'culture' and mean any behaviour learned from others, whereas the horticulture of leaf cutting ants is no 'culture' to them because the behaviour is inborn (see sections 2.3 and 2.4). Sociobiologists start by using every-day words within quotation marks in order to indicate that they have given them a special connotation, then omit the quotation marks because it is too tedious continually to use them, and finally they are inclined to mix up the ordinary and the special meaning of the words.

'The trouble about this is that it is simply not possible to use words of strong everyday import in a private and peculiar sense,' writes Mary Midgley (1981). 'The whole nature of language prevents such a detachment of meaning from habitual background. Anyone using words like this *must* mislead his audience. What is still more serious, unless he is exceptionally sharp and sophisticated, he will certainly *mislead himself*, slipping into the everyday opinions which he supposes are no part of his scientific business. It is clear that this has happened in sociobiology.'

Sociobiologists often do not differentiate clearly between the *intention* and the *result* of a certain behaviour. Of course, one cannot repeat in every other sentence that natural selection puts a premium on instinctive behaviour that ensures maximum reproductive success and that hence... The temptation to use incorrect 'teleological' language – i.e. a language imputing to an animal intentions it really does not have – is strong when writing on such topics. Maybe a critical reader of this book has occasionally found examples where I too have slipped in this direction. But sociobiologists should at least try to avoid such wrong and misleading use of words and concentrate on making clear what they really want to say. In Barash's book (1977, p. 180), to give one striking example, one can read that animal parents, when they '*insist*' on having progeny that need intense brood care, '*have no choice*' but to produce fewer of them. Here the incorrect use of language is very evident.

On the other hand a fuzzy teleological language can well serve to obfuscate the fact that the real delimitations between intention and instinct are not always easy to draw. What, for instance, is the exact meaning of 'maternal manipulation' when applied to social insects?

A bee queen has a gland that produces a sterilizing substance and bee workers are innately programmed to be addicted to this substance (see section 1.14). In many ant species the same effect, however, comes about in quite a different way: the queen eats or destroys eggs laid by the workers. Is such a queen genetically preprogrammed to behave in that way following blindly her instinct 'without realising what she does'? Or does she have a certain 'intention'? Can an ant have 'intentions', anyway? And if not, on which evolutionary level can one assume such a capability? Does an ape have 'intentions'? And, conversely, might not a person too who believes that he or she is deciding freely in reality be merely following instinct?

Biologists do not always answer such questions very clearly. Sometimes it is not easy to recognize whether they really think in a teleological way or, rather, use a confusing 'simplifying' language. But this applies not only to sociobiology. The idea of 'manipulation' by the queen in social insects was brought up by zoologists who are rather critical towards sociobiology. Critics from the realms of social sciences or the humanities ought to realize that philosophers and psychologists too do not always make it clear what they think about these problems. For it obviously is a difficult question whether man – not to mention apes and other animals – does really have something like a 'free will'.

Words like 'egoism' and 'altruism' too have their special connotations as sociobiological technical terms. When they are used in everyday language one thinks of the intentions of the actor. Sociobiologists, on the other hand, look solely at the result and thus they can speak about 'unselfish' corals of amoebae (see section 1.12), 'altruistic' viruses (Wilson, 1975, p. 116) and devise a book title like Richard Dawkins' well known *Selfish Gene*.

Yet this gene to which Dawkins imputes selfishness is not the gene of molecular biologists either. It is not a recipe for the production of an enzyme, nor an individual regulating gene, but, as Dawkins (1976, p. 30) puts it, paraphrasing G. C. Williams, 'any portion of chromosomal material which potentially lasts for enough generations to to serve as a unit of natural selection'. Gunther Stent quite appropriately sneers (1981) that Dawkins' selfish gene 'is neither selfish, in the context of morality, nor is it a gene, in the context of genetics'.

Wilson, too uses the term 'gene' rather loosely. Referring to man he writes about genes for spite, homosexuality and conformism

(1975, pp. 119, 555, 562). Of course, he knows very well that if there is any genetic influence at all on such traits, it is the result of the combined effects of many genes that are not necessarily inherited together. On the other hand the working group of the Dahlem Conference on the Evolution of Social Behaviour mentioned in the last chapter (Oster *et al.*, 1980) considers such simplification as justified. Even if there are many genes influencing a specific trait one can assume that in the long run natural selection can change the frequency of the individual genes contributing to such a trait in accordance with its selective advantage or otherwise. But whether there really are such things as genes causing an inborn tendency towards conformism remains a matter of dispute.

Critics of sociobiology argue that using terms of everyday language with special, technical connotations is particularly questionable when comparing animals with man (see Allen *et al.*, 1976; Solomon *et al.*, 1978). 'Slavery' in ants is something other than slavery in man, and one should not simply 'omit the quotation marks' without checking whether the two phenomena are in any way comparable (see section 2.11). On the other hand Maynard Smith and other participants at the Dahlem Conference on Morality as a Biological Phenomenon were no less justified in pointing out that too much linguistic purism might restrain creative thought, since man often thinks in loose anãlogies. Or, as the Oxford philosopher B. A. O. Williams put it in the final session of the conference: what is seen as 'slippage' of terms by some might be the first step to a valuable generalization for others.

Konrad Lorenz repeatedly has been put down as an anthropomorphizing romantic for imputing 'motives' and 'intentions' to his geese and sticklebacks. Sociobiologists try to avoid this reproach by looking solely at the results and not at the intention of an act when speaking about the 'altruistic' behaviour of an animal. But man as well can behave 'altruistically' in this sociobiological sense, and there is not always a clear border line between altruism with and without quotation marks.

This is not really surprising either, for what critics of sociobiology, in my view, do not sufficiently pay attention to is the fact that man, after all, is a descendant of animals and that human behaviour must have evolved from animal behaviour. Man is less influenced by his instincts than an ape who in turn is less dependent on them than an ant, but these are differences in degree and not in principle. There is no Great Wall of China between human and animal behaviour.

There are slight differences *within* our species as well. As Mary Midgley repeatedly points out there are children of diverse ages and stages of development. There are psychologically deviant criminals. But even in the case of a normal and fully responsible person a judge may acknowledge that he or she acted under the influence of an 'irresistible force' and grant mitigating circumstances.

While arguing whether there really are genes for this or that behaviour pattern found in animals or men, proponents as well as critics of sociobiology sometimes apparently neglect an aspect that seems very important to me: *sociobiology is not a mere genetical theory* but, according to Wilson's definition, 'the systematic study of the biological basis of all social behaviour' (1975, p. 3). Part of this basis certainly is the *learning ability* of animal, and still more of human, societies. A troop of baboons, macaques or chimpanzees is able to develop new 'cultural traditions' (see section 2.4) and to adapt in this way much quicker than by genetic evolution to changed external circumstances. This applies even more so to man. The immense diversity of human societies cannot be explained by genetic differences, but mainly by cultural differences. Sociobiologists might have avoided a lot of trouble had they always emphasized that with the required clarity.

4.3 *Is Wilson really a fascist?*

In the introduction of her book *Le Fait Feminin* (1978) Evelyne Sullerot, certainly not a reactionary but a progressive, reports on the many difficulties she had to face when preparing her conference (see also section 3.12 of this book). 'The fear of being considered as reactionary if one dares to speak of genetics or if one does not use exclusively the analytical methods and the vocabulary of feminism, as has become customary in the universities as well as in public discussions, induced many [of the scientists invited to attend] to use all sorts of evasions and excuses.' People advised her to desist from the idea of this conference and some tried to intimidate her. When she told all this to Jacques Monod his determination was only reinforced all the more. 'He was much too progressive in his thoughts as well as in his actions to let himself be stopped by taboos, even if in this case they came from the left. Moreover he detested any abuse of science for dogmatic purposes just as well as dubious teleological arguments serving reactionary thinking. Even more he rejected the arrogant method of putting forward claims without proof or without at least attempts to obtain proof while, simultaneously, intimidating those who look for the truth.'

Sociobiology often has to suffer under a similar intolerance of doctrinaire left-wingers who consider themselves to be the only true guardians of the Holy Grail of progressive thought and are all too quickly prepared to call everything not fitting into their preconceived notions as 'reactionary', 'racist' or 'fascist'.

'At Harvard I taught sociobiology in 1979 and 1980,' Paul Harvey, an ethologist and ecologist, told me, 'Wilson couldn't; he would be shouted down by the students.'

At the annual meeting of the American Association for the Advancement of Science (AAAS) in February 1978, a symposium on sociobiology was held. As Wilson was announced to speak in the final public session a group of fifteen young people ran onto the podium with a poster declaring Wilson to be 'the racist and fascist scientist of the year'. One of them tipped a jug of water over Wilson's head (*New Scientist*, 1978).

When I was young such methods of 'discussion' were themselves considered as fascist and were mainly practised by radicals of the right, not of those of the left. But there is more to this than the mere question of methods. Sometimes I wonder whether these young left radicals, who so loosely use terms like 'fascist' or 'fascistoid', actually have any idea what a real fascist is like – or whether this term too has been 'generalized' so much that it lost any real meaning.

For me fascism is not a mere theoretical notion; I have practical experience. I was born in Vienna in 1919 and went to school in Austria in the years between the two World Wars. I have experienced what the intellectual climate of a country is like when extremely reactionary, chauvinistic, revanchistic, racist and indeed fascist ideas are expounded at its universities and higher schools which intrude into most of the school books and into the heads of many teachers, students and pupils. I know very well the phrasing and the accent of racists and fascists and still have a good ear for it. And I know what it is like when fascism conquers power.

231

Wilson is reproached for 'racism' and occasionally it is mentioned that he was born in the deep south of the USA. I cannot judge whether he is influenced by sentiments widely rampant there. I did not notice anything like that in his books, but readers might just as well form their own opinion of the following passage from *On Human Nature* (1978a, p. 136):

'In the United States, slave families were frequently broken up during sales. African customs were disregarded, and neither marriage nor parenthood were given legal protection. Yet kin groups survived for generations, individual kin were classified, children were assigned familial surnames, and incest taboos were observed faithfully. The Africans' attachment to their families remained deep and emotional. . . According to the historian Herbert G. Gutman [1976], networks of this kind, many unknown to the slave owners, extended throughout the South. Today, they persist with little or no dilution in the most impoverished ghettos. As Carol Stack has shown in her remarkable book *All Our Kin* [1974], detailed knowledge of relatives and an unquestioning code of mutual loyalty are the very basis of survival among the poorest American blacks.'

I have never seen a supporter of Nazi race theory write in a similar vein about Jews.

Whoever wants to know what a pseudo-science that indeed can be called racist and fascist is like ought to look into the standard work of 'race theory' published in Germany as early as the twenties: *Menschliche Erblehre und Rassenhygiene* (Human hereditary theory and race hygiene) by E. Baur, E. Fischer and F. Lenz. The first two of them were well-known geneticists, but in this book they misused their authority to confer some scientific prestige on a book expounding racist and political prejudices.

The main content of this race theory is a glorification of the so-called 'Nordic race' which, it is claimed, 'marches in the vanguard of humanity as concerns intellectual gifts' (p. 737). It is to this race 'that ancient Greece ows its golden age, . . . to it the world is indebted for the German cultural achievements' (p. 316). One should note the fine distinction: the world has to be thankful for German culture, whereas the Greeks have to be thankful to the Nordic race. 'The Nordic man,' one reads, 'is the one least dedicated to the moment, he is superior to all other races by the energy of his will. . . Whenever

232

trouble is to be mitigated by a bold attack, the Nordic man is there' (p. 737).

It is rather a tough job to translate this bombastic rhetoric, but I want to try to give to English speaking readers at least a faint idea of what was considered a 'science' in Germany many years before Hitler's advent to power. There are no proofs offered for the claims of this 'theory', nor criteria for its value judgements. 'If we consider our race as unique and without anything equal to it, such a judgement can neither be proven nor refuted,' writes Lenz. Neither, of course, can he prove his claim that the population of southern Europe is intellectually inferior to that of northern Europe, and that of eastern Europe to that of western Europe (p. 729).

The Slavs, in particular, are inferior. Said to originate from a mixture of Europeans and Mongols, they are 'of little intellectual activity, bound to tradition and dissolving in the community; they are a fertile ground for mass suggestion and mandarinism' (p. 725). Hence, of course, they are quite the reverse of the Nordic Germans who just in that period showed how little they are susceptible to mass suggestion and Führer cult!

Special scorn is reserved by the race theorists for the Jews: 'They detest hard bodily work. Hardly any of them work on the land. Considering their small talents and little inclination for primary production a state consisting solely of Jews seems impossible' (p. 749). As can be seen in Israel, where, whatever one may think about Zionism, young people have proved that Jews certainly are capable of transforming desert into blossoming gardens.

'The Jewish race', writes Lenz, 'has been described as a race of parasites. Undoubtedly Jews can become a grave danger to their host people.' One ought to read these sentences twice to realize their abysmal inhumanity. The notion of 'host' is borrowed from parasitology. People are compared here to pests that ought to be anihilated.

Hitler later practised what these 'race theorists' had preached. Millions of Jews, Gypsies, Slavs and members of other 'inferior races' were brought to the gas chambers to be killed – with a poison declared to be an insecticide – how fittingly!

Millions of people were killed, not because they had *done* anything; their whole 'guilt' had been to belong to a wrong 'race'. Such is the real face of fascism.

Whatever objections there might be against Wilson and socio-biology in general, I think it is making fascism look rather harmless to use the term in this context. The orders of magnitude simply do not fit.

Such absurd and, at the very least, highly inflated reproaches must first of all be removed before one can seriously discuss the question whether Wilson and/or other sociobiologists are indeed expounding reactionary ideas; or whether the whole sociobiological enterprise inherently must lead to conclusions liable to be abused for propping up reactionary ideologies.

4.4 *Unscientific comparisons*

In 1940, when 'race theory' was rampant in Nazi Germany, the later Nobel laureate Konrad Lorenz published a paper claiming that a rather large number of inheritable traits to be observed in 'super-civilized inhabitants of large cities' can be compared with domestication effects in animals. According to what he wrote at that time 'healthy' members of a species as a rule have an inborn sense of beauty preventing them from mating a degenerated individual. Hence degeneracy would not spread within the species. When looking for the 'socially most valuable' member of a group of greylag geese, Lorenz claimed, one would hardly make a mistake when selecting the most beautiful.

In man, too, he wrote, this rule originally had been valid. 'As long as a tribe or a people has a high degree of racial uniformity, it is possible and justified to judge an individual according to his outwardly visible traits only and to deduce from them his inner norms of behaviour.' In modern city-dwellers, however, this mechanism seemed threatened to Lorenz: 'Our species-specific sensitivity to the beauty and ugliness of members of our species is intimately connected with symptoms of degeneration caused by domestication, which threaten our race.'

How a Hitler or a Goebbels corresponded to the natural sense of beauty in 'our race', Lorenz cautiously refrained from analysing. He dwelt instead on the then popular topic of 'decadent art', on the 'high reproductive rate of the moral imbecile', whatever that may mean, and on the 'people's physician' who had to cull 'socially inferior human material' – meaning at that time that the insane and imbecilic were sent to the gas chambers, as well as members of 'inferior races'.

There also is a disapproving reference to 'some nations' that 'curiously still reject the racial idea, even consider efforts of racial biology to balance bodily traits as offending the dignity of man, and that do not object to the mixing of races in man whereas they are very keen on racial purity and long pedigrees as soon as not men but domestic animals are concerned.'

'The selection for toughness, heroism, and social utility,' Lorenz concludes, 'must be accomplished by some human institution if mankind, in default of selective factors, is not to be ruined by dom-estication-induced degeneracy. The racial idea as the basis of our state has already accomplished much in this respect. The Nordic movement always intuitively opposed the 'domestication' of man. . . The most effective race-preserving measure is the greatest support of the natural defences. We must – and should – rely in this respect on the healthy feelings of our Best and charge them with the selection which will determine the prosperity or decay of our people.'

Of course, Lorenz later disclaimed the ideas expounded in this paper, but actually it is not an exaggeration to call them racist and fascist. Moreover they are a veritable paradigm of a superficial and unscientific argument. Within one sentence Lorenz speaks of 'members of our *species*', a term which, when used by a biologist, evidently must mean '*all* men' including Gypsies, Jews and members of other 'inferior races', and then, suddenly, he jumps to 'domes-tication threatening our *race*'. Mentioning 'racial purity' he dodges the issue of this being *not* a natural state in wild animals but some-thing enforced onto domesticated animals by man; a state which, moreover, breaks down as soon as the animals have a chance of free choice. Quite in line with the Nazi myths of '*Blut und Boden*' (blood and soil) Lorenz refers to the big cities as centres of degeneration side-stepping the fact that – apart from the high nobility – it is mainly in small mostly inbreeding populations of remote villages, valleys or islands and *not* in the panmictic great centres of popula-tion where real and obvious human degeneracy can be found. All this can only be classified as an attempt to adapt in content as well as in phraseology to a pseudo-science then in vogue in Nazi Germany.

Only three years later, in 1943, *Science* in the USA published a paper of the ethologist W. C. Allee, discussing implications of biological thinking on the ideas for the world order after the end of the war. His basic claim is 'that the idea of a ruthless struggle for existence is not the whole, or even the major contribution of current biology to social philosophy and social ethics'. In his view not only selfish but also co-operative forces influence animal behaviour; hence it could be assumed that not only selfish tendencies in man but also human altruistic drives and 'our tendencies toward goodness' are innate and 'as firmly based on an animal ancestry as is man himself.'

I am not quite sure whether everything Allee wrote in this paper is perfectly sound scientifically. Nevertheless I found it very gratifying reading; for the claims of 'social Darwinism' (see section 2.2), which are criticized by Allee, certainly are scientifically and philosophically much more questionable.

Basing himself on ideas of a Christian humanism Allee declared 'that the data of biology, if properly understood, do not furnish sound support for a social philosophy based primarily on the idea that might makes right in interpersonal contacts or in international relations'. He then presented several proposals for the post-war order, not necessarily designed to make himself popular with the ruling circles of his own country: disarmament, relief to *all* suffering peoples in Europe without any political preconditions, no punishment for defeated *peoples* which by no means should be treated as Nazi Germany had treated her victims.

A world organization based on dominance and subordination is somewhat like a peck order in the hen-house, Allee claims. Yet, 'solidly as the peck-right system is grounded in animal behaviour, it is not the only pattern for human action that biology has to offer... The difficulties in the transition from the power politics of the international peck order system to a system based on international cooperation are impressive. The change is possible... We must remember always that in such matters the idealist with the long-range view is frequently the true realist.'

As I see it, the conviction expressed here deserves to be regarded highly and with the warmest sympathy; and there hardly will be anybody who would criticize Allee for 'abusing science for humanistic purposes'. Nevertheless it seems to me that his comparison of the pecking order in the hen-house with the power politics among nations is somewhat questionable. Unscientific comparisons are not a privilege for reactionaries and fascists only.

In sociobiological writings, as far as I know them, I never found anything expounding racist or fascist ideas in a similar vein to that of Lorenz's above-mentioned paper. On the other hand I repeatedly read analogies between animals and man which to me seemed not to be well founded. Wilson has emphasized more than once that it will not be possible to judge properly the value of sociobiology for the study of man until there are workers trained in social sciences who try to integrate sociobiological ideas into their own fields. Hitherto there are very few who have done so. All the greater is the temptation for sociobiologists to draw the detailed investigation of human social behaviour into their own field of research – and by doing so they understandably do not just meet with unequivocal approval of social and human scientists.

A good example for such an incursion into a foreign field is Hamilton's paper on *Innate Social Aptitudes of Man* (1975). The basic idea is that in modern society people mainly interact with unrelated individuals (non-kin), and this is why Hamilton thinks that altruism must be reduced. Such a theoretical expectation might be right or wrong, and nobody would have blamed the author if he had confined himself to just state it and had left it to sociologists or historians to check whether the facts fit to this theory – for evidently he, as a theoretical biologist, is not in a proper position to do so. Yet, unfortunately, Hamilton did not go for wise restraint. Rather he dealt at length with this idea and in a way which, to quote the anthropologist S. L. Washburn (1978a), 'illustrates what may happen when a person who has made major contributions to the theory of natural selection discusses human evolution'. The following is a passage from Hamilton's paper:

'The incursions of barbaric pastoralists seem to do civilizations less harm in the long run than one might expect. Indeed, two dark ages and renaissances in Europe suggest a recurring pattern in which a renaissance follows an incursion by about 800 years. It may even be suggested that certain genes or traditions of the pastoralists revitalize the conquered people with an ingredient of progress which tends to die out in a large panmictic population for the reasons already discussed. I have in mind altruism itself, or the part of altruism which is perhaps better described as selfsacrificial daring. By the time of the renaissance it may be that the mixing of genes and cultures (or of cultures alone if these are the only vehicles, which I doubt) has continued long enough to bring the old mercantilic thoughtfulness and the infused daring into conjunction in a few individuals who then find courage for all kinds of inventive innovation against the resistance of established thought and practice. Often however, the cost in fitness of such altruism and sublimated pugnacity to the individuals concerned is by no means metaphorical, and the benefits to the fitness, such as they are, go to a mass of individuals whose genetic correlation with the innovator must be slight indeed. Thus civilization probably slowly reduces its altruism of all kinds, including the kinds needed for cultural creativity.'

In my view one cannot but agree with Washburn when he calls this passage an 'absurdity'. Characterizing the whole of Hamilton's paper he says that it consists of: '(1) useful genetic theory, briefly presented and clearly discussed; (2) practically no effort to uncover the facts of human evolution, of recent human history, or of animal behaviour; (3) conclusions which are personal biases, stemming from neither facts nor theories.' This, he continues, 'is the general form through which sociobiology is applied to the interpretation of human behaviour.'

But what is claimed in the last sentence cannot be proved by merely quoting a few examples. And even if Washburn were able to show that *everything* stated by sociobiologists on man so far is no more than superficial and unscientific nonsense, it would still not prove that sociobiological ideas used by scientists properly trained in the fields investigating man and his society could not help to get valuable new insights.

Nevertheless scholars in these fields have ample reason to be worried. If even a scientist of the rank of W. D. Hamilton can present such evident nonsense with the true ring of a scientific authority, how can one prevent such utterances being declared as 'science' and used for the justification of all sorts of preconceived ideas? And how can one be sure *that nonsense is always recognized as such* if perhaps it is not as evident as in the above-mentioned examples?

It is much easier to ask such questions than to answer them. Not only sociobiologists occasionally produce nonsense, but also

238

representatives of other fields of natural and social sciences which nevertheless cannot all be declared to be pseudo-sciences. On the other hand many really great new insights were not recognized as such at first and were declared to be 'nonsense' by many contemporaries including eminent scientists. Often it takes quite a long time to find out who was right and who was not. How many reproaches and abuses were thrown at Darwin in his time? Mendel was spared the same fate only because he was not recognized as a serious scientist by his contemporaries. When he died as a highly respected abbot of the Brno monastery not one of the speakers at his funeral mentioned his scientific work – which now makes him immortal.

To prove formally that an idea is unscientific is often very difficult. All the more so in a new discipline like sociobiology which in the course of its development must create its own new standards of quality and testing methods. Interdisciplinary co-operation cannot always solve such problems, since the ideas and the methods used in different fields are often widely different.

A good illustration is the dispute about the incest taboo (see section 3.15). Biologists claim that there are behaviour patterns resulting in incest avoidance in practically all higher animals; that such behaviour is biologically reasonable and that hence one would expect it to be favoured by natural selection; thus there is every reason to assume that man too would have similar *inborn* behavioural tendencies. Anthropologists consider that to be a crude simplification. In their view human incest taboos can be understood only in a cultural context.

To me the arguments of the biologists who do not exclude a cultural superstructure over an inborn behavioural tendency seem convincing. But perhaps this is just my personal bias, since usually my work is concerned rather more with biology than with anthropology. There are no simple rules of thumb to find an 'objective' solution to such disputes, and in many instances both sides contribute part of the truth. Neither are there really reliable criteria for an unfailing separation of scientific and pseudo-scientific claims.

Any simplifying black-and-white-approach cannot do justice to a much more complex situation. There is no such thing as good guys who are true scientists on the one side and bad guys who are reactionary, racist and fascist pseudo-scientists on the other. The scienti-

239

fic achievements of a scholar cannot be judged by his ideological position, and even an occasional slip into pseudo-scientific ideas does not prove a general scientific incompetence. Astronomy originated as an ancillary science to astrology, and Johannes Kepler was still searching for a mystical 'harmony of the spheres' – but that does not reduce the validity of the laws of planetary motion which he discovered.

Genetics, though it did not originate as an auxiliary to race theory, easily can be linked with it. Eugen Fischer, one of the authors of the standard work of 'scientific' German racism mentioned in the preceding section, became known by a book published in 1913 on studies in a mulatto village in the then German colony of South West Africa (Namibia) – one of the first scientific investigations applying Mendelian genetics to man. Reading it today one finds a curious hotch-potch of very interesting scientific facts and an abominable attitude of 'white man's superiority'. Yet, such an attitude is not just a special trend of German genetics; it can be found in writings of geneticists of other nations just as well. On the other hand it is *not inherent* in genetics as can be seen in the work of Haldane or of Dobzhansky, to quote but two eminent geneticists mentioned in this book.

Lorenz's above-mentioned 1940 paper does not make ethology into a discipline with a 'fascist bias', and even Lorenz himself – in spite of his adaptations to the 'spirit' of that time – is nevertheless an eminent scientist in his discipline who well deserved the Noble prize. Similarly many questionable utterances of Wilson, Hamilton Trivers and other sociobiologists cannot justify a general disqualification of this discipline.

4.5 *Are genes a reactionary invention?*

Evelyne Sullerot, at that time professor of sociology at the University of Paris-Nanterre, writes in her book on female phenomena (1978) about the preconceived notions of 'an environmentalistic neoprogressivism, which considers that individuals are *only* influenced by society and the education given to them'. Most of her students, she reports, 'professed to this religion . . . and they knew how to silence anybody who would have dared to speak about chromosomes'.

The University of Nanterre was a well-known citadel of the New Left, but the approach described here of calling everybody who only mentions genes in the context with human behaviour a reactionary can be found far beyond the circles of radical students. Of course, nobody today would dismiss the mere notion of genes and chromosomes as 'reactionary inventions' as did Trofim D. Lyssenko, president of the Soviet academy for agricultural sciences in the days of Stalin. Today it seems to be generally agreed that traits of the body, such as red hair or blue eyes, are genetically determined and similarly certain diseases like colour blindness or sickle cell anaemia. What is in dispute is whether there is any significant influence of genes on 'higher' human qualities like intelligence – or criminality.

The New Left and others, who react to the claim that genes have an influence on human behaviour somewhat like a bull to a red rag, consider themselves to be materialists in the philosophical sense; some of them claim to be Marxists. They know that one needs a human brain to be able to think in a human way; that a certain species-specific structure of the human brain is a precondition for the structure of the human intellect; and that the 'blueprints' for the wiring of our brain cannot be other than encoded in our genes. But what happens if an error – a mutation – slips into these blueprints? This is one of the instances when even students of sociology adhering to the New Left will hardly be able to deny a certain influence of genes on behaviour and/or intelligence.

A well-known example is a disease called phenylketonuria. Its cause is a faulty gene coding for an enzyme needed for the decomposition of the amino acid phenylalanine. About one person in 30 000 by an unfortunate coincidence inherits this faulty gene from *both* parents. As a consequence, an intermediate product of phenylalanine decomposition accumulates in his or her body and this substance interferes with the normal wiring process in the brain in early childhood, resulting in incurable imbecility. Since all this is known one can recognize the disease by a simple routine test with the urine of new-born children, and as phenylalanine is a rather rare building block in the proteins the child can be fed with a diet containing very little of this amino acid. In this way the accumulation of its dangerous decomposition products in the body can be prevented. A child who would have become an idiot thus grows up to be a normal individual, and after the sixth year when the wiring of the

241

nerves in the brain is practically finished there is no further need to continue with the special diet.

There can hardly be any doubt that such medical applications of genetics are beneficial. But as soon as this is recognized it is, logically, only a small step to assume that there might be variations in the wiring of the brain of healthy persons as well, influencing the capabilities of individuals to learn certain things more easily or with more difficulty. Why is it that just this sort of reasoning – which is perfectly 'materialistic' in a philosophical sense – raises such violent and strongly emotional opposition from the Left?

'I think that is quite easy to see' Maynard Smith told me. 'Whoever wants to change society can only hope to alter acquired characters but not innate ones. What is inborn cannot be changed by social reform.' To put it in another way: the greater the influence of the genes, the smaller the range where social reform or revolution can effect any change at all.

But no serious biologist ever denied that the individual characters of an animal or a man (his phenotype) are influenced by the *combined effects* of genes *and* environment, of inborn behavioural tendencies *and* learning processes (see section 1.2). Recognizing this as a fact still leaves ample room for useful reform of society.

Certainly it is true that by a proper knowledge of inborn traits one can be spared pursuing futile efforts such as some of the unsuccessful vocational training projects for girls described by Evelyne Sullerot (see section 3.12). Yet, on the other hand it is no less true that any reference to inborn differences might be used by reactionary forces to justify existing inequalities: discrimination against women in professional life, discrimination against children of the less well-to-do in education, discrimination against coloured people (or 'aliens' generally) in every sphere of life.

'I am not implying that [the Conservatives] engaged a team of sociobiologists to write the Thatcher scripts,' writes Steven Rose (1979b), a British biologist sympathizing with the New Left and a harsh critic of sociobiology; anyway, he is not the only one struck by the coincidence of a new fashionable scientific theory with a political trend. In her election campaign Margaret Thatcher repeatedly said that all men are unequal and had a right to be so; that parents should be given the opportunity to choose their children's education, etc.

242

But what is the result of Conservative politicians demanding 'better education for gifted children'? Even if it was not their intention, such an educational system inevitably will result in a situation where it is not the most talented children who go to the best schools, but the children of the most privileged – and this applies not only to capitalistic countries. On the other hand, the creed of many progressive pedagogues that any child is talented if it is only helped and motivated in the right way does not solve the problems of a teacher who is confronted with a class of pupils with a wide scatter of individual talents: either the most untalented will not be able to grasp what he teaches, or the brightest will be bored and be deprived of the opportunity to fully develop their talents.

'The notion that we "have a nature", far from threatening the concept of freedom, is absolutely essential to it,' writes Mary Midgley (1978/80, p. 18). 'If we were genuinely plastic and indeterminate at birth, there could be no reason why society should not stamp us into any shape that might suit it.' The reason people view suggestions about inborn tendencies with such indiscriminate horror, she continues, seems to be that they think exclusively of reactionaries abusing such ideas for their ends. But actually progressive theorists need them just as much. 'Rousseau's trumpet call, "Man is born free, but everywhere he is in chains", makes sense only as a description of our innate constitution as something positive, already determined, and conflicting with what society does to us.' Similarily Marx' ideas of Alienation and Dehumanisation are based on a covert premise of a human nature.

A remarkable contribution to this discussion comes from a member of the Boston 'Science-for-the-people' group, gathered around the well-known population geneticist Richard Lewontin, a group that was very active in criticizing Wilson. According to Lawrence G. Miller (1976) a mere dichotomy of either genes or environment must be rejected since 'determinist theories, whether genetic or environmental, serve to inculcate an ethos of passivity and thus render us susceptible to active manipulation by others. . . We view humans as *active* agents, striving to shape lives and destinies.'

This, of course, is a position deviating considerably from the above-mentioned credo of the environmentalistic neoprogressivistic students of sociology in Nanterre, and here we have a real and profound problem. Theories relieving man from responsibility for his own actions make us feel very uneasy indeed, since they are in contradiction to our own impression that we can decide freely, as well as to our assumption – considered to be obvious in every day life – that others with whom we interact are responsible for their actions too.

Purely deterministic theories could not be accepted by any society – *even if they were true.* In a certain sense and to a certain degree it might well be true that *every* criminal is a victim – of his genes, of his education, of his environment or of other external factors. Nevertheless the legal system must be based on the assumption that an adult healthy and normal person can and must be held responsible for what he or she does – otherwise an orderly co-existence in a society would be impossible.

We are touching here the thorny problem of 'free will' that has been occupying philosophers for more than 2000 years; its solution certainly is not the task of sociobiology. Hence we might confine ourselves to what has been repeated in this book several times: that even a greylag goose is by no means a pre-programmed automaton and still less an ape, and that man certainly has a still far larger range of free choice.

As I see it, we are indeed – within limits – active subjects responsible for our actions and do not just imagine ourselves to be so. But this does not exclude that inborn tendencies, education, previous experiences and other factors do have certain influences on what we do. Or should we consider human behaviour as a mere 'super-structure' floating freely in space without any biological or social basis?

4.6 *What the New Left might learn from old Engels*

In his review of Wilson's book *On Human Nature* mentioned in section 3.9 Steven Rose (1978) writes that Wilson, 'while he has clearly read the Bible, shows little evidence of even having read Marx for Beginners'. I would think that this assertion is correct; yet I wonder what might be inferred from it. The same probably could be said of Martin Luther King, Dom Helder Camara, and Adolfo Perez Esquivel who recently got the Nobel Peace Prize, and yet there can be no doubt that these are very progressive persons.

Marxism is mentioned in Wilson's book several times, not

always with great insight, but the main point Wilson makes, though criticized by Rose, seems correct to me: Marxism indeed has become a sort of secular equivalent of religion for many of its adherents. This has been pointed out by people who should know, and who have not changed over into the reactionary camp; a recent example is Zdenek Mlynar, secretary of the Central Committee of the Communist Party of Czechoslovakia in the era of the 'Prague Spring', who emigrated to Austria in 1977 after signing Charta 77 (Mlynar, 1980).

If I had to write a review of Wilson's book I would put my finger on quite another problem. As far as I can see Wilson knows much more about insect societies than about human society. His book on human nature is far less impressive than his monumental volume *Sociobiology – the New Synthesis* which deals mainly with animal societies; and this is not merely a question of size. The new book, though containing some remarkable thoughts, clearly illustrates what Wilson has repeatedly stressed himself: that the value of sociobiology for the investigation of human behaviour cannot be properly judged as long as there are no well-trained experts in human and social sciences who try to apply the ideas of the new discipline in their own field.

If you are looking for a Marxist interpretation of human nature you probably will not exactly study Wilson's book – but this does not mean that it would not be a rewarding reading for a Marxist. The value of a scientific publication cannot be judged by the political or philosophical position of the author. Friedrich Engels, anyway, was much more liberal in this respect than many doctrinaire left-wingers of our days. He was, to give an example, by no means uncritical towards Bachofen. In the preface to the fourth edition of his *Origin of the Family*... he even wrote that occasionally one is led to think that Bachofen himself believed just as much in the Erinnyes, Apollo and Athene as Aeschylus did. Yet, nevertheless, Engels did justice to Bachofen and recognized the great importance of his pioneering work in the study of the history of the family.

I have mentioned Engels several times in this book and pointed out that most of the scientific sources he used are obsolete nowadays. Hence many of his conclusions based on the scientific knowledge of his time are by now obsolete as well. Nevertheless I consider his *Origin of the Family*... still worth reading today. One will find ideas

245

there that are still valuable in our time, but what seems most important to me, and what would be well worth the emulation of left-
wingers of our days is Engels' openmindedness – the great interest
that he, and Marx as well, showed in the scientific achievements of
their epoch.

This interest was by no means confined to preparatory work for
The Origin of the Family... In other works of Engels, scientific
topics are repeatedly mentioned too, and after his death fragments,
drafts and notes for a book on *Dialectics of Nature* were found
among his writings. For the English edition of this book J. B. S.
Haldane wrote the preface and notes referring to scientific developments since Engels' death. 'Had his remarks on Darwinism been
generally known, I for one would have been saved a certain amount
of muddled thinking,' Haldane writes (Engels, 1940/1946, p. 14).

That Engels had indeed a very modern approach to science can be
seen in his remark, not at all obvious in his days, 'that we by no
means rule over nature like a conqueror over a foreign people ...
but that we, with flesh, blood, and brain, belong to nature and exist
in its midst, and that all our mastery of it consists in the fact that
we have the advantage over all other beings of being able to know and
correctly apply its laws' (*ibid.* p. 292). Since we belong to nature we
are subject to its laws of heredity and evolution, and it seems that
Engels would have been better able to grasp this than many calling
themselves Marxists today.

This great interest in science unfortunately has not been preserved in the Marxist movement after Engels' death. To quote the well-
known Hungarian Marxist philosopher Georg Lukacs (1964): 'Marx
and Engels used to incorporate new achievements of science into
Marxism... We must revive this Marxist method in order that
Marxism should preserve its vitality. What, for example, did Marx
and Engels do with the theory of Darwin? Of course, nobody would
repeat verbatim today what Darwin said. But we are concerned
with the essence of things, and seen in this way, the incorpora-
tion of Darwin by Marx was a methodological feat that must not be
lost.'

Still more pointedly the philosopher Wolfgang Harich of East
Berlin reproaches 'quasi-Marxistic trends in Western philosophy'
and in particular the so-called 'Frankfurt School' (Horkheimer,
Adorno and others) of 'reducing Marxism to a mere theory of
society'. In his view they are 'neglecting large fields of philosophical

investigation – especially those fields that do not interest an intellectual trained one-sidedly only in the humanistic disciplines' and
'eliminating the dialectics of nature to which end they continually
oppose an ostensibly authentic Marx against the universal philoso-
phic interests of Engels' (1975, p. 17).

Whatever objections one may raise against Harich's general
views, I think that this critique is not quite unjustified – though, of
course, it is rather absurd to restrict it to Marxist schools in the
West. As clearly emphasized in the above-quoted passage of Lukacs
it applies just as well to most of what is called Marxist thinking in
the East.

Progress of science since Engels' death is impressive indeed and
sociobiology is but a tiny stone in this grand mosaic. Yet, the question of how human behaviour did evolve from animal behaviour is
perfectly legitimate and 'materialistic' (in the philosophical sense)
and would well deserve serious attention by Marxist philosophers.
The political views of individual sociobiologists are of no relevance
here. Anyhow it might be worth noting that some of the most basic
ideas of this new discipline can be traced back to the very same
J. B. S. Haldane who wrote the preface and the notes for the
English edition of Engels' *Dialectics of Nature.*

Some of these ideas were first published in popular scientific
articles that Haldane regularly contributed to the *Daily Worker*,
the newspaper of the Communist Party of Great Britain; later he
incorporated them into his scientific publications. A few years after
the Second World War Haldane left the Communist Party – mainly
to protest against the persecution of highly esteemed geneticists in
the Soviet-Union who had dared to oppose to the pseudo-scientific
ideas of Lyssenko.

That Haldane, one of the founders of population genetics and of
the Neo-Darwinistic 'Modern Synthesis' (see section 2.1) was a
left-winger does not indicate anything about the correctness or
otherwise of his scientific ideas. But it might reasonably be assumed
that his views were not *politically* reactionary. To him it seemed fully
compatible to be a geneticist and a Marxist simultaneously.

4.7 *Of twins and XYY-men*

'Are we going to have twins?' asked my wife, who is herself a twin,
two months before the birth of our son; there was so much turmoil

going on in her womb. Two years later, when she was in the same state again she expressed fears that our second child might have died before birth – so little did she feel of its movements.

The differences in temperament of our two children, manifesting themselves already many weeks before birth, were clearly observable in a very different behaviour on the swaddling table, in the pram or in the bath tub – and they are still in evidence now, 25 years later. For me they were always a piece of hard evidence that there are some inborn characteristics already present when they obviously cannot as yet be a product of education or environmental influences. But what can be inferred from this?

In principle I feel sure that genes do indeed influence our 'higher' traits. Yet to what extent such phenomena can be investigated at the present state of the art is quite another question. I, for one, have considerable doubts when reading claims that heritability (i.e. genetic determination) of intelligence is something like 70–80% (see for instance, Eysenck, 1979). It is not just that to my 'gut feeling' this percentage seems rather high. Much more important seems to me the question whether we really do possess the scientific tools to make such a statement with such a high degree of exactness. There are scientists claiming that we can. There are others who doubt it – even among those who do not reject *per se* the idea of a genetic influence on intelligence.

To go into the details of the IQ dispute would be beyond the scope of this book. What needs emphasizing, however, is the fact that all this has nothing to do with sociobiology, even though some of its critics tend to lump all these things together. The scientists studying the heritability of human intelligence are psychologists working solely with human beings; comparisons with animals are none of their business. What they have in common with the sociobiologists is only the assumption that genes do influence higher human traits.

The main difficulty in investigating such phenomena is the fact that the most important scientific tool of genetics, controlled cross-breeding experiments, cannot be applied to man for obvious reasons. Moreover behaviour and intelligence are most probably influenced not just by a few genes but by many. Thus the genetic influences on higher human traits are complex and as a rule not straightforward, and they can be studied only by indirect methods, like comparing twins or true children with adopted children, or by observing the development of behaviour in handicapped (blind, deaf) children.

Twin research is based on the fact that there are identical and non-identical twins. The latter come from two egg cells fertilized independently of each other; they are not more closely related to each other than other siblings. Identical twins, on the other hand, come from one egg cell that divided after fertilization. They have identical genes. As a rule it turns out that identical twins show much more similarity in all traits than non-identical twins – even in cases where identical twins have been separated for one reason or another and have grown up in different families.

This, of course, is strong evidence for a considerable genetical influence on traits like behaviour, intelligence and so on, though it might be premature to calculate such influence in percentages. And this sort of evidence is not weakened by the fact that one of the basic assumptions of twin research – the existence of a similar environment when twins grow up together – is in my view questionable. For in a certain sense twins growing up together live in radically different and even diametrically opposed environments.

As a rule the first born twin will also be the first to learn walking and speaking, and he or she nearly always will be one step before the other in development; in girls the first born of a pair of identical twins usually will be the first to have her monthly menstruation periods and so on. In terms of dominance the first born is nearly always an 'alpha' individual holding the higher rank. Since twins usually go to the same school class and spend much more time together than other siblings such differences have strong psychological effects.

I can see this time and again when comparing my wife to her sister. They are identical twins and outwardly they are so similar that after being married for 30 years I still have difficulty in distinguishing them at a distance. But their characters are very different. I am not the only one to know this; many of our friends have noticed it. And I know other twins too with similar specific differences in character between the first and second born.

One need not be married to a twin for 30 years to recognize these differences. For me they are evidence of the fact that genes are not the only factor influencing the behaviour and 'nature' of a human being, but that even with identical genes, diverging outer conditions

249

might induce a very different individual development. Yet, as a rule, this aspect is little emphasized in twin research. Reading such papers one often gets the impression that the authors gave much more attention to discovering similarities than dissimilarities – though the latter are of no less scientific interest.

One reason why many social scientists are rather sceptical about applying human genetics beyond the strictly medical field is their well-founded apprehension that premature conclusions might be drawn from insufficiently tested premises. A typical example is the fuss about the so-called XYY-men, i.e. men that have an additional Y-chromosome. It is an established fact that the proportion of such XYY-men in closed institutions for mentally disturbed criminals is much above the average. It is, however, much less known that about one man in a thousand (according to other sources one in about 2000 to 3000) has such an extra Y-chromosome and that *a large majority of them are neither criminal nor mentally disturbed* (see for instance Hook, 1973; Witkin *et al.*, 1976). Nearly all XYY-men are rather tall and often they look a bit bizarre. On the average their IQs are below the general level. It might well be that their criminality rate is not above the average, but that they are more frequently detected because of their extravagant outer appearance and/or their lower intelligence (see Beckwith and King, 1974).

Originally it was claimed that XYY-men are particularly aggressive. Actually, those confined in closed institutions nearly always had committed property offences. In a large investigation in Copenhagen, Witkin and collaborators (1976) checked more than 4000 men taller than 184 cm born in the years of 1944 to 1947. Twelve among them were XYY-men. Seven of them did not appear in the penal register, three had committed one or two minor criminal acts as adolescents or in their early twenties, one was a chronic thief and burglar who had spent 9 to 15 years of his adult life in prison but had never suffered a higher penalty than a few months for any one of his criminal acts, and the twelfth had been a welfare child and had spent only 3 years outside institutions for the mentally retarded; this man too had been an episodic thief and burglar. None of them had committed serious acts of violence.

After publication of the first reports on XYY-men in closed institutions some of the North American states started screening male juvenile criminals for an extra Y-chromosome. Sociologists and biologists of the above mentioned 'Science-for-the-people' group conducted a long campaign against this practice and finally were able to effect a ruling that results of chromosome tests must not be handed to the courts. Their main argument was that a higher criminality rate for XYY-men had not been proven and that anyway the majority of them are not criminals; thus one might create a prejudice against an innocent person if it became known to judges or jurors that a defendant had this chromosomal anomaly (Beckwith and King, 1974).

Similarly it was argued that parents ought not to be informed about an additional Y-chromosome found in their child; for this too might create prejudices, leading to a self-fulfilling prophecy that might drive the child onto a criminal path. On the other hand there are counter arguments as well. If among these children there is an increased rate of debility and, on the average, a lower level of intelligence, it might be helpful for the parents to know this in order to start in time with preventive and adjusting measures and not to present the child with expectations it cannot live up to.

It must be acknowledged that Wilson in his book on human nature (1978a, p. 43) deals with this question in an objective and competent manner. He quotes the above mentioned Copenhagen study extensively, making the reservation, however, that one such investigations is not sufficient to finally disprove that there is a correlation between an extra Y-chromosome and some predisposition to criminality. While this might be true, there is certainly so far no convincing evidence to the contrary. The question is open and premature applications of unproven theories in the law courts or in penal institutions would most probably cause much more harm than good and create unnecessary human tragedies.

4.8 *The 'atmosphere' of sociobiology*

The cover of the German edition of Richard Dawkins' much discussed book *The Selfish Gene* shows a puppet hanging on strings that lead to the word 'gene'. Presumably the author has not seen and approved the design of this cover before it was printed. For on p. 205 of the English edition he writes quite clearly 'that, for an understanding of modern man, we must begin by throwing out the gene as the sole basis of our ideas on evolution'; and the whole last chapter of the book deals with non-genetical mechanisms of (cultural) evolution.

Thus Dawkins has, as it were, an 'alibi'. It is not his fault that the designer of this impressive cover did not read the book right to the end – nor, perhaps, the manager of the publishing house who had to decide on accepting or rejecting the draft of this cover. Title and cover must first of all help publicity – never mind if they are a bit simplified. But certainly those who decided on this cover were under the impression that it reflected, at least to some extent, the contents of the book. Were they really mistaken all along?

Dawkins has his 'alibi', but in my view he nevertheless is not quite innocent. The disclaimer on page 205 is not sufficient to counterbalance the total impression given by his book; and this disclaimer refers to men only. But actually animals too are not just puppets on the strings of their genes, and men even less so. Of course, Dawkins knows that the behaviour of an animal is the result of the concerted action of inborn tendencies, environmental influences and learning processes. Maybe one can find a paragraph in his book where he expressly says so. But the idea is superseded by a brilliantly written popular presentation which gives the *main emphasis* on depicting organisms as 'gene machines'. Dawkins' presentation is not *balanced*. It is not a mere coincidence that it creates misunderstandings in the head of the reader.

Whereas a scientist may not be responsible for the abuse of his theories or its gross misrepresentations, he or she is responsible for what might be called 'the atmosphere' created by a theory, said the American anthropologist Clifford Geertz in the discussions of the Dahlem Workshop on Morality as a Biological Phenomenon (see Solomon *et al.*, 1978). The 'atmosphere' of sociobiology seems to be conducive to simplifications and misunderstandings tending in a certain particular direction. This is not only imputed by its critics; it presents itself very clearly when people who obviously do not intend to draw a caricature of this new discipline try to describe its basic ideas for a broad audience.

One such typical example is a film entitled 'Sociobiology: doing what comes naturally', designed for high school and college students. Based mainly on interviews with Wilson, DeVore, and Trivers, it makes, according to Maynard Smith (1978*a*) 'a crude use of sociobiological images (one could hardly call them arguments) to justify such views as that a woman's place is in the nursery and in bed, and a man's in the boardroom and on the football field'.

But is this film merely misrepresenting sociobiology or does it depict, in a crude and simplified form, ideas that are indeed in the heads of some sociobiologists? And if so, are these just personal views held by individual representatives of the new discipline, or are they part of a tendency inherent in this field?

A film might give a wrong impression, but David Barash's book *Sociobiology and Behaviour* (1977) is, according to Wilson's preface, 'an excellent primer that can serve well in biology courses but is also particularly suitable as an introduction to the subject for social scientists'. Thus one must assume that this is an authentic account.

The final chapter of that book deals with applying sociobiology to man. Barash himself calls this chapter 'speculating' and starts by saying that 'at this point no one knows whether the perspective of evolutionary biology will shed light on our own social behaviour, but it seems worth trying' (p. 276). I, for one, found his efforts not very convincing.

According to Barash the main reason 'why women have almost universally found themselves relegated to the nursery while men derive their greatest satisfaction from their jobs' is 'that males of virtually all animal species must have less confidence in their paternity than females do in their maternity' (pp. 300–1). Even for animals this is a very simplifying and one-sided argument not paying attention to many of the interesting sociobiological ideas dealt with in the third chapter of this book. Moreover, the statement is simply false when speaking of 'virtually *all* animal species', for, as Barash himself writes in another passage (p. 190), paternity can be fairly certain in many species with external fertilization; hence such species, for instance many fishes, are particularly likely to have paternal brood care (see the example of the stickleback mentioned in section 3.4).

To explain paternal behaviour in man with this argument seems absurd to me. But Barash does not confine himself to the father. He uses the same argument to explain grandparental behaviour as well (p. 302): 'For the same reason that men and women differ in the confidence of their genetic relatedness to their offspring, grandparents or, rather, grandmothers are certain to be related to the offspring of their daughters, whereas they must rely upon the honour of their daughters-in-law for the offspring of their sons. Grand-parents would therefore be predicted to invest more heavily in their daughters than in their daughters-in-law. Why is it usually the mother's parents who help out most when the new baby arrives?'

Yes, why indeed? Might it not be that the young mother prefers the help of her own mother to that of her mother-in-law? And this, perhaps, has much less to do with genes, than with the bond of familiarity connecting mother and daughter, whereas the mother-in-law is a stranger at first – and moreover might be a little jealous of the woman that has 'taken away her son', as reputedly often happens.

I have my humble doubts whether Barash's book really is a good introduction to sociobiology, and particularly for social scientists who can only feel confirmed in all their preconceived notions about this discipline when reading such a text. But there is even worse to come.

Starting from the idea of 'parental investment' that we have described in sections 3.2 of this book, Barash holds that in man too 'parental solicitude should vary directly with the extent to which the assisted child will benefit reproductively by each investment. Thus, a deformed or defective child should generally receive little investment or even suffer infanticide" (p. 299).

Now it cannot be denied that such phenomena do exist, in parti-cular amongst people living on the verge of starvation; and even in well-to-do societies instances of such behaviour might be found. Thus, one case of murder of a thalidomide baby has become known. But it simply is not true that this is a *general* tendency of human behaviour. There are a multitude of parents that do not act according to Barash's cost–benefit calculations, but rather invest extra amounts of love and care into a deformed or 'defective' child. They do it even though they know very well that such investments pro-bably will be 'lost' since the child presumably never will have child-ren of its own to pass on the genes of its parents to future generations.

Yet, the case of the deformed child does not seem to be sufficient for Barash. To make quite sure that the reader does get the right idea of what he means he further invents an example of two women, 'pregnant for the first time, and both hypothetically faced with the choice of saving themselves or their baby. One woman is 19 and the other is 38 years old. Most women in these situations would probably save themselves, but older women should also be significantly more inclined to save their baby than would younger women'. The young woman can have another baby later in her life, whereas the older woman 'would likely be sacrificing her only reproductive potential and should be reluctant to do so... The presence of other, dependent offspring introduces complications: it should reduce the likelihood of maternal self-sacrifice. It would be adaptive to sacrifice the infant if the failure to do so would endanger the ultimate success of the other children to whom the mother is equally related' (pp. 299–300).

I do not intend to discuss the question whether such deliberations are correctly applying the theory of 'parental investment'; and only as an aside might it be noted that in Barash's language 'should' does not mean a moral 'ought' but solely a statistical probability according to the theory of natural selection. What worries me in this passage is the manner in which this hypothetical example is treated, the tone of the writing – in short, 'the atmosphere'. The cold-bloodedness with which Barash first constructs a human tragedy – fortunately very unlikely to occur in real life – and then goes on to treat it without any personal engagement, just as an example for a genetical cost–benefit calculation, seems frightening to me. It shows how science can become dehumanized.

The participants of one of the working groups of the Dahlem workshop on Morality as a Biological Phenomenon (Solomon et al., 1978), most of them philosophers or anthropologists, held that such an attitude of demoting the individual is not a coincidence. '*Any* approach to moral issues which takes a considerably larger (or smaller, e.g. individual genes) unit than the individual will *tend* to neglect individual concerns and rights,' they state. 'For example, Hegel's philosophy of the State, because it takes "the State" to be the "real" entity in question tends to make individual concerns secondary or derivative of the concerns of the larger entity. Thus the bias of sociobiology away from the individual ... is inherent in the very nature of the enterprise.'

4.9 *A dangerous combination*

Could a crude and simplified form of sociobiology serve as a popular 'ideology'? According to what Steven Rose wrote about Margaret

Thatcher's election speeches (see section 4.5) it already does so, and it ought to be realized that this is a dangerous trend. Speaking at the final session of the Dahlem workshop on Morality as a Biological Phenomenon, the Oxford philosopher B. A. O. Williams pointed out that 'scientism' itself is an ideology in our present intellectual environment and that there are good reasons for that. Science has given us a better knowledge of the universe, and also has given us the chance to apply laws of nature to our own advantage. Science therefore has prestige, and the consequence is not less superstitious beliefs but superstitions in the form of pseudo-science.

On the other hand, Williams continued (1978, pp. 319–20), this has been counterbalanced recently by an extreme degree of anti-technical and antimanipulative alarm. More and more people are becoming aware of how technology can destroy our environment and how science is developing ever-more sophisticated tools for manipulating man. This causes fear – not only of totalitarian power but also of a future governed by a wholly impersonal, technocratic and computerized bureaucracy.

In such a situation, Williams thinks, vulgarized sociobiology could easily become an ideology appealing to many people because it is 'scientific' and conservative at the same time. 'It combines the notion of being based on scientific explanation with a fundamentally . . . conservative "keeping what is found natural" approach to various social institutions. In the present ideological climate, one can predict that that is an extraordinarily potent combination of characteristics. Most conservative outlooks are antiscientific, and therefore treated with distrust because they seem to leave aside the paradigm of modern knowledge. Many scientistic outlooks, on the other hand, are deeply radical. . . People do not like either for various old-fashioned reasons. When you have an outlook which can be at once scientistic and conservative, it can speak to quite a lot of our needs, and therefore . . . I think that, on the whole, we had better watch out.'

Another aspect of the 'atmosphere' of sociobiology has been noted mainly by critics on the left. According to them, sociobiology considers certain phenomena that are typical for the profit-orientated capitalistic society as characteristic for *any* human society and as part of 'human nature', and then applies this kind of thinking to the animal world as well. To Hobbes in the seventeenth century, man was seen as a wolf to man, and later 'social Darwinism' tried to justify conditions of early capitalism by declaring them 'natural'. But sociobiology, it is claimed, goes even further. 'Since they would now extend the same folk conception of capitalism to the animal kingdom as a whole, for sociobiologists it is also true that the wolf is a man to other wolves' (Sahlins, 1976, p. 99).

Trivers, in particular, introduced a very profit-orientated approach into analysing the relations between sexual partners (1972) and between parents and children (1974; for reasons of space I cannot go into this topic here). But the very idea of a genetic 'cost—benefit calculation', one of the basic propositions of sociobiology, is 'capitalistic' as well. Yet, does this prove that the idea is false? Haldane never used the *expression* of 'cost—benefit relation', but the *idea* is clearly present in his *bon mot* about being prepared to sacrifice his life for two brothers or eight cousins; and Haldane certainly was not orientated to capitalistic ideology.

After listening to the discussions of the Dahlem workshop on Animal and Human Mind for a couple of days the American psychologist Henry Gleitman asked whether all biologists are economists. The question shows a deep insight, and in a certain sense the answer is 'yes' – though, of course, most biologists are *not only* economists. Living in a capitalistic society and addressing an audience that lives there as well, socio- and other biologists often use a metaphorical language pertaining to this well-known social environment. Of course, nobody really assumes that an animal does make genetical cost—benefit computations in its head. Nor does anybody depict 'Natural Selection' as a wicked fairy thinking in capitalistic terms. But the mechanisms described by the term 'natural selection' result, in the long run, in only those traits persisting that help to pass on one's genes – in other words, that are bringing 'genetical profit'.

Capitalism has its specific forms of social organization and a language mirroring them. In other kinds of societies exploitation has other forms and a different language is used – but does this mean that there is no exploitation in non-capitalistic societies? Men, as a rule, tend to look after their own interests – and, by the way, so do animals. This is not a special feature of the capitalistic system.

The wolf becomes a man to other wolves. . . Animals, too, are 'not better' than ourselves. They are not indeed, and romantic illusions ought to be cast aside (see section 1.6). Of course, even for animals, all-too-radical generalizations should be avoided. The behaviour of Lorenz's greylag goose that maintains matrimonial fidelity to a partner even long beyond its death and sometimes for the rest of its life, cannot be explained by a simple genetical cost–benefit calculation. They 'should', as Barash would say, try instead to maximize their 'fitness' (i.e. their reproductive success) and strive to get a new mate *as soon as possible*. The friendship between a chimp girl and a baboon girl described by Jane Goodall (1971, p. 152, 193) did not bring them any direct or indirect 'genetic benefit' but dangers. But such phenomena are exceptions; they are individual cases and not behaviour patterns typical for a whole species. On the whole sociobiologists do portray animals realistically and do not paint them as being 'worse' than they are – if such a notion of moral value can be applied to animals at all.

Nevertheless I think that the uneasiness with the 'atmosphere' of sociobiology as felt by Sahlins and many others is not wholly unjustified; rather, it seems to me, it is not spelled out in a clear and proper way. The trouble is not that sociobiologists draw a false picture of the wolf, but rather that they present a false – or rather a biased and one-sided – picture of man. As I see it, the root of the evil is not that sociobiology 'justifies an evil status quo of existing society' – though it can all too easily be abused for that purpose too; nor is it the equation of phenomena of capitalistic society with the essence of human society *per se* or with human nature. For me the main weakness of sociobiology is in the ethical realm.

'In my opinion, most critics of sociobiology, Sahlins included, have erred in attacking sociobiology on either political or scientific grounds.' writes Gunther Stent (1981). 'For on those grounds sociobiology is not dramatically weaker than most other so-called "human sciences". In so far as the application of biology to the understanding of human social behaviour is concerned, it is not so much the case that the sociobiological project is intrinsically impossible. Rather, it is the case that many sociobiologists, by virtue of philosophical and political näiveté, lack of sociological insights, and overbearing exuberance, have greatly overblown the significance and scope of their findings. On their part, many humanists, social anthropologists, and Marxist-oriented biologists have overreacted to these exaggerated claims. In their, not wholly unjustified, fear of the political consequences of the work of sociobiological would-be social engineers, these critics of sociobiology have gone too far by dismissing as completely worthless also what there is of value in the sociobiological approach to animal societies. I think that if there is to be effective criticism of the claims of sociobiology with regard to human social affairs, then this criticism has to be made on philosophical grounds, and in particular on moral philosophical grounds.'

The uneasiness with the 'atmosphere' of sociobiology can, in my view, be reduced to one central question: sociobiology does not take notice of the fact that man – and only man – can identify with any conspecific and feel sympathy with him; and that this can be a source of emotions that cannot be explained or even dealt with within a system of genetical cost–benefit relations (see section 2.15). This most human ability might well be applied with much more generosity in any society, also in those countries that call themselves 'socialistic'. But our capability to feel sympathy does exist and can be seen again and again – in capitalistic societies too.

4.10 *The human dimension*

Jane Godall is a scientist who really loves her chimpanzees. She calls them by names, she uses words like 'boy', 'girl', 'child', etc. when writing about them, she knows many of them 'personally'. Her fascinating book *In the Shadow of Man* (1971) is dedicated to her husband, to her mother, to professor Leakey who opened the way to her career, and 'to the memory of David Greybeard' – a chimp with whom she was on especially good terms. He was the first to tolerate her presence; he even permitted her to touch him, and once when she sat next to him he gently and reassuringly took her hand. 'When I was with David,' she writes, 'I sometimes felt that our relationship came closer to friendship than I would have thought possible with a completely free wild creature' (p. 240).

Her sympathy is not confined to chimps only. With moving words she describes the tragedy of a young baboon female who, when still a girl, had been for many months a good friend of a chimp girl and who later had her baby robbed and eaten by the chimps (*ibid.*, p. 152, 193–4).

For Jane Goodall there can be no doubt that she must help a chimp when it is ill and not just leave it alone and watch how the disease develops under natural conditions. It is all the more obvious to her that she cannot merely observe without interferring when chimps that have turned cannibal (see section 1.6) are trying to hunt a baby. She describes how she followed these cannibals whom she called Passion, Pom and Prof, as they approached a young mother called Little Bee (1979, p. 619):

'Cautiously Pom reached a hand toward the infant, then glanced down at Passion. I could see what was going to happen. So apparently could Little Bee, who had already lost one, probably two, infants. Uttering squeks of fear, she began to edge away toward a tall tree close by. I looked again at the baby, almost hidden in the mother's embrace, and picked up a big stick. Feeling totally inadequate, I reached up and tapped Pom's arm with my stick. She pushed it away in an irritated manner, scarcely giving me a glance. At that instant Little Bee leaped into the next tree, Pom and Prof close behind. Passion was already racing up the trunk. Helplessly I shouted and threw things, but the second tree was tall, and already screaming and fighting had erupted high above. I do believe, though, that the commotion I made added to the general confusion and helped Little Bee escape. Passion and Pom searched for a full hour before moving on, but they did not find her. We decided to have Passion and her family followed every day for several weeks.'

One might object that 'seen from a strictly scientific angle' Jane Goodall's behaviour might be considered questionable. After all she did not interfere when the chimps hunted baboon children, though she did feel sympathy with the prey. So why interfere in this special case? It might have been very interesting to see how things would have gone on in undisturbed natural conditions and to find out whether the chimps themselves would have been able, sooner or later, to put an end to this cannibalism. (Actually there were no more babies robbed after Passion herself had got a new child soon afterwards; see section 1.6.)

In my view such a 'strictly scientific' attitude must be rejected. One must not demand from a scientist that he should extinguish in his heart any trace of sympathy with the animals he studies and remain only a cool and distant observer –else one would eventually develop a completely dehumanized science. Jane Goodall behaved

260

as a psychologist working with humans would have done if, say, in an experiment with children, a dangerous situation did arise. In such circumstances he or she cannot just observe but must interfere. Behaving in the same way when observing chimps is, I think, not a fault, but a merit.

Yet just because Jane Goodall has such a profoundly humanistic attitude she never loses sight of the difference between man and animals. 'Humans ... can be genuinely sorry for someone,' she writes. 'It is unlikely that a chimpanzee acts from feelings quite like these' (1971, p. 221; see also section 2.15 of this book). And in another passage: 'I cannot conceive chimpanzees developing emotions, one for the other, comparable in any way to the tenderness, the protectiveness, the tolerance, and the spiritual exhilaration which are the hallmarks of human love in its truest and deepest sense' (ibid., p. 178; see also section 3.9 of this book).

I cannot remember ever having read a statement of similar clarity in any sociobiological publication. In these the differences between man and animal usually are reduced mainly to a much stronger influence of culture on human behaviour, to higher human intelligence and to language. The fact that only man is able to identify with any of his conspecifics is not dealt with either by sociobiologists or by most of its critics. Whether one calls this most human ability loving one's neighbour, or solidarity, or humanism, does not seem very important to me. It is something that must be understood, as it were, by brain and heart. It is the very essence of what makes us really human.

Wilson continually struggles with the problem of evolution of human ethics. He believes that with further scientific progress eventually a time will come when it will be possible to define 'a genetically accurate and hence completely fair code of ethics' (1975, p. 575). But then, he thinks, we will be faced with a 'dilemma' (1978, pp. 2–6; 196–8). Once we have uncovered the evolutionary roots of our ethics and know how our value systems and norms have come about, he thinks, that 'we will have to decide how human we wish to remain'. But which of the then uncovered and explained value systems shall we use? From where are we going to take the norms with which to evaluate the norms inherent in our 'nature' as a result of human evolution?

Wilson apparently does not realize that any effort to find a natural and hence 'completely fair' ethical code is bound to fail because different people, for example men and women, *naturally* have diverging interests which cannot both be fully met – as shown in the third part of this book, particularly in section 3.10. Moreover as Wilson himself repeatedly points out (see for example 1975, p. 4; p. 380–3) there are bound to be real clashes of interest between individual and group, individual and family, and family and group in all vertebrate societies at least. Ethics cannot do more than help to achieve a more or less viable compromise that might be acceptable to all concerned (see also Midgley, 1981).

Further, there are not only contradictions among different people; there are also contradictory tendencies *within* each individual. Wilson (1978a, p. 165–6) quotes a moving passage of Alexander Solzhenitsyn, stating that the line dividing good and evil cuts right through the heart of every human being. But he does not really make use of this idea and does not try to explain how this state was arrived at in the course of human evolution.

Reading Dawkins I also had the impression that occasionally he himself feels a bit uneasy about depicting man in such a one-sided manner as being motivated *only* by egoism. Thus he writes in the first chapter of his book *The Selfish Gene* (1976, p. 3): 'This book is mainly intended to be interesting, but if you would extract a moral from it, read it as a warning. Be warned that if you wish, as I do, to build a society in which individuals co-operate generously and unselfishly towards a common good, you can expect little help from biological nature. Let us try to *teach* generosity and altruism, because we are born selfish. Let us understand what our own selfish genes are up to, because we may then at least have the chance to upset their designs, something which no other species has ever aspired to.'

In the very last paragraph of his book Dawkins returns to this question: 'It is possible,' he writes, 'that yet another unique quality of man is a capacity for genuine, disinterested, true altruism. I hope so, but I am not going to argue the case one way or the other. . . We have at least the mental equipment to foster our long-term selfish interests rather than merely our short-term selfish interests. . . We have the power to defy the selfish genes of our birth and, if necessary the selfish memes [Dawkins' term for smallest units of cultural evolution] of our indoctrination. . . We are built as gene machines

262

and cultured as meme machines, but we have the power to turn against our creators. We, alone on earth, can rebel against the tyranny of the selfish replicators.'

But *why* should we do so? Where would our motivation come from? Is it really only the intellectual realization of our long-term selfish interests? For what reasons does Dawkins *wish* 'to build a society in which individuals co-operate generously and unselfishly towards a common good', if it is true that such a desire is in contradiction to his inborn human nature?

I think that in this decisive issue W. C. Allee whom we mentioned in section 4.2 comes nearer to truth. Even if some of his agruments might be questionable in detail I think that his basic idea is correct: *our tendencies towards goodness are just as innate as our egoistic tendencies.* If we want to rebel against our selfish genes, we can rely in this task not only on our intelligence but also on other genes, just as inherent in our nature, that confer on us the capability to feel sympathy for and identify with any fellow man.

The line dividing good and evil cuts right through the heart of every one of us. Sociobiologists are certainly correct in stating that man like any other creature has an inborn tendency to look after his own interests. This includes many kinds of behaviour that usually are not considered as 'evil' but as obvious and reasonable. Sociobiologists are also correct when pointing out that a tendency for many actions generally considered to be 'good' – as, for example, caring affectionately for one's children – is *inborn* in us because it is beneficial to ourselves in a genetical sense, i.e. it increases our chance to pass on our genes to future generations. There are, however, instances when our inborn and, as a rule, educationally reinforced capability to identify with any other man does motivate us to do 'good deeds' that cannot be explained within the framework of genetical cost–benefit relations. This is the other side of man which is also part of his 'nature' and as long as sociobiology overlooks this side and fails to deal with it, it is lacking a truly humanistic dimension.

When I started to prepare the work on this book I did not yet realize this. And I think that there are many critics of sociobiology who somehow are vaguely aware of this problem without spelling it out clearly. Of course, the uniqueness of man is *not only* defined by his ability to feel sympathy, but all the achievements of our intelligence and of our culture are in danger of becoming *dehumanized* if they lack this truly human attitude.

There is no point in reproaching sociobiology for studying the influence of genes on human behaviour. There might have been exaggerations or premature conclusions in some instances, but in principle there can be no doubt that such an influence does exist, and to investigate it is one of the main tasks of this discipline. It is, however, in no way inherent to sociobiology that in doing so it must neglect the unique capability of man to identify with any conspecific. Quite to the contrary, the question of how such a capability could evolve, as it were, in contradiction to the principles of genetical cost–benefit calculations, is one of the basic problems of applying sociobiological ideas to man.

If workers from the realm of social and human sciences could contribute to the solution of this problem by applying sociobiological ideas they might be able to build a very important bridge between biology and the sciences dealing with man and his society. Then sociobiology would indeed have gained its truly human dimension.

Literature

Abegglen, J. J., 1976: On Socialisation in Hamadryas Baboons. Doctoral Thesis, University of Zürich.

Agarwal, A., 1980: A decade of clean water. *New Scientist*, **88**, 356–59.

Alexander, R. D. and P. W. Sherman, 1977: Local mate competition and parental investment in social insects. *Science*, **196**, 494–500.

Allee, W. C., 1943: Where angels fear to tread: a contribution from general sociology to human ethics. *Science*, **97**, 517–25.

– N. E. Collias and Catherine Z. Lutherman, 1939: Modification of the social order in flocks of hens by the injection of testosterone propionate. *Physiological Zoology*, **12**, 412–40.

Allen, E. *et al.*, 1976: Sociobiology – another biological determinism. *BioScience*, **26**. (Reprinted in A. L. Caplan (Ed.), pp. 280–90.)

Altmann, S. A. and Jeanne Altmann, 1970: *Baboon Ecology: African Field Research*. Chicago: University of Chicago Press.

Angst, W., 1980: *Aggression bei Affen und Menschen*. Berlin, Heidelberg, New York: Springer-Verlag.

Ardrey, R., 1970: *The Social Contract*. New York: Atheneum.

Ayala, F. J., 1980: Genetic and evolutionary relationships of apes and humans. In: H. Markl (Ed.), pp. 147–62.

Bachmann, C. and H. Kummer, 1980: Male assessment of female choice in hamadryas baboons. *Behavioral Ecology and Sociobiology*, **6**, 315–21.

Bachofen, J. J., 1861: *Das Mutterrecht*. Stuttgart.

Baker, M. C. and P. Marler, 1980: Behavioral adaptations that constrain the gene pool in vertebrates. In H. Markl (Ed.), pp. 59–80.

Barash, D. P., 1977: *Sociobiology and Behavior*. New York: Elsevier.

Bateman, A. J., 1948: Intra-sexual selection in *Drosophila*. *Heredity*, **2**, 349–68.

Bateson, P. P. G., 1976: Specificity and the origins of behaviour. In: J. S. Rosenblatt *et al.* (Eds.), *Advances in the Study of Behaviour*, pp. 1–20. New York: Academic Press.

– 1978: Sexual imprinting and optimal outbreeding. *Nature, London*, **273**, 659–60.

Baulieu, E., and France Haour, 1979: Die physiologischen und pathologischen Unterschiede zwischen Mann und Frau. In: E. Sullerot (Ed.), pp. 155–85.

Baur, E., E. Fischer and F. Lenz, 1927 *et seq.*: *Menschliche Erblehre und Rassenhygiene*. München: J. F. Lehmann.

Beckwith, J. and J. King, 1974: The XYY syndrome: a dangerous myth. *New Scientist*, **64**, 474–6.

Berghe, P. L. van den, 1978: Bridging the paradigms. *Society*, **15**, pp. 42–9.

– and D. P. Barash, 1977: Inclusive fitness and human family structure. *American Anthropologist*, **79**, 809–23.

Bertram, B. C. R., 1976: Kin selection in lions and in evolution. In: P. P. G. Bateson and R. A. Hinde (Eds.), *Growing Points in Ethology*. Cambridge University Press.

Bischof N., 1975: Comparative ethology in incest avoidance. In: R. Fox (Ed.), *Biosocial Anthropology* pp. 37–67. London: Malaby Press.

– 1978: On the phylogeny of human morality. In: G. S. Stent (Ed.), pp. 53–73.

–1979: Der biologische Zweck der Zweigeschlechtlichkeit. In: E. Sullerot (Ed.), pp. 38–59.

Bonner, J. T., 1967: *The Cellular Slime Molds*, 2nd edn. Princeton University Press.

– 1979: The biological basis of culture. *Proceedings of the American Philosophical Society*, **123**, 219–21.

Boulding, K. E., 1978: Sociobiology or Biosociology? *Society*, **15**, 28–34.

Bray, O., J. Kenelly and J. Guarino, 1975: Fertility of eggs produced on territories of vasectomized redwing blackbirds. In: *Wil. Bull.* 87, S. 187–95.

Brock, V. E., and R. H. Riffenburg, 1960: Fish schooling: a possible factor in reducing predation. *Journal du Conseil Permanent International pour l'Exploration de la Mer*, **25**, 307–17.

Brown, L. H., 1970: *Eagles*. London: A. Barker (quoted after Wickler, 1971).

Burian, R. M., 1978: A methodological critique of sociobiology. In: A. L. Caplan (Ed.), pp. 376–95.

Burnet, F. M., 1971: 'Self-recognition' in colonial marine forms and flowering plants in relation to the evolution of immunity. *Nature, London*, **232**, 230–5.

Campbell, B. (Ed.), 1972: *Sexual Selection and the Descent of Man 1871–1971*. London: Heinemann.

Campbell, D. T., 1978: Social morality norms as evidence of conflict between biological human nature and social systems requirements. In: G. S. Stent (Ed.), pp. 75–92.

Caplan, A. L., 1978: *The Sociobiology Debate: Readings on the Ethical and Scientific Issues Concerning Sociobiology.* New York: Harper and Row.

Chagnon, N. A., 1979. Mate competition favoring close kin and village fissioning among the Yanomamö Indians. In: N. A. Chagnon and W. Irons (Eds.), *Evolutionary Biology and Human Social Behavior: an Anthropological Perspective*, pp. 86–132. North Scituate, Mass: Duxbury Press.

Chance, M. R. A., and C. J. Jolly, 1970: *Social Groups of Monkeys, Apes and Men.* New York: E. P. Dutton.

Charnov, E. L., 1978: Evolution of eusocial behaviour: offspring choice or parental parasitism. *Journal of Theoretical Biology*, 75, 457–65.

Chepko-Sade, Bonita Diane, 1979: Monkey group splits up. *New Scientist*, 82, 348–50.

Cherfas, J., 1977: The games animals play. *New Scientist*, 75, 672–3.

–1980: Voices in the wilderness: monkey screams are words of warning. *New Scientist*, 86, 303–6.

Crook, J. H., 1972: Sexual selection, dimorphism, and social organization in primates. In: B. Campbell (Ed.), pp. 231–81.

– 1980: Social change in Indian Tibet. In: *Social Science Information*, 19, pp. 139–166.

Crozier, R. H., 1980: Genetical structure of social insect populations. In: H. Markl (Ed.), pp. 129–45.

Dahlberg, Frances, (Ed.), 1981: *Woman the Gatherer.* New Haven and London: Yale University Press.

Daly, M., and Margo Wilson, 1979: Sex and strategy. In: *New Scientist*, 81, 15–17.

Darwin, C., 1871: *The Descent of Man and Selection in Relation to Sex.* London: Murray.

Dawkins, Marion E., et al. (group report), 1981: Evolutionary ecology of thinking. In: D. R. Griffin (Ed.), pp. 355–73.

Dawkins, R., 1976: *The Selfish Gene.* Oxford University Press.

Denham, W. W., 1971: Energy relations and some basic properties of primate social organisation. In: *American Anthropologist*, 73, 77–95.

DeVore, I., and K. R. L. Hall, 1965: Baboon ecology. In: I. DeVore (Ed.), *Primate Behaviour*, New York: Holt, Rinehart and Winston.

Dobzhansky, T., 1972: Genetics and the races of man. In: B. Campbell (Ed.), pp. 59–86.

Dumpert, K., 1978: *Das Sozialleben der Ameisen.* Berlin, Hamburg: Parey.

Dyer, K., 1977: Female athletes are catching up. *New Scientist*, 75, 722–3.

Eibl-Eibesfeldt, I., 1950: Über die Jugendentwicklung des Verhalten eines männlichen Dachses. *Zeitschrift für Tierpsychologie*, 7, 327–55.

Eisenberg, L., 1978: Die differentielle Verteilung der psychiatrischen Störungen auf die Geschlechter. In: E. Sullerot (Ed.), pp. 377–403.

Ely, D., 1981: *Physiology and Behaviour*, 26, 655 (cited in: *New Scientist*, 91, 286).

Emlen, S. T., 1976: An alternative case for sociobiology. *Science*, **192**, 736–8.

– 1981: Altruism, kinship, and reciprocity in the White-fronted Bee-eater. In: Alexander and Tinkle (Eds.), *Natural Selection and Social Behavior*, pp. 217–30. Chiron Press.

–and L. W. Oring, 1977: Ecology, sexual selection, and the evolution of mating systems. *Science*, **197**, 215–23.

Engels, F., 1884: *Der Ursprung der Familie, des Privanteigentums und des Staats.* (English: *The Origin of the Family, of Private Property and the State.*)

– 1940 (posthumous publication): *Dialectics of Nature.* Translated and edited by Clemens Dutt, with a preface by J. B. S. Haldane, London: Lawrence and Wishart, (reprinted 1946).

Estioko-Griffin, Agnes, and P. B. Griffin, 1981: Woman the hunter: the Agta. In: F. Dahlberg (Ed.).

Eylmann, E., 1902: Das Feuermachen der Eingeborenen der Colonie Süd-Australien. *Zeitschrift für Ethnologie*, **34**, 89–94.

Eysenck, H., 1979: Race, intelligence and education, (discussion with S. Rose). *New Scientist*, **82**, 849–52.

Feldman, M. W. *et al.* (group report), 1980: Genetics and Social Behaviour. In: H. Markl (Ed.), pp. 221–32.

Fisher, R. A., 1930: *The Genetical Theory of Natural Selection.* Oxford: Clarendon Press.

Flad-Schnorrenberg, Beatrice, 1978: *Der wahre Unterschied: Frau sein-angeboren oder angelernt?* Freiburg: Herder.

Fossey, Dian, 1972: Living with mountain gorillas. In: P. R. Marler (Ed.), *The Marvels of Animal Behavior*, pp. 209–29. Washington: National Geographic Society.

Fox, R., 1972: Alliance and constraint: sexual selection and the evolution of human kinship systems. In: B. Campbell (Ed.), pp. 282–331.

Gallup, G. G., Jr., 1970: Chimpanzees: self-recognition. *Science*, **167** 86–7.

Gardner, R. A., and Beatrice T. Gardner, 1978: Comparative psychology and language acquisition. *Annals of the New York Academy of Sciences*, **309**, 37–76.

Goodall, Jane (van Lawick-Goodall), 1968: The behavior of free-living chimpanzees in the Gombe stream area. *Animal Behaviour Monographs*, **1**, 161–311.

–1971: *In the Shadow of Man.* London: Collins.

–1979: Life and death at Gombe. *National Geographic Magazine*, **155**, 591–621.

Gösswald, K., 1951: *Die Rote Waldameise im Dienste der Waldhygienie.* Lüneburg: Metta Kinau. (Cited by K. Dumpert.)

–and K. Bier, 1954: Untersuchungen zur Kastendetermination in der Gattung Formica, *Naturwissenschaften*, **40**, 38–9.

Goy, R. W., 1966: The role of androgenes in the establishment and regulation of behavioral sex differences in mammals. *Journal of Animal Science*, **25**, 21–31.

Greenberg, L., 1979: Genetic component of bee odor in kin recognition. In: *Science*, **206**, 1095–7.

Griffin, D. R. (Ed.), 1981: *Animal Mind - Human Mind*. Dahlem-Konferenzen. Berlin, Heidelberg, New York: Springer-Verlog.

Guhl, A. M., 1950: Social dominance and receptivity in domestic fowl. *Physiological Zoology*, **23**, 361–6.

Gutman, H. G., 1976: *The Black Family in Slavery and Freedom 1750–1925*. New York: Pantheon.

Haldane, J. B. S., 1932: *The Causes of Evolution*. London: Longmans Green.

– 1955: Population genetics. *New Biology*, **18**, 34–51.

Hamilton, W. D., 1964: The genetical theory of social behaviour. *Journal of Theoretical Biology*, **7**, 1–52.

– 1967: Extraordinary sex ratios. *Science*, **156**, 477–88.

–1975: Innate social aptitudes of man: an approach from evolutionary genetics. In: R. Fox (Ed.), *Biosocial Anthropology*. London: Malaby Press.

Hamilton, W. J. III, and W. M. Gilbert, 1969: Starling dispersal from a winter roost. *Ecology*, **50**, 886–98.

Harcourt, A. H., and K. J. Stewart, 1977: Apes, sex and societies. *New Scientist*, **76**, 160–2.

Harich, W., 1975: *Kommunismus ohne Wachstum? Babeuf und der 'Club of Rome'*. Six Interviews with F. Duwe. Reinbeck bei Hamburg: Rowohlt.

Hart, M., 1979, In: *Icarus*, 37, 351.

Harvey, P. H., *et al.*, (group report), 1980: Mechanisms of kin-correlated behavior. In: H. Markl (Ed.), 183–202.

Hausfather, G., 1975: Dominance and reproduction in baboons. *(Papio cyanocephalus)*: a quantitative analysis. In: *Contrib. Primatol.*, 7, Basel: Karger.

Hayes, C., 1951: *The Ape in our House*. New York: Harper and Brothers.

Helm, June, 1968: The nature of the Dogrib socioterritorial groups. In: R. B. Lee and I. DeVore (Eds.), pp. 118–25.

Héritier, Françoise, 1979: Die Frau in den ideologischen Systemen. Ein Gespräch mit Evelyne Sullerot. In: E. Sullerot (Ed.), pp. 482–92.

Hiatt, L. R., 1968: Gidjingali marriage arrangements. In: R. B. Lee and I. DeVore (Eds.), pp. 165–75.

Hölldobler, B., 1976: Tournaments and slavery in a desert ant. *Science*, **192**, 912–14.

–and C. D. Michener, 1980: Mechanisms of identification and discrimination in social Hymenoptera. In: H. Markl (Ed.), pp. 35–57.

Horn, H. S., 1968: The adaptive significance of colonial nesting in the Brewer's Blackbird (*Euphagus cyanocephalus*). *Ecology*, **49**, 682–94.

Hook, E. 1973: Behavioral implications of the human XYY genotype. *Science*, **179**, 139–50.

Imanishi, K., 1963: Social behaviour in Japanese monkeys, *Macaca fuscata*. pp. 47–54. Princeton: Van Nostrand.

Itani, J., and A. Suzuki, 1967: The social unit of the chimpanzees. *Primates*, **8**, 355–81.

Jenni, D., 1979: Female chauvinist birds: swapping sex roles – the birds did it first. In: *New Scientist*, **82**, 896–9.

Kalmus, H. and C. R. Ribbands, 1952: The origin of the odours by which honeybees distinguish their companions. *Proceedings of the Royal Society*, **B 140**, 50–9.

Kawai, M., 1965: Newly acquired pre-cultural behaviour of the natural troop of Japanese monkeys on Koshima Islet. *Primates*, **6**, 1–30.

Kennedy, G. E., 1978: Hominoid habitat shifts in the Miocene. In: *Nature, London*, **271**, 11–12.

King, M. C. and A. C. Wilson, 1975: Evolution at two levels: molecular similarities and biological differences between humans and chimpanzees. *Science*, **188**, 107–16.

Kolata, Gina B., 1977: Human evolution: Hominoids of the Miocene. Science, **197**, 244–5, 294.

Krebs, J. R., *et al.*, (group report), 1980: Measuring fitness in social systems. In: H. Markl (Ed.), pp. 205–18.

Kruuk, H., 1972: *The Spotted Hyena: a Study of Predation and Social Behavior*. Chicago: University of Chicago Press.

Kummer, H., 1968: *Social Organisation of Hamadryas Baboons: a Field Study*. Chicago: University of Chicago Press.

– 1971: *Primate Societies*. Chicago: Aldine Publishing.

– 1976 In: K. Bättig and E. Ermetz (Eds.): *Lebensqualität*: Ein Gespräch zwischen Wissenschaftlern. Basel and Stuttgart: Birkhäuser.

– 1978: Analogs of morality among nonhuman primates. In: G. S. Stent (Ed.), pp. 35–52.

– 1981: Social knowledge in free-ranging primates. In: D. R. Griffin (Ed.).

Lack D., 1968: *Ecological Adaptations for Breeding in Birds*. London: Methuen.

Laughlin, W. S., 1968: Hunting: an integrated biobehaviour system and its evolutionary importance. In: Lee and DeVore (Eds.), pp. 304–20.

Lawick-Goodall, Jane van, *see* Goodall, Jane.

Le Boeuf, B. J., 1974: Male–male competition and reproductive success in elephant seals. *American Zoologist*, **14**, 163–76.

Lee, R. B., 1968: What hunters do for a living, or, how to make out in scarce resources. In: R. B. Lee and I. DeVore (Eds.), pp. 30–48.

– and I. DeVore (Eds.)., 1968: *Man the Hunter*. Proceedings of a symposium at the University of Chicago. Chicago: Aldine Publishing.

Lévi-Strauss, C., 1949: *Les structures élémentaires de la parenté*. Paris: Presses Universitaires de France.

– 1966: The scope of anthropology. *Current Anthropology*, **7**, 112–23.

– 1968: The concept of primitiveness. In: R. B. Lee and I. DeVore (Eds.), pp. 349–52.

Lewontin, R. C., 1977: Sociobiology – a caricature of Darwinism. In: P. Asquith and F. Suppe (Eds.); *The Philosophy of Science Association, 1976*, pp. 22–31.

– 1978: Adaptation. *Scientific American*, **239** (September), 156–69.

Lorenz, K., 1940: Durch Domestikation verursachte Störungen des arteigenen Verhaltens. *Zeitschrift für Angewandte Psychologie und Charakterkunde*, **59**, 2.

– 1963: Das sogenannte Böse: Zur Naturgeschichte der Aggression. Vienna: Borotha-Schoeller Verlag. English translation: *On Aggression*. London: Methuen, 1966.

– 1965: *Evolution and Modification of Behavior*. Chicago: University of Chicago Press.

Lukacs, G., 1964: Interview with '*Literarny Noviny*', Prague, 18 January.

Maccoby, Eleanor, 1979: Die Psychologie der Geschlechter: Implikationen für die Erwachsenenrolle. In: E. Sullerot (Ed.), pp. 284–306.

Mackie, G. O. 1973: Coordinated behavior in hydrozoan colonies. In: R. S. Boardman *et al.* (eds.), *Animal Colonies: Development and Function through Time*, pp. 95–106. Stroudsburg, Pa: Dowden, Hutchinson and Ross.

McLaren, Anne, 1970: Biological regulation of reproduction. In: K. Elliot (Ed.): *The Family and its Future*, A Ciba Foundation Blueprint. London: J. and A. Churchill, pp. 101–9.

Markl, H., 1971: Von Eigennutz des Uneigennützigen. In: *Naturwissenschaftliche Rundschau*, **24**, pp. 281–9.

– 1976: *Aggression und Altruismus: Coevolution der Gegensätze im Verhalten der Tiere*. Konstanz: Universitätsverlag.

– (Ed.), 1980: *Evolution of Social Behavior: Hypotheses and Empirical Tests*. Berlin: Dahlem Konferenzen; Weinheim: Verlag Chemie.

Martin, P. S., 1966: Africa and the Pleistocene overkill. *Nature, London*, **212**, 339–342.

– 1973: The discovery of America. *Science*, **179**, 969–74.

Maynard Smith, J., 1964: Group Selection and Kin Selection. *Nature, London*, **201**, 1145–7.

– 1975: Survival through suicide. In: *New Scientist*, **67**, pp. 496–7. (review of E. O. Wilson: *Sociobiology – the New Synthesis*).

– 1978a: The concepts of sociobiology. In: G. S. Stent (Ed.), pp. 23–34.

– 1978b: The evolution of behavior. *Scientific American*, **239** (September), 136–45.

– and G. R. Price, 1973: The logic of animal conflict. *Nature, London*, **246**, 15–18.

– and M. G. Ridpath, 1972: Wife sharing in the Tasmanian native hen, *Tribonyx mortierii*: a case of kin selection? *American Naturalist*, **106**, 447–452.

Mayr, E., 1972: Sexual selection and natural selection. In: B. Campbell (Ed.), pp. 87–104.

Mead, Margaret, 1949: *Male and Female*. New York: Morrow.

Menzel, E. W., Jr., 1975: Natural language of young chimpanzees. *New Scientist*, **65**, 127–30.

– 1978a: Implications of chimpanzee language-training experiments for primate field studies. In: D. J. Chivers and J. Herbert (Eds.), *Recent*

Advances in Primatology, vol. 1, London: Academic Press.
- 1978*b*: Cognitive mapping in chimpanzees. In: S. H. Hulse *et al.* (Ed.), *Cognitive Processes in Animal Behavior*, New York: L. Erlbaum Ass.
Metcalf, R. A., 1980: Measuring fitness in social insects. In: H. Markl (Ed.), pp. 81–95.
Michener, C. D., 1974: *The Social Behaviour of the Bees: a Comparative Study*. Cambridge, Mass.: Belknap Press of Harvard University.
Midgley, Mary, 1978: *Beast and Man: The Roots of Human Nature*. Cornell University Press; reprinted New York: New American Library, 1980.
- 1981: The limits of individualism. In: *How Humans Adapt: a Biocultural Odyssey*. Smithsonian Institution (in press).
Miller, L. G., 1976: Philosophy, dichotomies, and sociobiology. In: *Hastings Center Report*, (October), 20–5.
Mlynar, Z., 1980: *Night Frost in Prague: the End of Human Socialism*. London: C. Hurst.
Moehlman, Patricia D., 1979: Jackal helpers and pup survival. *Nature, London*, **277**, 382–3.
Mohr, H. 1960: Zum Erkennen von Raubvögeln, insbesondere von Sperber und Baumfalk, durch Kleinvögel. In: *Zeitschrift für Tierpsychologie*, **17**, 686–99.
Money, J. and Anke A. Erhardt, 1972: *Man and Woman, Boy and Girl*. Baltimore: Johns Hopkins University Press.
Morgan, L. H., 1877: *Ancient Society or Researches in the Lines of Human Progress from Savagery through Barbarism to Civilisation*. London.
Morris, D., 1967: *The Naked Ape: a Zoologist's Study of the Human Animal*. New York: McGraw Hill.
Murdock, G. P., 1968: The current status of the world's hunting and gathering peoples. In: R. B. Lee and I. DeVore (Eds.), pp 13–20.
Murton, R. K., 1968. Some predator – prey relationships in bird damage and population control. In: R. K. Murton and E. N. Wright (Eds.), *The Problems of Birds as Pests*, pp. 157–69. New York: Academic Press.
Nagel, U., 1973: A comparison of anubis baboons, hamadryas baboons, and their hybrids at a species border in Ethiopia. In: *Folia Primatologica*, **19**, 104–65.
New Scientist (anonymous), 1978: Throwing cold water on sociobiology. **77**, 486.
-1982: Quails find their cousins convenient mates. **93**, 642.
Norton-Griffiths, M. N., 1969: The organisation, control and development of parental feeding in the oystercatcher (*Haemotopus ostralegus*). In: Behaviour, **34**, 55–144.
Orians, G. H., 1969: On the evolution of mating systems in birds and mammals. In: *American Naturalist*, **103**, 589–603.
Oster, G. F. *et al.* (group report), 1980: Methodology and sociobiology modelling. In: H. Markl (Ed.), pp. 165–80.
Packer, C., 1977: Reciprocal altruism in *Papio anubis*. *Nature, London*, **265**, 441–43.

- 1979: Intertroop transfer and inbreeding avoidance *in Papio anubis*. *Animal Behavior*, **27**, 1–36.

Parker, G. A., K. K. Baker, and V. G. F. Smith, 1972: The Origin and Evolution of Genetic Dimorphism and the Male–Female Phenomenon. *Journal of Theoretical Biology*, **36**, 529–53.

Premack, D., 1971: Language in chimpanzee? *Science*, **172**, 808–22.

- 1976: Language and intelligence in ape and man. *American Scientist*, **64**, 674–83.

Reinisch, June M. and W. G. Karow, 1977: Prenatal exposure to synthetic progestins and estrogenes: effects on human development. *Archives of Sexual Behavior*, **6**, 257–88.

Rensch, B., 1965: Die höchsten Hirnleistungen der Tiere. *Naturwissenschaftliche Rundschau*, **18**, 91–101.

Reyer, H. U., 1980: Flexible helper structure as an ecological adaptation in the Pied Kingfisher. *Behavioral Ecology and Sociobiology*, **6**, 219–28.

Richards, O. W., 1927: Sexual selection and allied problems in the insects. *Biological Reviews, Cambridge Philosophical Society*, **2**, 298–364.

Richter, C. P., 1953: Experimentally produced reactions to food poisoning in wild and domesticated rats. *Annals of the New York Academy of Sciences*, **56**, 225–39.

Ristau, Carolyn A. and D. Robbins, 1981: Cognitive aspects of ape language experiments. In: D. R. Griffin (Ed.), pp. 299—330.

Rose, F. G. G., 1968: Australian marriage, land-owning groups, and initiations. In: R. B. Lee and I. DeVore (Eds.), pp. 200–8.

Rose, S., 1978: Pre-copernican sociobiology? (review of E. O. Wilson: *On Human Nature.*) *New Scientist*, **80**, 45.

- 1979*a*: Race, intelligence and education. (Discussion with H. Eysenck.) *New Scientist*, **82**, 849–52.

- 1979*b*: The Thatcher view of human nature. *New Scientist*, **82**, 575.

Rowell, Thelma E., 1971: Organisation of caged groups of *Ceropithecus* monkeys. *Animal Behaviour*, **19**, 625–45.

Rozin, P., 1976: The selection of food by rats, humans, and other animals. In: *Advances in the Study of Behavior*, **6**, 21–76.

Rumbaugh, D. M., (Ed.), 1977: *Language Learning by a Chimpanzee: the Lana Project.* New York: Academic Press.

Sade, D. S., 1980: Can 'fitness' be measured in primate populations? In: H. Markl (Ed.), pp. 97–114.

Sahlins, M. D., 1976: *The Use and Abuse of Biology: an Anthropological Critique of Sociobiology.* London: Tavistock Publications.

Sauer, E. G. F. and Eleonore M. Sauer, 1967: Verhaltensforschung an wilden Straussen in Südwestafrika. *Umschau*, **67**, 652–57.

Savage-Rumbaugh, E. Sue, D. M. Rumbaugh and Sally Boyen, 1978: Symbolic communications between two chimpanzees. *Science*, **201**, 641–4.

- 1980*a*: Do apes use language? *American Scientist*, **68**, 49–61.

Savage-Rumbaugh, E. Sue, D. M. Rumbaugh, S. T. Smith and J. Lawson, 1980*b*: Reference: the linguistic essential. *Science*, **210**, 922–4.

Schaller, G. B., 1963: *The Mountain Gorilla: Ecology and Behavior*. Chicago: University of Chicago Press.

−1972: *The Serengeti Lion: a Study of Predator−Prey Relations*. Chicago: University of Chicago Press.

Schjelderup-Ebbe, T., 1922: Beiträge zur Sozialpsychologie des Haushuhns. *Zeitschrift für Psychologie*, **92**, 60−87.

Schrödinger, E., 1943: *What Is Life? The Physical Aspect of the Living Cell*. Cambridge University Press, 1948.

Sebeok, T. A. and J. Umiker-Sebeok, 1979: Performing Animals: secrets of the trade. *Psychology Today*, **13**, 78−91.

Seemanova, Eva, 1972; cited in *Time*, 9 Oktober, 1972, 58.

Selander, R. K., 1972: Sexual selection and dimorphism in birds. In: B. Campbell (Ed.), pp. 180−230.

Seyfarth, R. M., Dorothy L. Cheney and P. Marler, 1980: Monkey responses to three different alarm calls: evidence of predator classification and semantic communication. *Science*, **210**, 801−3.

Seyfarth, R. M. *et al.* (group report), 1981: Communications as evidence of thinking. In: D. R. Griffin (Ed.), pp. 391−406.

Shepher, J., 1971: Mate selection among second-generation kibbutz adolescents and adults: incest avoidance and negative imprinting. *Archives of Sexual Behavior*, **1**, 293−307.

Sherman, P. W., 1980: The limits of ground squirrel nepotism. In: G. W. Barlow, J. Silverberg (Eds.), *Sociobiology: Beyond Nature/Nurture?* pp. 505−44. AAAS Selected Symposium 35. Boulder, Colorado: Westview Press.

Simpson, G. G., 1966: The biological nature of man. In: *Science*, **152**, 472−8.

− 1972: The evolutionary concept of man. In: B. Campbell (Ed.), pp. 17−39.

Smith, S. M., 1978: The 'underworld' in a terrestrial sparrow: adaptive strategy for floaters. *American Naturalist*, **112**, 571−82.

Solomon, R. C., *et al.* (group report), 1978: Sociobiology, morality, and culture. In: G. S. Stent (Ed.), pp. 283−307.

Stack, Carol B., 1974: *All Our Kin*. New York: Harper and Row.

Steffens, L., 1931: *Autobiography*. New York: Harcourt, Brace.

Steinmann, E., 1976: Über die Nahorientierung solitärer Hymenopteren: Individuelle Markierung der Nesteingänge. *Mitteilungen der Schweizer Entomologischen Gesellschaft*, **49**, 253−8.

Stent, G. S., (Ed.), 1978: *Morality as a Biological Phenomenon*. Berlin: Dahlem Konferenzen.

− 1981: The limits of the naturalistic approach to morality. Preface to reprint of G. S. Stent (Ed.), 1978. University of California Press.

Stolba A., 1979: *Entscheidungsfindung in Verbänden von Papio Hamadryas*. Doctoral thesis, Universität Zürich.

Struhsaker, T. T., 1967: Auditory communication among vervet monkeys. In: S. A. Altmann (Ed.): *Social Communication among Primates*. Chicago: University of Chicago Press, S. 281−324.

Suarez, Susan and G. Gallup, Jr., 1981: *Journal of Human Evolution*, **10**, 175.

Sullerot, Evelyne, (Ed.), 1978: *Le Fait Feminin*. Paris: Librairie A. Fayard. German translation: *Die Wirklichkeit der Frau*. München: Steinhausen, 1979. (No English translation available.)

Suttles, W., 1968: Coping with abundance: subsistence on the Northwest Coast. In: R. B. Lee and I. DeVore (Eds.), pp. 56–68.

Talbot, Mary, 1943: Population studies of the ant *Prenolepis imparis Say*. *Ecology*, **24**, 31–44.

Tannenbaum, B., 1975: Reproductive strategies in the white-lined bat (*Saccopteryx bilineata*). Doctoral thesis, Cornell University, Ithaca, N.Y.

Teleki, G., 1973: *The Predatory Behavior of Wild Chimpanzees*. Lewisburg, Pa: Bucknell University Press.

Terrace, H. S., 1979a: *Nim*. New York: Knopf.

– 1979b: Is problem-solving language? *Journal of Experimental Analysis of Behaviour*, **31**, 161–75.

– et al., 1979: Can an ape create a sentence? *Science*, **206**, 891–902.

Tiger, L. and J. Shepher, 1975: *Women in the Kibbutz*. New York: Harcourt, Brace, Jovanovich.

Tinbergen, N., 1939: Field observations of east Greenland birds. *Transactions of the Linaean Society of New York*, **5**, 1–94.

– 1951: *The Study of Instinct*. Oxford: Clarendon Press.

Trivers, R. L., 1971: The evolution of reciprocal altruism. *Quarterly Review of Biology*, **46**, 35–57.

– 1972; Parental investment and sexual selection. In: B. Campbell (Ed.), pp. 136–79.

– 1974: *Parent–Offspring Conflict*. *American Zoologist*, **14**, 249–64.

– 1977 in: *Time*, 1 August, 1977, p. 54.

– and Hope Hare, 1976: Haplodiploidy and the evolution of the social insects. *Science*, **191**, 249–63.

Uyenoyama, M. and M. W. Feldman, 1980: Theories of kin and group selection: a population genetics perspective. *Theoretical Population Biology*, 1980.

Verner, J., 1965: Breeding biology of the long-billed marsh wren. *Condor*, **67**, 6–30.

Washburn, S. L., 1978a: Animal behavior and social anthropology. *Society*, **15**, 35–41.

– 1978b: The evolution of man. *Scientific American*, **239** (September), 146–54.

– and C. S. Lancaster, 1968: The evolution of hunting. In: R. B. Lee and I. DeVore (Eds.), pp. 293–303.

Watanabe, H., 1968: Subsistence and ecology of northern food gatherers with special reference to the Ainu. In: Lee and DeVore (Eds.), pp. 69–77.

Watson, J. D., 1968: *The Double Helix: a Personal Account of the Discovery of the Structure of DNA*. London: Weidenfeld and Nicolson.

275

Welsh, D. A., 1975: Savannah sparrow breeding and territoriality on a Nova Scotia dune beach. *Auk*, **92**, 235–51.

White, J. P. and J. F. O'Connell, 1979: Australian prehistory: new aspects of antiquity. *Science*, **203**, 21–8.

Wickler W., 1969: *Sind wir Sünder? Naturgesetze der Ehe*. München: Droemer Knaur.

– and Uta Seibt, 1977: *Das Prinzip Eigennutz: Ursachen und Konsequenzen des sozialen Verhaltens*. Hamburg: Hoffmann and Campe.

Wiley, R. H., 1973: Territoriality and non-random mating in sage grouse. *Animal Behaviour Monographs*, **6**, 85–169.

Wilkins, M. H. F., 1963: Molecular configuration of nucleic acids (Nobel lecture) *Science*, **140**, pp. 941–50.

Williams, B. A. O., 1978: Conclusion. In: G. S. Stent (Ed.), 309–30.

Wilson, E. O., 1975: *Sociobiology: The New Synthesis*. Cambridge, Mass: The Belknap Press of Harvard University.

–1978a: *On Human Nature*: Cambridge, Mass: Harvard University Press.

– 1978b: What is Sociobiology? In: *Society*, **15**, 10–14.

Witelson, Sandra F., 1976: Sex and the single hemisphere: right hemisphere specialization for spatial processing. *Science*, **193**, 425–7.

– 1977: Developmental dyslexia: two right hemispheres and none left. In: *Science*, **195**, 309–11.

– 1978: Geschlechtsspezifische Unterschiede in der Neurologie der kognitiven Funktionen und ihere psychologischen, sozialen, edukativen und klinischen Implikationen. In: E. Sullerot (Ed.), 341–368.

Witkin, H. A. *et al.*, 1976: Criminality in XYY and XXY men. *Science*: **193**, 547–55.

Wolf, L. L., 1975: 'Prostitution' behavior in a tropical hummingbird. *Condor*, **77**, 140–44.

Woolfenden, G. E., 1973: Nesting and survival in a population of Florida scrub jays. *Living Bird*, **12**, 15–49.

– and J. W. Fitzpatrick, 1978: The inheritance of territory in group-breeding birds. *BioScience*, **28**, 104–8.

Wright, S., 1931: Evolution in Mendelian populations. *Genetics*, **16**, 97–158.

– 1945: Tempo and mode in evolution: a critical review. In: *Ecology*, **26** 415–19.

– 1969: *Evolution and the Genetics of Populations*. Chicago: University of Chicago Press.

Wu, H. M. H. *et al.* 1980: Kin preference in infant *Macacca nemestrina*. *Nature, London*, **285**, 225–7.

Wynne-Edwards, V. C., 1962: *Animal Dispersion in Relation to Social Behavior*. Edinburgh: Oliver and Boyd.

Yengoyan, A. A., 1968: Demographic and ecological influences on aboriginal Australian marriage sections. In: R. B. Lee and I. DeVore (Eds.), pp. 185–99.

Zazzo, R. 1979: Einige Bemerkungen über die Unterschiede in der Psychologie der Geschlechter. In: E. Sullerot (Ed.), pp. 311–21.

Zweig, A., 1959: Tierpsychologische Beiträge zur Phylogenese der Ich/ Über-Ich-Instanzen. In: *Schweizerische Zeitschrift für Psychologie*, Supplement 37.

Name index

Abegglen, J. J., 164, 172
Adorno, T. W., 246
Agarwal, A., 194
Alexander, R. D., 38–9, 64
Allee, W. C., 215, 236, 263
Allen, E., 223, 229
Altmann, S. A., 2
Altmann, Jeanne, 2
Angst, W., 139, 156
Ardrey, R., 73
Avery, O. T., 78
Ayala, F. J., xvii, 12, 112–13,

Bachmann, C., 108, 163–4, 187–8
Bachofen, J. J., 217–18, 245
Baker, M. C., 18
Barash, D. P., 157–9, 161, 165, 180,
  216, 225–7, 253–5, 258
Bateman, A. J., 148
Bateson, P. P. G., xvii, 9, 210
Baulieu, E., 199
Baur, E., 232
Beaumarchais, P. A., 180
Beckwith, J., 250–1
Beethoven, L. van, 137
Berghe, P. L. van den, 140, 180
Bertram, B. C. R., 35
Bier, K., 65
Bischof, N., 134–5, 145, 156, 177–8,
  181, 208, 210, 212
Bonner, J. T., xvii, 52, 86
Boulding, K. E., 81
Bray, O., 18
Brock, V. E., 5
Brown, L. H., 28
Burian, R. M., 222–3
Burnet, F. M., 69

Camara, Dom Helder, 244
Campbell, B., 85

Campbell, D. T., 136
Caplan, A. L., 223
Caruso, Enrico, 150
Chagnon, N. A., 208
Chance, M. R. A., 107
Charnov, E. L., 63
Cheney, Dorothy, 97
Chepko-Sade, Bonita Diane, 43, 171,
  208
Cherfas, J., 26, 97
Clutton-Brock, T., 26
Crick, F. H. C., 79
Crook, J. H., 115, 176, 179, 197
Crozier, R. H., 59
Curie, Marie, 203

Dahlberg, Frances, 218
Daly, M., 179–80, 193–4
Darwin, Charles, ix, xiii, 59, 71, 87,
  91, 161, 225–6, 239, 246
Dawkins, Marion E., 90
Dawkins, R., 59, 65, 177–8, 225–6,
  228, 251–2, 262–3
Denham, W. W., 165
DeVore, I., 122, 125, 180, 188–90,
  194, 205–6, 252
Dobzhansky, T., 14, 82, 240
Dumpert, K., 65, 121
Dyer, Ken, 199–200

Eibl-Eibesfeldt, I., 11
Eisenberg, L., 198
Ely, D., 215
Emlen, S. T., xvii, 50, 155, 166–8, 175
Engels, F., xi, 119–20, 210, 220,
  245–7
Erdmann, B., 140
Erhardt, Anke A., 192
Esquivel, A. P., 244
Estioko-Griffin, Agnes, 194

279

Eylmann, E., 188
Eysenck, H., 248

Feldman, M., xvii, 49, 209–10
Fischer, E., 232, 240
Fischer, Helga, 17
Fisher, R. A., 30, 71, 148, 151
Fitzpatrick, J. W., 37, 41
Flad-Schnorrenberg, Beatrice, 192
Fossey, Dian, 18
Fox, R., 211
Freud, Sigmund, 81
Frisch, K. von, 4

Gallup, G. G., Jr., 105
Gardner, R. A., 100
Gardner, Beatrice T., 100
Geertz, C., 212, 252
Gilbert, W. M., 5
Gleitman, H., 257
Goethe, J. W., 156
Goodall, Jane, xvii, 19, 27, 36, 45, 90,
   109, 115, 131, 138–9, 163, 170–1,
   175, 181, 191, 209, 215, 258–61
Gösswald, K., 65
Goy, R. W., 192
Greenberg, L., 46
Griffin, D. R., 194
Guhl, A. M., 216
Gutman, H. G., 205, 232

Haldane, J. B. S., xii, 30, 33–4, 48,
   71, 240, 246–7
Hall, K. R. L., 125
Hamilton W. J., III, 5
Haour, France, 199
Hare, Hope, 39, 59, 63–5, 223
Harcourt, A. H., 163, 170, 175
Harich, W., 246–7
Hart, M., 47
Harvey, P. H., xvii, 35, 43, 59, 61, 209,
   231
Hausfather, G., 152
Hayes, C., 99
Hegel, Georg W. F., 81, 140, 255
Helm, June, 180, 206
Héritier, Françoise, 217–18
Hiatt, L. R., 188–9, 205
Hitler, Adolf, xi, 78, 81, 233–4
Hobbes, Thomas, 257
Hölldobler, B., xvii, 25, 27, 39, 46–7,
   65, 86
Hook, E., 250
Horkheimer, M., 246
Horn, H. S., 165

Imanishi, K., 90
Isaiah, 137
Itani, J., 115

Jarvis, Jennifer, 38
Jenner, F. A., 212
Jenni, D., 155
Jesus Christ, 137
Johannsen, W., 11
Jolly, C. J., 107

Kalmus, H., 46
Karow, W. G., 192
Kawai, M., 90
Kennedy, G. E., 113
Kepler, Johannes, 240
King, J., 250–1
King, M. C., 112
King, Martin Luther, 244
Kishon, E., 180
Kolata, Gina B., 114
Krebs, J. R., 41, 61
Kruuk, H., 27
Kummer, H., xvii, 2, 5, 20, 84, 91–3,
   95, 105–9, 120, 129–31, 136, 138,
   163–7, 172–3, 176, 184, 187–8,
   191–2, 214–15, 265

Lack, D., 168
Lagerlöf, Selma, 203
Lancaster, C. S., 81, 118, 124–5, 212
Laughlin, W. S., 122
Leaky, Louis, 19
Le Boeuf, B. J., 152
Lee, R. B., 122–5, 180, 188–90, 194,
   205–6
Lenz, F., 232–3
Lévi-Strauss, C., 119, 188–9, 211
Levy, Jerre, 201
Lewontin, R. C., 23, 223, 243
Livi-Bacci, M., 177–8
Lorenz, K., xi, 1–5, 10, 17, 26, 29–30,
   33, 43, 72–3, 89, 157, 229, 234–5,
   237, 240
Lukacs, G., 246–7
Lumsden, C., xvii
Lyssenko, T. D., 241, 247

Maccoby, Eleanor, 191
Mackie, G. O., 54
McLaren, Anne, 149
Mann, Thomas, 213
Markl, H., xvii, 5, 27, 31, 56, 60, 107
Marler, P., xvii, 18, 97, 265
Martin, P. S., 126–7
Marx, Karl, xi, xiii, 119, 140, 243–7

280

281

Subject index

adaptation, 22–3, 48, 84–5, 124, 133, 167, 183, 186, 210, 230
'adultery' (in animals), 18, 40, 42, 129–30, 153, 157, 161, 184–5
agriculture, 80, 119–20, 123–7
amoeba, 51–3, 228
anonymous crowd, 5
ant, 27, 45–6, 55–6, 60, 63–6, 69–70, 85–6, 119, 230; see also honey-pot ant, leaf-cutting ant
antelope, 127
anthropology, xiii, xv, 73–7, 80, 119, 188–90, 194, 205–7, 217, 239, 255, 258
anubis baboon, 49–50, 130–1, 171–2, 209
ape, 19, 42–3, 49, 55, 81–3, 86, 100–2, 104–9, 112–18, 133–4, 138–42, 168–71, 175–7, 191, 207, 209, 219, 228–9, 244
aphid, 145
Argus pheasant, 163
artificial insemination, 149
asexual reproduction, 52–3, 144–6, 151
Ausralopithecus, 114, 117, 133

baboon, 2, 5–6, 25, 84, 89, 91, 108, 110, 115–6, 120, 125, 138, 230, 258–60; see also anubis b.; hamadryas b.
'baby sitter' (helper), 37, 40–1, 50, 60, 62, 120
bachelor groups, 43, 169, 171–2
badger, 10–11, 168
Barbary macaque, 110
bat, 18
bear, 118
beaver, 85, 109, 119, 127
bee, 25, 27, 45–6, 51, 55, 62–3, 69–70, 90, 117; see also honey bee

bee-eater, 50
Belding's ground squirrel, 42
bigamy, 18, 84, 154, 157
bison, 216
bryozoans, 53, 66
budding, 53–4, 68
bug, 57
buffalo, 2
bumble-bee, 63
bushbuck, 115

camel, 127
cannibalism, 27, 131, 260
capuchin monkey, 44
cat, 88, 128–9
cattle farming, 119–20, 127
chaffinch, 10
chess, 200
chimpanzee, xiii, 12, 14, 19, 27, 36, 42, 45, 49, 83, 90, 97–117, 122, 131–4, 138–42, 151, 153, 163–4, 167, 169–71, 173–5, 179, 181, 191, 207, 209, 214–15, 218–19, 221, 230, 258–61
chromosomes, 13, 57, 112, 197, 240, 250–1
cockroach, 56, 60
coelenterates, 53–4, 144
compassion, see sympathy
corals, 51, 53, 66, 68, 70, 228
cost/benefit calculation (analysis, ratio), genetical, 31–2, 35–6, 39, 59, 63, 137, 206, 254–5, 263–4
cuckoo, 6–7, 10, 13, 16, 42, 88, 145
culture, 23, 77, 80, 84–92, 141, 227, 230

Dahlem workshops, xvi, 31, 38–9, 44, 59, 65, 86, 102, 201, 212, 224, 229, 255–7

283

Darwin finch, 87–8, 141
Darwinism, ix, xii–xiv, 39, 71–5,
    81, 137, 226–7, 246–7
DNA, 12–15, 78–9
dog, xiii, 10, 42, 88, 96, 128–9, 141;
    see also shepherd's dog
dominance (pecking order), 67,
    213–17, 220, 236, 249
dove, see pigeon
Dryopithecus, 111

eagle, 28, 35, 97, 161, 168, 217
earthworm, 147
ecological niche, 20, 47–8, 85, 183
elephant, 2, 25, 36, 42–3, 67, 92, 110,
    150, 169
elephant seal, 152, 162
ethics, 73–6, 137–9, 258, 261–2
ethology, xi, xv, 38, 71, 84, 147, 227,
    240
evolution, xi–xii, xvi, 6, 25, 33, 47, 55,
    72, 75, 80, 91, 133, 140–1, 147, 223,
    237, 261
Evolutionarily Stable Strategy (ESS),
    31–3
existential anxiety, 135

falcon, 3–4
fascism, xi, xiii, 230–4, 239–40
feminism (womens' movement), 156,
    187, 195–7, 201, 218, 221, 230
fish, 5, 7, 26, 118, 159, 253
fishing, 118, 122, 125, 194
'free love', see promiscuity
fox, xiii, 16, 109

game theory, 30–1
gatherers (gathering, forage), 117, 119,
    122–5, 173, 190, 194, 205, 220–1
gelada, 84, 115, 172–4, 214, 218–19
gene, x, xvi, 7, 11–16, 23, 33–5, 58–9,
    68, 78, 82, 112–3, 132–3, 136, 144–7,
    151, 160–1, 209, 223, 228–9, 237,
    240–4, 248, 251–5, 262–4
gerontocracy, 188
gibbon, 105, 110–12, 150, 153, 168,
    170, 173–4, 177, 219
giraffe, 126
goat, 129, 162
goose, 10, 162, 208, 229; see also
    greylag goose
gorilla, 19, 29–30, 99, 105–6, 108,
    110–13, 115, 118, 125, 164, 170, 173,
    175, 177, 184, 209, 218–19
greylag goose, 16–18, 133–4, 153,

156–7, 168, 177, 179, 182, 184, 234,
    244, 258
group selection, 48–9, 136, 223
gull, 166

hamadryas baboon, 20, 43, 49, 92–5,
    115, 129–31, 152, 154, 162–9, 166,
    172–7, 184–5, 187–91, 214, 218
hamster, 109
hare, 168
harem, 40, 43, 92, 129–31, 153–5, 157,
    164–8, 170, 172, 176–9, 187, 208, 226
helper, see baby sitter
hen, see poultry
herd, 1–6, 18, 24, 166
heron, 97
herring, 3, 21
Homo sapiens, see man
honey bee, 56, 59, 63, 65, 150, 228
honey-pot ant, 25
horse, 127
hummingbird, 159
hunting (hunter), 115–16, 119, 122–7,
    136, 173, 194, 205, 214, 220–1
hybrids, 82, 157
hyena, 4, 27, 97, 215
hymenoptera, 55–65, 68–9, 223

identification, see sympathy
imprinting, 10, 47
incest, 84, 206, 208–13, 239
insects, 7, 28, 45, 55, 86; see also
    social insects
instinct, 6–9, 30, 134, 136
IQ-test, 201–2, 248
islam, 177, 184–5
ius primae noctis, 180, 182

jacana, 155–6, 182
jackal, 4, 37, 153, 168
jackdaw, 89
jay, 37, 41
jelly fish, 53–4

kangaroo, 168
kibbutz, 193, 212
kin selection, 34–44, 49, 57, 59,
    62–5, 68, 136, 204–8, 223
kingfisher, pied, 41, 120
kleptogyny, 160–1

language, 95–104, 141, 261
lateralization (of brain) 200–1
leaf-cutting ant, 85–6, 227
lek, 162
leopard, 2, 4, 97, 116

284

lion, 3–4, 27, 35–6, 42–3, 120–1, 126, 152, 164–6, 173, 216

macaque, 90–1, 105, 108–9, 118, 141, 230
male sex hormone, *see* testosterone
mammals, 21, 26, 29, 36, 57, 67–70, 126–7, 133, 136, 149–50, 156, 165, 168–9, 173, 178, 190, 209, 215
mammoth, 127
man (*Homo sapiens*), xi, xiii–xvi, 8–10, 28–9, 66–70, 73–7, 80–8, 94–6, 103–4, 106, 108, 110–14, 116–28, 130, 133–43, 147–50, 159, 169, 174, 176–208, 210–13, 217–21, 228–30, 234–40, 243–4, 248–51, 253–5, 257–9, 261–4
manipulation (of daughters by social insect queens), 62, 64, 223, 227–8
mantis, 226
mantis shrimp, 25
marten, 216
Marxism, 81, 119, 241, 244–7, 258
mastodon, 127
matriarchy, 217–21
mirror experiments, 105
mole rat, 37–8
monkeys, 2, 42–3, 49, 55, 81–3, 89, 105–10, 115, 118, 120, 138–9, 141–2 168–72, 175, 177, 191–2, 207, 209, 216–19
monogamy, 17–8, 36, 40, 84, 153, 157–8, 161, 165–8, 173, 176–9, 182–7, 219,
moose, 216
Mormons, 151, 177
mountain bluebird, 157–8
mouse, 105, 129, 210, 215
mule, 157
murder, 26–9, 66
musk-oxen, 2
mutation, 15–16, 24, 34, 48–9, 63, 145

natural selection, xii, xvi, 6, 20–5, 30–5, 59, 62, 67, 132, 136, 223, 227, 237, 257

oestrus, 174–5
operational sex ratio, 175
orang–utan, 99, 106, 110–12, 150, 156, 170, 173, 219
ostrich, 208
oyster, 144, 149
oystercatcher, 87, 141

parental investment, 64, 148–9, 152, 154, 158, 183, 254–5
parrot, 10
partnership, 150, 153, 194, 221
partridge, red-legged, 155
patas monkey, 167, 215
paternity, 40, 43, 171, 204, 217–20, 253
peacock, 162–3, 177
pecking order, *see* dominance
pheasant, 162
phenotype, 12, 242
phenylketonuria, 241
phytognomy, 222
pigeon (dove) 4, 29–30, 101
pigtail macaque, 44
polyandry, 155–6, 179
polygamy (polygyny), 153–4, 159, 161–2, 166, 168, 175–9, 181, 183–4, 187, 218–20
polygyny (bigamy) threshold, 166, 168
polyp, 53
poultry (domestic fowl, hen), 129, 154, 162, 214, 216
predator, 2–6, 88, 90, 94, 97, 108, 116, 126–7, 150, 166, 172–3
pre-humans (proto-h., semi-h., half-men), xvi, 83, 91, 116–8, 136, 141, 169, 173, 179, 221
primates, 95, 106–9, 152, 163, 167, 169–74, 191
promiscuity ('free love'), 153, 162–3, 171, 179, 217–20
prostitution, 159, 180, 185, 189
python, 97

quail, 210

rabbit, 168
racism, xi, 82, 231–5, 239–40
Ramapithecus, 114
rape, 156, 180, 182, 213
rat, 26, 42–3, 88, 156, 210
rattlesnake, 25
raven, 30
reciprocal altruism, 49–50, 136, 223
redwing blackbird, 18, 40, 184–5
reptiles, 7, 26, 149
rhesus monkey, 40, 43, 50, 108, 171, 192, 208–9, 216
rhinoceros, 23, 110
ritualized combat, 26, 29, 32–3
rodents, 109, 117
role, 191, 193, 204, 211, 220

sage grouse, *see* wildfowl